The Psalms Companion

The Psalms Companion

The Ways and Means of Faith in Everyday Life

A Handbook

Nancy Johnston

Trilogy Christian Publishers

A Wholly Owned Subsidary of Trinity Broadcasting Network

2442 Michelle Drive

Tustin, CA 92780

Copyright © 2024 by Nancy Johnston

Unless otherwise noted, all Scripture quotations are taken from the King James Version of the Bible. Public domain. Scripture quotations marked ESV are taken from the ESV® Bible (The Holy Bible, English Standard Version®), copyright © 2001 by Crossway Bibles, a publishing ministry of Good News Publishers. Used by permission. All rights reserved.

All rights reserved, including the right to reproduce this book or portions thereof in any form whatsoever.

For information, address Trilogy Christian Publishing

Rights Department, 2442 Michelle Drive, Tustin, Ca 92780.

Trilogy Christian Publishing/ TBN and colophon are trademarks of Trinity Broadcasting Network.

For information about special discounts for bulk purchases, please contact Trilogy Christian Publishing.

Trilogy Disclaimer: The views and content expressed in this book are those of the author and may not necessarily reflect the views and doctrine of Trilogy Christian Publishing or the Trinity Broadcasting Network.

10 9 8 7 6 5 4 3 2 1

Library of Congress Cataloging-in-Publication Data is available.

ISBN 979-8-89333-221-6

ISBN 979-8-89333-222-3 (ebook)

This book is dedicated to the memory of John and Marie Brosky.
A special thanks to Colleen Elliot.

Psalm 26:7, "That I may publish with the voice of thanksgiving, and tell of all thy wondrous works."

Table of Contents

Introduction 16
Psalm 1: The Two Ways—the Blessed and the Ungodly 18
   Worksheet: Examination of Your Own Spiritual Nature. 20
Psalm 2: Blessed Are They Who Trust in the Lord. 22
Psalm 3: For the Lord Sustained Me. 24
   Study: What Is Meekness? 25
Psalm 4: Put Your Trust in the Lord 27
Psalm 5: The Lord Wilt Bless the Righteous. 29
   Worksheet: Our Current Daily Habits 31
Psalm 6: Have Mercy upon Me, O Lord, for I Am Weak. . . 33
Psalm 7: The Lord Shall Judge the People. 35
Psalm 8: Oh Lord, Our Lord, How Excellent Is Thy
   Name in All the Earth. 38
Psalm 9: I Will Shew Forth All Thy Marvelous Works. 41
Psalm 10: Arise, O LORD; Forget Not the Humble 44
Psalm 11: For the Lord Trieth the Righteous 47
   Worksheet: Life's Hardships 49
Psalm 12: The Words of the Lord Are Pure Words. 51
Psalm 13: I Will Sing unto the Lord because He
   Hath Dealt Bountifully with Me. 54
   Study: The Role of Sacrifice 55
Psalm 14: God Is in the Generation of the Righteous 57
Psalm 15: Who Shall Dwell in Thy Holy Hill? 59
   Study: Fear of the Lord 60
Psalm 16: Preserve Me, O God: For in Thee Do I
   Put My Trust. 62
Psalm 17: Keep Me on Your Path 65
Psalm 18: God Saves Us from Our Enemies 67
Psalm 19: O Lord, My Strength, and My Redeemer. 73
Psalm 20: I Now Know That the Lord Saveth His
   Anointed 76
   Worksheet: How Has God Saved You? What
      Would You Like God to Save You From? 77
Psalm 21: The Lord Has Strength That None Can

Overcome 78
Study: Wrath. 79
Psalm 22: David Speaks as the Messiah 81
Psalm 23: The Lord Is My Shepherd. 85
Psalm 24: Who Is the King of Glory?. 88
Psalm 25: Shew Me Thy Ways, O Lord; Teach Me
   Thy Paths. 90
Psalm 26: Examine Me, O Lord 93
   Worksheet: Where Do I Slide Back in My Own
      Life, and What Can I Do about It?. 95
Psalm 27: The Lord Is the Strength of My Life 97
   Contemplation: Strength through Faith 98
Psalm 28: Give unto Them According to Their Deeds 100
Psalm 29: Give unto the Lord Glory and Strength. 103
Psalm 30: O Lord My God, I Cried unto Thee, and
   Thou Hast Healed Me. 105
   Worksheet: Lessons Learned in the Waiting 106
Psalm 31: Into Thine Hand, I Commit My Spirit. 107
   Study: Hope 109
Psalm 32: I Acknowledge My Sin unto Thee 111
   Study: Iniquity 112
Psalm 33: Sing unto Him a New Song 114
Psalm 34: The Lord Redeemeth the Soul of His Servants . 117
   Study: Redemption 118
Psalm 35: Lord, How Long Wilt Thou Look On? 121
Psalm 36: O Continue Thy Lovingkindness unto
   Them That Know Thee. 124
   Worksheet: Where Are You Today?. 126
Psalm 37: The Lord Shall Give Thee the Desires
   of Thine Heart. 127
Psalm 38: For I Will Declare Mine Iniquity; I Will
   Be Sorry for My Sin 131
Psalm 39: Verily Every Man at His Best State Is
   Altogether Vanity 134
Psalm 40: And He Put a New Song in My Mouth. 136
Psalm 41: Thou Upholdest Me in Mine Integrity 139

    Worksheet: Cultivating Discernment 141
Psalm 42: I Shall Praise God; He Is the Health of
    My Countenance. 143
    Study: Countenance 145
Psalm 43: O Deliver Me from the Deceitful and
    Unjust Man. 147
Psalm 44: My Confusion Is Continually Before Me. 149
Psalm 45: When We Enter the King's Palace 153
Psalm 46: God Is Our Refuge and Strength, a Very
    Present Help in Trouble. 158
Psalm 47: For the LORD Most High Is Terrible;
    He Is a Great King over All the Earth 160
    Study: God Is Terrible; What Does It Mean?. 161
Psalm 48: The City of the Great King 163
Psalm 49: Man That Is in Honour, and Understandeth
    Not, Is Like the Beasts That Perish 166
Psalm 50: Our God Shall Come, and Shall Not
    Keep Silence 169
    Worksheet: How Is Your Life Going Right Now? 172
Psalm 51: Restore unto Me the Joy of Thy Salvation. 173
Psalm 52: I Will Wait on Thy Name; for It Is Good
    before Thy Saints. 177
Psalm 53: The Fool Hath Said in His Heart, There
    Is No God 179
Psalm 54: Behold, God Is Mine Helper 182
    Worksheet: Help Me, O Lord! 183
Psalm 55: For It Was Not an Enemy That Reproached
    Me. 184
    Worksheet: How Do I Betray the Will of God in
        My Daily Life? 187
Psalm 56: In God Have I Put My Trust: I Will Not
    Be Afraid What Man Can Do unto Me 188
Psalm 57: In the Shadow of Thy Wings Will I Make
    My Refuge. 191
Psalm 58: A Man Shall Say, Verily, There Is a Reward
    for the Righteous. 194

Contemplation: How Words Are Life............... 195
Psalm 59: God Is My Defence, and the God of
    My Mercy..................................... 197
Psalm 60: Give Us Help from Trouble: For Vain Is
    the Help of Man................................ 200
Psalm 61: Hear My Cry, O God; Attend unto My Prayer.. 203
Psalm 62: For Thou Renderest to Every Man According
    to His Work.................................... 206
    Worksheet: Examination of Where I Imagine I
        Am Powerful............................... 207
Psalm 63: My Flesh Longeth for Thee in a Dry and
    Thirsty Land................................... 210
    Study: The Living Water......................... 211
Psalm 64: O God, Preserve My Life from Fear of the
    Enemy... 214
Psalm 65: Blessed Is the Man Whom Thou Choosest..... 217
Psalm 66: I Will Declare What He Hath Done for
    My Soul!....................................... 220
Psalm 67: O Let the Nations Be Glad and Sing for Joy ... 222
Psalm 68: The Earth Shook, the Heavens Also Dropped
    at the Presence of God.......................... 224
Psalm 69: O God, in the Multitude of Thy Mercy,
    Hear Me....................................... 228
    Study: Who Was David?......................... 231
Psalm 70: O God, Thou Art My Help and My Deliverer.. 234
    Examination of Conscience...................... 234
Psalm 71: Cast Me Not Off in the Time of Old Age..... 237
Psalm 72: Blessed Be the Lord God, the God of
    Israel, Who Only Doeth Wondrous Things.......... 241
Psalm 73: So Foolish Was I…: I Was as a Beast
    before Thee.................................... 244
    Study: The Biblical Cycle of Redemption
        and Renewal.............................. 246
Psalm 74: O God, How Long Shall the Adversary
    Reproach?..................................... 249
    Study: The Adversary........................... 250

Psalm 75: Unto Thee, O God, Do We Give Thanks 253
Psalm 76: When God Arose to Judgment, to Save
    All the Meek of the Earth..........................255
    Study: Zion...256
Psalm 77: In the Day of My Trouble I Sought the Lord...259
    Worksheet: Help in Our Time of Trouble............262
Psalm 78: That They Might Set Their Hope in God,
    and Not Forget the Works of God 263
Psalm 79: O Remember Not against Us Former Iniquities.269
Psalm 80: Turn Us Again, O Lord God of Hosts,
    Cause Thy Face to Shine; and We Shall Be Saved.....273
Psalm 81: Oh That My People Had Hearkened unto Me..276
    Contemplation: What Do I Put above God in
    My Own Life?.......................................278
Psalm 82: He Judgeth among the Gods 280
Psalm 83: Hold Not Thy Peace, and Be Not Still,
    O God..281
Psalm 84: For the Lord God Is a Sun and Shield!.........284
    Study: Ways That Our God Is the Sun and the
    Shield..285
Psalm 85: Turn Us, O God of Our Salvation 287
Psalm 86: For Thou Art Great, and Doest Wondrous
    Things: Thou Art God Alone.......................289
    Study: How God Has Proven Himself to Be Great?...290
    Worksheet: How Has God Shown His Greatness
    in Your Life? 290
Psalm 87: The Lord Loveth the Gates of Zion 292
    Study: Rahab.......................................292
Psalm 88: For My Soul Is Full of Troubles; My
    Life Draweth Nigh unto the Grave.................294
Psalm 89: The Covenant between God and His People....297
Psalm 90: Thou Turnest Man Destruction and Sayest,
    Return Ye Children of Men........................302
Psalm 91: He That Dwelleth in the Secret Place of
    the Most High Shall Abide under the Shadow
    of the Almighty....................................305

Psalm 92: O Lord, How Great Are Thy Works! And Thy
    Thoughts Are Very Deep..................307
Psalm 93: The Lord Reigneth 309
    Contemplation: The Lord Allows and He Restores. . . . 309
Psalm 94: O God, to Whom Vengeance Belongeth,
    Shew Thyself..........................311
Psalm 95: For the Lord Is a Great God, and a King
    above All.............................313
Psalm 96: O Sing unto the Lord a New Song: Sing
    unto the Lord 315
    Study: Sing a New Song 316
Psalm 97: The Lord Reigneth 320
Psalm 98: The Lord Hath Made Known His Salvation. . . . 322
Psalm 99: Let Them Praise Thy Great and Terrible
    Name; for It Is Holy 326
    Study: Holiness 326
Psalm 100: It Is He Hath Made Us................330
Psalm 101: I Will Behave Myself Wisely in a Perfect Way. 332
    Worksheet: Examination of Our Relationships.......334
Psalm 102: Hide Not Thy Face from Me in the Day
    When I Am in Trouble 336
Psalm 103: The Lord Is Merciful and Gracious,
    Slow to Anger, and Plenteous in Mercy 340
    Study: So, Why Does God Show Mercy toward
        His Children? 342
Psalm 104: O Lord, How Manifold Are Thy Works!*......345
Psalm 105: He Is the Lord Our God: His Judgments
    Are in All the Earth 350
Psalm 106: Many Times Did He Deliver Them 355
    The Biblical Cycle of God's Mercy, Grace, and
        Redemption......................359
Psalm 107: He Sent His Word, and Healed Them,
    and Delivered Them from Their Destructions 360
    The Biblical Cycle of Satan's Destruction and
        Everlasting Death 363
Psalm 108: Give Us Help from Trouble; for Vain

Is the Help of Man 366
    Worksheet: God's Perfect Justice in My Own Life 368
Psalm 109: He Shall Be Judged. 369
Psalm 110: Sit Thou at My Right Hand 373
    Study: The Messiah 374
Psalm 111: I Will Praise the Lord with My Whole Heart . 379
    Worksheet: Psalm 111 and Verse 10 381
Psalm 112: Blessed Is He That Delighteth Greatly
    in His Commandments. 382
Psalm 113: He Raiseth up the Poor Out of the Dust 384
Psalm 114: Tremble, Thou Earth, at the Presence
    of the Lord 387
    Study: The Lord Dwells among His People 387
Psalm 115: Not unto Us, O Lord, but unto Thy
    Name Give Glory 391
Psalm 116: I Was Brought Low, and He Helped Me 394
Psalm 117: For His Merciful Kindness Is Great
    toward Us 397
    Study: Mercy. 397
Psalm 118: This Is the Day Which the Lord Hath Made . . 400
    Study: Jesus as the Mercy of God 402
Psalm 119: How to Remain Righteous in an Unrighteous
    World 405
    Highlights: The Precepts Contained in Psalm 119 413
Psalm 120: I Am for Peace: But When I Speak, They
    Are for War 415
Psalm 121: The Lord Is Thy Keeper …He Shall Preserve
    Thy Soul 417
Psalm 122: Our Feet Shall Stand within Thy Gates,
    O Jerusalem. 419
    Study: Jerusalem 419
Psalm 123: So Our Eyes Wait upon the Lord Our God. . . 424
    Worksheet: Give It to the Lord and Let It Go 425
Psalm 124: Blessed Be the Lord, Who Hath Not
    Given Us as a Prey. 427
    Worksheet: Times When We Were Delivered from

Becoming Someone's Prey 428
Psalm 125: Do Good, O Lord, unto Those That Be Good . 430
Psalm 126: They That Sow in Tears Shall Reap in Joy 432
Psalm 127: The Fruit of the Womb Is His Reward 434
Psalm 128: Blessed Is Every One That Feareth the Lord . . 437
   Study: God's Purpose for Israel Was Multifaceted 438
Psalm 129: Many a Time Have They Afflicted Me
   from My Youth 439
   Worksheet: Affliction 440
Psalm 130: If Thou, Lord, Shouldest Mark Iniquities,
   O Lord, Who Shall Stand? 442
Psalm 131: Lord, My Heart Is Not Haughty, Nor
   My Eyes Lofty. 444
Psalm 132: Lord, Remember David, and All His
   Afflictions 446
Psalm 133: It Is Good to Dwell Together in
   Brotherly Unity 449
Psalm 134: Behold, Bless Ye the Lord, All Ye Servants
   of the Lord 451
Psalm 135: For the Lord Will Judge His People,
   and He Will Repent Himself Concerning
   His Servants 453
Psalm 136: For His Mercy Endureth Forever 456
   Worksheet: God's Mercy in My Life. 459
Psalm 137: By the Rivers of Babylon, There We
   Sat Down. 461
   Study: Brief Biblical History of Babylon. 462
Psalm 138: The Lord Will Perfect That Which
   Concerneth Me 464
Psalm 139: O Lord, Thou Hast Searched Me, and
   Known Me 466
   Study: How Does the Lord Search and Know Us? 468
Psalm 140: Deliver me, O Lord, from the Evil Man 471
Psalm 141: Incline Not My Heart to Any Evil Thing 474
Psalm 142: No Man Cared for My Soul 477
Psalm 143: Cause Me to Know the Way Wherein

  I Should Walk 479
Psalm 144: How to Separate from Strange Children 481
  Worksheet: How Has God Encouraged You in
    Your Own Life? 484
Psalm 145: A Psalm of Praise 486
Psalm 146: The Lord Loveth the Righteous…but the
  Way of the Wicked He Turneth Upside Down. 489
  Study: Who Are the Wicked and What Do They Do? . 490
Psalm 147: Praise Ye the Lord, for It Is Good to
  Sing Praises unto Our Lord! 493
Psalm 148: Praise Ye the Lord. Praise Ye the Lord
  from the Heavens: Praise Him in the Heights 496
Psalm 149: Sing unto the Lord a New Song! 499
  Study: Vengeance. 501
Psalm 150: Let Every Thing That Hath Breath Praise the
  Lord. 503
  List All the Wonderful Things of God 504
  Contemplation: Praise of All Things Created 506

Introduction

It is well known and understood that the Proverbs contain practical wisdom for people of faith to learn and use in their everyday lives. In fact, chapter one of the Proverbs sets out with the clear purpose of the book in verses 1–7,

> The proverbs of Solomon the son of David, king of Israel; To know wisdom and instruction; to perceive the words of understanding; To receive the instruction of wisdom, justice, and judgment, and equity; To give subtilty to the simple, to the young man knowledge and discretion. A wise man will hear, and will increase learning; and a man of understanding shall attain unto wise counsels: To understand a proverb, and the interpretation; the words of the wise, and their dark sayings. The fear of the Lord is the beginning of knowledge: but fools despise wisdom and instruction.

As a reader, we can read the purpose of Proverbs from the very first verses and can begin to focus our minds on the direction of discussing biblical wisdom and what that means. For someone who is new to the book of Proverbs or is reading them again after some time, this setup is very helpful.

The book of Psalms, on the other hand, does not give the reader the same overarching introductory verses. In Psalm one, as we will see, we are introduced to the "two ways," which can be summed up as follows in verse 6, "For the LORD knoweth the way of the righteous: but the way of the ungodly shall perish."

In a way, that sounds foreboding and a little intimidating, especially to the less seasoned faithful and those who are just starting on their journey in faith. The Lord knows who follows His ways and who does not. And those who do not follow His ways will perish. *Bum bum bum…*(cue a mighty drum roll).

Fear not! As we make our way through the Psalms, we are going to see that, as scary as that might seem, it is very good information to know. It is also just one facet of the Psalms that is discussed along with a whole host of other topics and issues. As someone who has studied the Psalms, I can say firsthand that we are about to embark on the most interesting and thrilling roller coaster of knowledge in, dare I say, the entire biblical canon.

You see, the Psalms contain the ways and means of faith. Getting it. Practicing it. Staying in it even when times are hard.

Whether you are just starting on your journey or going through a difficult period and are curious about how faith can help, or maybe you are a lifelong believer and love the Psalms. Wherever you are right now in relationship to faith, we are about to explore how faith is practiced practically both from man to God and God toward man. As we will see throughout the Psalms, it is a two-way street.

In this book, we are going to discuss and contemplate the foundations of faith. We are going to look closely at our own lives, contemplate where we fit in right now, and explore areas of faith that are helpful to get through good times and bad. We are going to discuss how and why we praise God and why He is so merciful and kind. Ultimately, however, we are going to learn how to stay in faith as we make our way up the good path to heaven and everlasting life.

Come, let's take a journey through the Psalms and enjoy the fruit of the wisdom and knowledge they contain so that we may prepare ourselves for life in faith with the creator of all things, our Father in heaven.

Psalm 1: The Two Ways—the Blessed and the Ungodly

> Blessed is the man that walketh not in the counsel of the ungodly, nor standeth in the way of sinners, nor sitteth in the seat of the scornful. But his delight is in the law of the LORD; and in his law doth he meditate day and night. And he shall be like a tree planted by the rivers of water, that bringeth forth his fruit in his season; his leaf also shall not wither; and whatsoever he doeth shall prosper. The ungodly are not so: but are like the chaff which the wind driveth away. Therefore, the ungodly shall not stand in judgment, nor sinners in the congregation of the righteous. For the LORD knoweth the way of the righteous: but the way of the ungodly shall perish.

Here, we see that the first Psalm, right out of the gate, compares those who are blessed with those who are ungodly. It is apparent that this concept is an important one in the Psalms because we need to know right away that there are distinguishing characteristics between those whom God blesses and those who are ungodly.

In Psalm 1, we see that we are blessed when:

1. We do not take counsel from the ungodly.
2. We do not have sinful ways like those who are on a sinful path.
3. We do not keep company and sit with those who are mocking or expressing contempt for others.
4. We follow God's laws.
5. We think carefully about His law day and night.

When we live in this way:

1. We are a delight to the Lord.

2. We will be like a fruit tree that sits on a riverbank, bearing an abundance of the best quality and most healthy fruit.
3. We will not wither.
4. Whatsoever we do will prosper.

However, when we are ungodly and live in an opposite way than above, it is a different story.

1. The fruit of our lives will be fleeting like chaff, which the wind drives away.
2. We will not stand within the judgment or counsel of the righteous.
3. We will not be where the righteous come together.

For the Lord knows and is familiar with the ways of the righteous, but He also knows and is familiar with how the ungodly perish.

Second Chronicles 19:2 further illustrates the biblical sentiments of the ungodly,

> And Jehu the son of Hanani the seer went out to meet him, and said to king Jehoshaphat, Shouldest thou help the ungodly, and love them that hate the LORD? therefore is wrath upon thee from before the LORD.

Unlike the blessed, the ungodly hate the Lord. An important point to remember as we make our way through the Psalms.

Worksheet: Examination of Your Own Spiritual Nature

Take time to consider your interior spiritual health at this time and make a list of those things within you that you feel are part of your blessed nature and those that may be part of your ungodly nature. It is good to be able to take a true account of our souls. Knowing your true self will be very helpful as we make our way through the rest of the Psalms. As you learn more, come back here, revisit these lists, and make edits or add to them.

My Blessed Nature

_____

_____

_____

_____

_____

_____

My Ungodly Nature

_____

_____

_____

_____

_____

_____

Notes:

Psalm 2: Blessed Are They Who Trust in the Lord

Why do the heathen rage, and the people imagine a vain thing? The kings of the earth set themselves, and the rulers take counsel together, against the LORD, and against his anointed, saying, Let us break their bands asunder, and cast away their cords from us. He that sitteth in the heavens shall laugh: the Lord shall have them in derision. Then shall he speak unto them in his wrath, and vex them in his sore displeasure. Yet have I set my king upon my holy hill of Zion. I will declare the decree: the LORD hath said unto me, Thou art my Son; this day have I begotten thee. Ask of me, and I shall give thee the heathen for thine inheritance, and the uttermost parts of the earth for thy possession. Thou shalt break them with a rod of iron; thou shalt dash them in pieces like a potter's vessel. Be wise now therefore, O ye kings: be instructed, ye judges of the earth. Serve the LORD with fear, and rejoice with trembling. Kiss the Son, lest he be angry, and ye perish from the way, when his wrath is kindled but a little. Blessed are all those that put their trust in him.

On one level, in Psalm 2, David is ruminating about the vanity of those who worship false idols, which is mainly what a heathen is in the Bible. Even the most powerful rulers congregate and conspire against the Lord and His anointed to devise a plan to cast them out of their kingdoms.

To David, this is a foolish endeavor because God is in charge, and He laughs at the plans of the powerful of this earth. In fact, at the end of the day, all David must do is ask, and it will be God who will vex the heathen. In His displeasure, the Lord will take all the land of the heathens to become the inheritance of His children, even those plots of land in faraway places. God is that powerful.

In the end, Psalm 2 becomes good counsel and a warning to all to be wise and to serve the Lord with fear and rejoice with trembling, lest He uses even a little of His wrath to push His children off His path. Instead, blessed are those who trust in the Lord.

On another level, Psalm 2 could be foreshadowing the life of Christ Jesus, the Son of God. Here we see David using very similar language as we see when the apostles discuss Jesus' life in the Gospels.

Psalm 2:7, "I will declare the decree: the LORD hath said unto me, Thou art my Son; this day have I begotten thee."

One cannot help but hear the words of John when describing the Son of God, Jesus Christ, "For God so loved the world, that he gave his only begotten Son, that whosoever believeth in him should not perish, but have everlasting life" (John 3:16).

And then here again in Psalm 2:12, "Kiss the Son, lest he be angry, and ye perish from the way, when his wrath is kindled but a little. Blessed are all those that put their trust in him."

One cannot help but read that the "him" we should put our trust in is the very same Son whose wrath can be kindled. It's pretty obvious that this verse is speaking about the Son of God, Christ Jesus, but you can be the judge of that for yourself.

Psalm 2 becomes a sort of cross-section between David, a son of God, and Jesus, *the* Son of God. Both are true and whole in themselves. It is as if we are to recognize within our faith that Christ was always with us, even in the Psalms of David, and we are presented with this revelation at the beginning of the book of Psalms to prepare for future reference.

Thank You, Lord, for reminding us that God is a powerful and everlasting God as we begin our journey into the faith that the Psalms reveal. Praise and glory to You!

Psalm 3: For the Lord Sustained Me

> LORD, how have they increased that trouble me! many are they that rise up against me. Many there be which say of my soul, There is no help for him in God. Selah. But thou, O LORD, art a shield for me; my glory, and the lifter up of mine head. I cried unto the LORD with my voice, and he heard me out of his holy hill. Selah. I laid me down and slept; I awaked; for the LORD sustained me. I will not be afraid of ten thousand people, that have set themselves against me round about. Arise, O LORD; save me, O my God: for thou hast smitten all mine enemies upon the cheek bone; thou hast broken the teeth of the ungodly. Salvation belongeth unto the LORD: thy blessing is upon thy people. Selah.

We have all had those moments in our lives where we have felt attacked by those people or circumstances that would harm us. There is an energy of anxiety and fear that accompanies these moments. Sometimes, we find out later that the real enemy was in the fearful and anxious thoughts we obsessed with and that there was no real basis for these feelings. Sometimes, reality revealed that our thoughts had a foundation, and it was wise for us to ponder such things. Psalm 3 begins to look at how faith moves within us to move through these anxious and trying times.

What does David do in this Psalm?

1. David prays to God about his enemies rather than taking matters into his own hands.
2. He trusts that God will protect and sustain him throughout his troubles.
3. He counts on God's blessings.
4. These acts show that David is acting in a righteous, humble, and patient manner, which is a definition of meekness.

Study: What Is Meekness?

Meekness is such an important theme to explore, for it is written about throughout the Bible, both in the Old and New Testaments:

Old Testament

1. Moses was meek. Meeker than any other man upon the face of the earth. This is why God chose him (Numbers 12:3).
2. The Psalms:
    a. People who are meek shall eat and be satisfied; they praise the Lord; their heart shall live forever (22:26).
    b. The meek will He guide in judgment; the meek will He teach His way (25:9).
    c. The meek shall inherit the earth and delight themselves in an abundance of peace (37:11).
    d. "For the LORD taketh pleasure in his people; he will beautify the meek with salvation" (149:4).
3. Isaiah:
    a. "The meek also shall increase their joy in the LORD" (29:19).
    b. The Lord will preach good tidings to the meek (61:1).

New Testament

1. Blessed are the meek, so they shall inherit the earth (Matthew 5:5).
2. Jesus is meek and lowly, and we can find rest in our souls. His yoke is easy, and His burden light (Matthew 11:29).
3. "But let it be the hidden man of the heart, in that which is not corruptible, even the ornament of a meek and quiet spirit, which is in the sight of God of great price" (1 Peter 3:4).

In conclusion, meekness is quiet strength in faith.

1. The meek are incorruptible.
2. The meek are teachable.
3. The meek, when they rule, bring peace.
4. Salvation shows in the beauty of the meek.
5. The meek will find more and more joy in the Lord.
6. The Lord will bring the meek into a peaceful place when He greets them.
7. To be meek is to be like Jesus.
8. It is a place of refreshment and a light burden.
9. It is a pleasure to God.

(Thank You.)

The world would have us believe that to be meek is to be weak. Do not believe it. Meekness has a quiet power that cannot be overcome. In fact, it is so necessary that it is a basic requirement of faith. As our faith deepens, we find ourselves becoming more and more meek and less arrogant and self-serving. Meekness is a gift from the Most High, for it is to become more like Him, and that pleases our Father.

Thank You, Father, for You are the Most High! Teach us Your ways in faith. Amen.

Psalm 4: Put Your Trust in the Lord

> Hear me when I call, O God of my righteousness: thou hast enlarged me when I was in distress; have mercy upon me, and hear my prayer. O ye sons of men, how long will ye turn my glory into shame? how long will ye love vanity, and seek after leasing? Selah. But know that the LORD hath set apart him that is godly for himself: the LORD will hear when I call unto him. Stand in awe, and sin not: commune with your own heart upon your bed, and be still. Selah. Offer the sacrifices of righteousness, and put your trust in the LORD. There be many that say, Who will shew us any good? LORD, lift thou up the light of thy countenance upon us. Thou hast put gladness in my heart, more than in the time that their corn and their wine increased. I will both lay me down in peace, and sleep: for thou, LORD, only makest me dwell in safety.

"Put your trust in the Lord."

Psalm 4 drives home the trust message of Psalms 2 even further, for though it is an easy thing to understand, "Trust in the Lord" is not an easy thing to do for many, many reasons. But it is a common theme, especially in the beginning chapters of the Psalms, because it is necessary to trust the Lord if we are to have an authentic faith in Him.

Consider this: can a person have an authentic relationship with another person if there is no authentic trust in that person? The very same concept applies to having an authentic relationship with God and even more so because He is not of this world and comes to us spiritually most times. Trust is a common sentiment within the Old Testament and the New Testament alike because it is among the most important factors of having real faith in the Lord.

Trust is certainly necessary for maneuvering the righteous path that a life with God will put us on. As Proverbs 28:26 so succinctly puts it, "He that trusteth in his own heart is a fool." The human heart is easily distracted, manipulated, overindulgent, and just plain wrong on so many occasions. Conversely, God never changes. What He says now was true at the beginning of creation and will be true at the end of all time. Trusting Him is a sure thing. He won't ever steer us wrong.

Are you ready to deepen your faith by trusting the Lord with your life?

Psalm 5: The Lord Wilt Bless the Righteous

Give ear to my words, O LORD, consider my meditation. Hearken unto the voice of my cry, my King, and my God: for unto thee will I pray. My voice shalt thou hear in the morning, O LORD; in the morning will I direct my prayer unto thee, and will look up. For thou art not a God that hath pleasure in wickedness: neither shall evil dwell with thee. The foolish shall not stand in thy sight: thou hatest all workers of iniquity. Thou shalt destroy them that speak leasing: the LORD will abhor the bloody and deceitful man. But as for me, I will come into thy house in the multitude of thy mercy: and in thy fear will I worship toward thy holy temple. [Note: John 2:19, "Jesus answered and said unto them, Destroy this temple, and in three days I will raise it up." He was talking about Himself in terms of being a temple in the same way Psalm 5 refers to God in this verse.] Lead me, O LORD, in thy righteousness because of mine enemies; make thy way straight before my face. For there is no faithfulness in their mouth; their inward part is very wicked; their throat is an open sepulcher; they flatter with their tongue. Destroy thou them, O God; let them fall by their own counsels; cast them out in the multitude of their transgressions; for they have rebelled against thee. But let all those that put their trust in thee rejoice: let them ever shout for joy, because thou defendest them: let them also that love thy name be joyful in thee. For thou, LORD, wilt bless the righteous; with favor wilt thou compass him as with a shield.

Psalm 5 is a blessing for the righteous faithful, but once again, we are presented with more character traits of the wicked and foolish:

1. God has no pleasure in wickedness.
2. Evil will not dwell with God.
3. The foolish will not stand before God.
4. The Lord hates the workers of gross injustice and immorality.
5. God will destroy those who are liars and deceitful.
6. They are the enemies of the righteous.
7. They do not speak of faith.
8. The words they speak are full of death.
9. They are flatterers.
10. They rebel against God.

On the other hand, the righteous:

1. Pray upon waking.
2. Come into the house of the Lord seeking mercy.
3. Worship with a reverential fear of God's holiness.
4. Those who put their trust in God will rejoice.
5. God defends His faithful.
6. Those who love God are joyful in Him.
7. The Lord will bless the righteous.
8. He will surround the righteous with favor.
9. He will protect them.

By examining how the wicked work and what good things will come to those who love God, we can begin to recognize and chisel out those people in our lives who will not support us in faith and, in fact, may seek to keep us on the wrong path. It is good to surround ourselves with faithful people when walking the righteous path.

But, more importantly, knowing the ways of those who are wicked helps us chisel out these traits we may find that exist within our own selves. It is so important that as we make our way in faith, we constantly examine our own will and where our faults lie. We all have them. It is in the nature of man to tend toward behavior that is sinful and offensive to God. There is no shame in admitting our poor behavior and seeking to do better. It is what this life is all about, and it is a lifelong pursuit.

Worksheet: Our Current Daily Habits

Using the lists above, honestly examine your life and write down those traits from both lists that make up your daily habits right now. Do you find yourself rebelling against God in your daily life? Do you feel that God is protecting you? Or do you have any of the other habits and traits of the foolish and the right living? What activities do you pursue? Etc. (It is not uncommon to have traits and activities from both sides).

_____

_____

_____

_____

_____

Now, in a similar fashion, write down the traits of those whom you surround yourself with in daily life.

_____

_____

_____

_____

_____

The most important part of this exercise is to be honest about yourself and others. Also, as you go through the Psalms, try to revisit this page from time to time to see if your daily life is evolving. You might be surprised how your life changes!

Thank You, Lord, for giving us a chance to change our behaviors.

Thank You for your mercy and understanding.

Thank You for blessing and protecting us as we make our way in faith.

Amen.

"I have asked to do God's will, so I must not be surprised when my life moves in a direction I have not anticipated nor understand. Trust in the Lord."

Psalm 6: Have Mercy upon Me, O Lord, for I Am Weak

> O LORD, rebuke me not in thine anger, neither chasten me in thy hot displeasure. Have mercy upon me, O LORD; for I am weak: O LORD, heal me; for my bones are vexed. My soul is also sore and vexed: but thou, O LORD, how long? Return, O LORD, deliver my soul: oh save me for thy mercies' sake. For in death there is no remembrance of thee: in the grave who shall give thee thanks? I am weary with my groaning; all the night make my bed to swim; I water my couch with my tears. Mine eye is consumed because of grief; it waxeth old because of all mine enemies. Depart from me, all ye workers of iniquity; for the LORD hath heard the voice of my weeping. The LORD hath heard my supplication; the LORD will receive my prayer. Let all mine enemies be ashamed and sore vexed: let them return and be ashamed suddenly.

Verse 5, "For in death there is no remembrance of thee: in the grave who shall give thee thanks?"

> Not every one that saith unto me, Lord, Lord, shall enter into the kingdom of heaven; but he that doeth the will of my Father which is in heaven. Many will say to me in that day, Lord, Lord, have we not prophesied in thy name? and in thy name have cast out devils? and in thy name done many wonderful works? And then will I profess unto them, I never knew you: depart from me, ye that work iniquity.
>
> Matthew 7:21–23

In Psalm 6, David is asking for mercy from the Lord. It appears that David is fearing death at his enemies' hands, and he is asking

God's mercy for his own iniquity/sins and asking, instead, that the Lord fill his enemies with shame for their wickedness and the harm they have caused him.

So often, we see our own sins as those things on which the Lord should have mercy. We pray that the Lord overlook our sins and not punish us for them. However, when we are confronted with the sins of people we consider an enemy, we want the full force of God put upon them. Not only do we want them punished, but we want them to be publicly shamed for their evil toward us.

Psalm 6 begins to set up the case for when, many centuries later, Jesus asks us to "forgive so that we may be forgiven" and to "pray for our enemies."

We are our enemies—in many ways. David recognizes his own sinful behavior and, at the same time, is consumed with aggravation at the evil behavior of his enemies.

We must not forget that, from their perspective, our enemies may feel aggrieved by us. Forgiveness covers a multitude of sins. And this is why Psalm 6 is a foreshadowing of Jesus' parable when the people meet Him in death and tell Him of all their good deeds. Jesus responds, "I never knew you." We draw closer to Him in forgiveness and prayer than we do in vain deeds. Thank You, Lord.

Therefore, the absolute heart of being a child of God in faith is that we pray for other people with the same expectation of mercy that we pray for ourselves. The heart of God is pure forgiveness, mercy, and compassion, even for those who harm Him. And this is the same heart that shows up in Christ when He walks this earth. God never changes.

Thank You, Lord, for showing us Your ways so that when we meet You in the afterlife, we may hear You say, "I know you."

Psalm 7: The Lord Shall Judge the People

O LORD my God, in thee do I put my trust: save me from all them that persecute me, and deliver me: Lest he tear my soul like a lion, rending it in pieces, while there is none to deliver. O LORD my God, if I have done this; if there be iniquity in my hands; If I have rewarded evil unto him that was at peace with me; (yea, I have delivered him that without cause is mine enemy:) Let the enemy persecute my soul, and take it; yea, let him tread down my life upon the earth, and lay mine honor in the dust. Selah. Arise, O LORD, in thine anger, lift up thyself because of the rage of mine enemies: and awake for me to the judgment that thou hast commanded. So shall the congregation of the people compass thee about: for their sakes therefore return thou on high. The LORD shall judge the people: judge me, O LORD, according to my righteousness, and according to mine integrity that is in me. Oh let the wickedness of the wicked come to an end; but establish the just: for the righteous God trieth the hearts and reins. My defense is of God, which saveth the upright in heart. God judgeth the righteous, and God is angry with the wicked every day. If he turns not, he will whet his sword; he hath bent his bow, and made it ready. He hath also prepared for him the instruments of death; he ordaineth his arrows against the persecutors. Behold, he travaileth with iniquity, and hath conceived mischief, and brought forth falsehood. He made a pit, and digged it, and is fallen into the ditch which he made. His mischief shall return upon his own head, and his violent dealing shall come down upon his own pate. I will praise the LORD according to his righteousness: and will sing praise to the name of the LORD most high.

Psalm 7 sets up David's prayer with what we discussed in Psalm 6: humbleness in one's own sin and iniquity.

Verses 3–5,

> O LORD my God, if I have done this; if there be iniquity in my hands; If I have rewarded evil unto him that was at peace with me; (yea, I have delivered him that without cause is mine enemy:) Let the enemy persecute my soul, and take it; yea, let him tread down my life upon the earth, and lay mine honor in the dust. Selah.

We see David actively requesting a punishment for himself if he has been unfair to those around him and has treated them as enemies when they only wished him peace. During times of distress, we can easily take our frustrations out on the innocent people around us. Sometimes, we accuse them of dreadful things or speak in anger to them when we are upset. It was wise for David to recognize that this may have been the case. We should always be open to considering that we are the ones who have done wrong in any situation. This is one of the ways of humility. It looks like David is coming to God with a humble heart in Psalm 7.

David also recognizes that God is the judge of all things, and He will judge the righteous and the wicked. It is not up to us to make that call. Consider verses 8–9 and 11,

> The LORD shall judge the people: judge me, O LORD, according to my righteousness, and according to mine integrity that is in me. Oh let the wickedness of the wicked come to an end; but establish the just: for the righteous God trieth the hearts and reins. …God judgeth the righteous, and God is angry with the wicked every day.

As we move forward in faith, it is important to remember to stay humble and recognize that it is God who makes the final judgment on all. In fact, our faith grows through our humble recognition that we, too, need to be judged for our own unrighteous behavior. We will never, ever be truly 100 percent righteous while we walk this earth, and that's okay. As long as we recognize our own shortcomings and work toward correcting them, God will judge us accordingly.

Thank You, Lord, for Your patience as we work on ourselves while we grow in faith.

We wish only to please You, but our nature is fallen and stained with sin while we walk this earth. Help us to become better so we may better serve You. With love and praise. Amen.

Notes:

_____

_____

_____

_____

_____

_____

_____

_____

_____

_____

_____

Psalm 8: Oh Lord, Our Lord, How Excellent Is Thy Name in All the Earth

> O Lord, our Lord, how excellent is thy name in all the earth! who hast set thy glory above the heavens. Out of the mouth of babes and sucklings hast thou ordained strength because of thine enemies, that thou mightest still the enemy and the avenger. When I consider thy heavens, the work of thy fingers, the moon and the stars, which thou hast ordained; What is man, that thou art mindful of him? and the son of man, that thou visitest him? For thou hast made him a little lower than the angels, and hast crowned him with glory and honour. Thou madest him to have dominion over the works of thy hands; thou hast put all things under his feet: All sheep and oxen, yea, and the beasts of the field; The fowl of the air, and the fish of the sea, and whatsoever passeth through the paths of the seas. O Lord our Lord, how excellent is thy name in all the earth!

Psalm 8 begins with praise for the Lord—whose name is excellent throughout the world! God is good, and it is right to give Him praise and glory. But who is man that God should consider him?

Verses 4–5, "What is man, that thou art mindful of him? and the son of man, that thou visitest him? For thou hast made him a little lower than the angels, and hast crowned him with glory and honour."

David asks about the value of man to God and acknowledges that man has been made with glory and honor by the creator. So far in the Psalms, we have learned about how the righteous live and what are the ways of the wicked. We've pondered how we have ungodly ways ourselves and why we should seek God to help us stay in faith and His good ways. We've examined our own hearts for evidence of fear and humility before God. For we are His children, and He is our Father who is above us.

Though it is right to become and stay humble, we must not forget that we were made in the image of God, and He made us a little lower than the angels. It is our inheritance to have dominion upon all things on Earth. We are glorious creations of the King of all things, who is also our heavenly Father, giving us a royal lineage. Our humility comes from knowing that God, whose name is excellent throughout the world, is in charge, but our strength comes from knowing that we are the children of the Most High King!

The enemy of God would love to see us in ruins and full of misery and low esteem. He wants us to think we are worthless and that it is not worth pursuing our God-given talents. And when we do follow where our talents lead us in God's will, the enemy would want us to believe that what we offer is not good enough or of no value.

It is when we understand that God offers us all good things, that it is our rightful inheritance as children of God to receive them, and that He finds pleasure in blessing us and providing for us that we gain confidence in who we are and what we have to offer. After all, the one who created all the beautiful things we see in nature and in the heavens created us. God is the creator of wondrous things and man was created just a little lower than the majestic angels that preside along our Most High Father. Isn't that inspiring?

So, don't let those who are stuck on their dead-end path toward ultimate destruction make you feel bad for being a wonderful creation in the image of God. Every person was created to be crowned with glory and honor alongside the Father. All we need to do is trust in the Lord and give our lives over to Him, putting our feet firmly on the righteous path that leads to heavenly salvation. It is available to every single one of us.

Are you ready to enjoy life as a faithful child of the King of kings and our heavenly Father? Believe it or not, He would like nothing more than to walk beside you. Let's go!

Psalm 9: I Will Shew Forth All Thy Marvelous Works

I will praise thee, O LORD, with my whole heart; I will shew forth all thy marvelous works. I will be glad and rejoice in thee: I will sing praise to thy name, O thou most High. When mine enemies are turned back, they shall fall and perish at thy presence. For thou hast maintained my right and my cause; thou sayest in the throne judging right. Thou hast rebuked the heathen, thou hast destroyed the wicked, thou hast put out their name for ever and ever. O thou enemy, destruction has come to a perpetual end: and thou hast destroyed cities; their memorial is perished with them. But the LORD shall endure for ever: he hath prepared his throne for judgment. And he shall judge the world in righteousness, he shall minister judgment to the people in uprightness. The LORD also will be a refuge for the oppressed, a refuge in times of trouble. And they that know thy name will put their trust in thee: for thou, LORD, hast not forsaken them that seek thee. Sing praises to the LORD, which dwelleth in Zion: declare among the people his doings. When he maketh inquisition for blood, he remembereth them: he forgetteth not the cry of the humble. Have mercy upon me, O LORD; consider my trouble which I suffer of them that hate me, thou that liftest me up from the gates of death: That I may shew forth all thy praise in the gates of the daughter of Zion: I will rejoice in thy salvation. The heathen is sunk down in the pit that they made: in the net which they hid is their own foot taken. The LORD is known by the judgment which he executeth: the wicked is snared in the work of his own hands. Higgaion. Selah. The wicked shall be turned into hell, and all the nations that forget God. For the needy shall not always be forgotten: the expectation of the poor shall not perish for ever. Arise, O LORD; let not man prevail: let the heathen be judged in thy sight. Put them in fear, O LORD: that the nations may know themselves to be but men. Selah.

Let us consider further the wonderful deeds of the Lord, lest we forget all the reasons to sing Him praise and glory! In Psalm 9, David sings again of God's marvelous works:

1. When God is present, the enemies of His children suffer ruin and destruction.
2. From His throne, He always judges righteously.
3. He reprimands the ungodly nations.
4. He destroys the wicked.
5. When He destroys an enemy nation, it comes to a perpetual end. Full stop.
6. The Lord will endure forever.
7. The Lord will never perish.
8. The Lord will continue to judge the world equitably.
9. He shall give the upright, righteous judgment.
10. He is a refuge for the oppressed.
11. He is a refuge in times of trouble.
12. All who truly know Him will put their trust in Him.
13. The Lord has and will not forsake those who trust in Him.
14. He does not forget the cry of the humble.
15. He lifts His children up from the gates of hell.
16. Those who do not believe in Him are sunk into a pit of their own making.
17. Unbelievers make a net for others but are snared in it themselves.
18. The Lord executes excellent judgment.
19. The needy shall not be forgotten.
20. The hope of the poor shall survive.

Over and over, the Psalms reveal the ways of God and present us with His greatness. Considering these things gives us the strength to begin to trust Him and to continue trusting Him even when things seem bleak. If we look at this in a certain manner, we can view knowing about the greatness of God as an actual device of His comfort and grace. It's as if He is saying, "Dear one, you can trust Me. As I have helped those before you, I will help you now. Come follow Me on My good path. It will be okay, I promise."

Perhaps you have come from a place where there was darkness all around you, and now you are not sure what to think or believe. Or maybe you have forgotten the God you once loved and need reminding of His wonderful ways. Maybe you bought into the ways of the world and thought of God as nothing more than a tyrant or an illusion. You may even be firmly on your righteous path and just love thinking about God's amazing works.

Wherever you are right now, God is here for you. He's been here for countless others before you and has proven that His Word is always true. He intends to keep His promise to give you strength and to be your refuge while you make your way down His path toward the everlasting life of salvation.

Will you trust Him?

Psalm 10: Arise, O LORD; Forget Not the Humble

Why standest thou afar off, O LORD? why hidest thou thyself in times of trouble? The wicked in his pride doth persecute the poor: let them be taken in the devices that they have imagined. For the wicked boasteth of his heart's desire, and blesseth the covetous, whom the LORD abhorreth. The wicked, through the pride of his countenance, will not seek after God: God is not in all his thoughts. His ways are always grievous; thy judgments are far above out of his sight: as for all his enemies, he puffeth at them. He hath said in his heart, I shall not be moved: for I shall never be in adversity. His mouth is full of cursing and deceit and fraud: under his tongue is mischief and vanity. He sitteth in the lurking places of the villages: in the secret places doth he murder the innocent: his eyes are privily set against the poor. He lieth in wait secretly as a lion in his den: he lieth in wait to catch the poor: he doth catch the poor, when he draweth him into his net. He croucheth, and humbleth himself, that the poor may fall by his strong ones. He hath said in his heart, God hath forgotten: he hideth his face; he will never see it. Arise, O LORD; O God, lift up thine hand: forget not the humble. Wherefore doth the wicked contempt God? he hath said in his heart, Thou wilt not require it. Thou hast seen it; for thou beholdest mischief and spite, to requite it with thy hand: the poor committeth himself unto thee; thou art the helper of the fatherless. Break thou the arm of the wicked and the evil man: seek out his wickedness till thou find none. The LORD is King for ever and ever: the heathen perished out of his land. LORD, thou hast heard the desire of the humble: thou wilt prepare their heart, thou wilt cause thine ear to hear: To judge the fatherless and the oppressed, that the man of the earth may no more oppress.

Psalm 10 lays out the miserable and contemptful ways of those who target the poor and those whom they see as lower than them. These are the people who:

1. In their vain pride, they imagine schemes that trap and persecute the poor.
2. They boast of their heart's desires and glorify the selfish and greedy.
3. In their vanity, they do not seek after God, and it shows in the prideful look on their faces.
4. They move through life without considering God in all their actions.
5. Their ways are always dishonorable.
6. In their low places, they cannot see God's ways, which are far above them.
7. They stand puffed up and proud in front of their enemies.
8. They harden their hearts in their ways because they do not think they will ever suffer.
9. They curse people.
10. They are deceivers and frauds.
11. Mischief and vanity are behind all they speak.
12. They hide in the shadows, lurking to murder the innocent.
13. They lie in wait to catch the poor to draw them into their net.
14. Their eyes are set against the poor.
15. They pretend to be low and humble to catch the poor.
16. They hide their faces and think God has forgotten them and will never see their ways.

This world is so filled with prideful, boastful people who seek to oppress and persecute the poor and poor in spirit. Many people have been ensnared by the reckless people who commit crimes against or oppress the innocent, impoverished, and poor at heart. And these actions create times of trouble in the lives of the victims and oppressed.

Psalm 10:1 asks, "Why standest thou afar off, O LORD? why hidest thou thyself in times of trouble?"

We all know what it means to be poor. It means to be living in a state of material poverty and all the emotional and psychological anxiety and desperation that entails. Poverty is deeply humbling for a person to live through. To be poor in spirit means to be humble as well by acknowledging our sins before God and recognizing that we need His mercy! The humble do not place themselves above others.

When times of trouble come to the poor and poor in spirit at the hands of the wicked in the ways it does in Psalm 10, it can feel like God has abandoned us and does not hear us in our afflictions and oppression. But we can be assured that "LORD, thou hast heard the desire of the humble" because He sees the mischief and spite of the oppressors. He also sees that His poor children have committed to and believe in Him. He will help us in our times of need.

"Thou wilt prepare their heart, thou wilt cause thine ear to hear."

Thank You, Lord. I trust in You to help me in my day of trouble. Praise and glory to You!

Psalm 11: For the Lord Trieth the Righteous

> In the LORD put in my trust: how say ye to my soul, Flee as a bird to your mountain? For, lo, the wicked bend their bow, they make ready their arrow upon the string, that they may privily shoot at the upright in heart. If the foundations are destroyed, what can the righteous do? The LORD is in his holy temple, the LORD'S throne is in heaven: his eyes behold, his eyelids try, the children of men. The LORD trieth the righteous: but the wicked and him that loveth violence his soul hateth. Upon the wicked he shall rain snares, fire and brimstone, and an horrible tempest: this shall be the portion of their cup. For the righteous LORD loveth righteousness; his countenance doth behold the upright.

Psalm 11 is very clear about how the Lord deals with the righteous and what the wicked can expect. In this way, we can see the distinct differences that separate the two camps in the sight of our Father. Sometimes, it is hard to see God's hand in a circumstance, and in our lack of understanding, we can falsely assume we are being punished for being wicked when, in fact, we are being tried in our faith.

God sees all things—even into the heart of man—from His throne. God is not one to be duped by anyone. So, when a season of hardship comes into our lives, it is prudent to search our own hearts. Are we making an effort not to offend God in our actions, or when we do, are we quick to repent? Is this hardship helping us to overcome obstacles or weak convictions in our lives? Do we trust in God? Throughout the Bible, God has tried the faith of men so He, as well as ourselves, can test the strength of our faith.

Consider one of the most famous examples of this:

Genesis 22: The offering of Abraham's son in burnt offering on the Mount.

> And it came to pass after these things, that God did tempt Abraham, and said unto him, Abraham: and he said, Behold, here I am. And he said, Take now thy son, thine only son Isaac, whom thou lovest, and get thee into the land of Moriah; and offer him there for a burnt offering upon one of the mountains which I will tell thee of. …And they came to the place which God had told him of; and Abraham built an altar there, and laid the wood in order, and bound Isaac his son, and laid him on the altar upon the wood. And Abraham stretched forth his hand, and took the knife to slay his son. … [Then God stopped Abraham and] saith the LORD, for because thou hast done this thing, and hast not withheld thy son, thine only son: …I will bless thee."
>
> Genesis 22:1–2, 9–10, 16–17

Being tried by God is not easy to go through, and many times, when a particularly difficult trial comes into our lives, our imperfect nature blames God for being mean to us, and we can become angry or, worse, turn away from the God we loved during good times. But, remember, the Lord trieth the righteous because He loves us.

1. James 1:12, "Blessed is the man that endureth temptation: for when he is tried, he shall receive the crown of life, which the Lord hath promised to him that love him."
2. And again, in Hebrews 2:18, God Himself tried even the most righteous, His Son, Jesus Christ, "For in that he himself hath suffered being tempted, he is able to succour them that are tempted."

God the Father tried His own Son so Christ would know firsthand how to assist and support in hardship and distress. Why?

Because He loves us.

As for the wicked, "He shall rain snares, fire and brimstone, and an horrible tempest: this shall be the portion of their cup."

There is a difference in outcomes for those who love God and trust in Him and those who don't. Even in times of trouble, lean into and trust the Lord, and He will bring blessings at the end of it.

Worksheet: Life's Hardships

Perhaps now is a good time to contemplate and list a few of the times when hardship came your way and how you dealt with it in the past. Consider how you could have done things differently.

(Example: My family member said something that hurt me. I stopped talking to them for years.)

_____

_____

_____

_____

_____

_____

_____

_____

_____

_____

_____

Now, list those hardships you are currently going through and vow to trust the Lord to help you through them. Come back later and write down the results of the situation you trusted God to help you overcome. What happened this time?

Notes:

Psalm 12: The Words of the Lord Are Pure Words

> Help, LORD; for the godly man ceaseth; for the faithful fail from among the children of men. They speak in vanity to every one with his neighbour: with flattering lips and with a double heart do they speak. The LORD shall cut off all flattering lips, and the tongue that speaketh proud things: Who has said, With our tongue will we prevail; our lips are our own: who is lord over us? For the oppression of the poor, for the sighing of the needy, now will I arise, saith the LORD; I will set him in safety from him that puffeth at him. The words of the LORD are pure words: as silver tried in a furnace of earth, purified seven times. Thou shalt keep them, O LORD, thou shalt preserve them from this generation for ever. The wicked walk on every side, when the vilest men are exalted.

Psalm 12 is lamenting about how the godly are ceasing and how the flatterers and double-hearted are all around. But God knows everything. It is vanity to think our humble knowledge is anything but a speck in the eye of God. Let God/Holy Spirit speak His knowledge into us.

That is real knowledge: Humble knowing through the Holy Spirit (aka, discernment).

In case we need to be reminded of the validity, truthfulness, and power behind the Word of God, here are a few verses from within the Bible:

1. God's Word is perfect. His Word is tried and true; He protects those who trust Him (Psalm 18:30).
2. God's Word is pure; His servants love His Word (Psalm

119:140).
3. Every word of God is pure. He is a shield unto him who trusts in the Lord (Proverbs 30:5).
4. "The words of the LORD are pure words: as silver tried in a furnace of earth, purified seven times" (Psalm 12:6).
5. "And the Word was made flesh, and dwelt among us, (and we beheld his glory, the glory as of the only begotten of the Father,) full of grace and truth" (John 1:14).

In other words, God's Word is pure. He never lies. What He said yesterday is true today and forever. His Word is like a shield to those who trust in Him. They will protect us. Sometimes, we just need to be reminded that our Father will always be true to His word. It is up to us to be patient while we wait for what He has promised to bear fruit.

While I was contemplating this psalm, I was moved by the Holy Spirit to remember that a loving parent would not lie to their child. Those parents make it very clear that their child is loved and that their needs will be taken care of while the child is living with them. It is difficult for some of us to fathom what it feels like to be in the care of a parent who gains pleasure in caring for and supporting us. Some of us have had the opposite type of parent: selfish and abusive. And it makes trusting the Father very difficult, even now.

Children of conscientious parents tend to feel secure in knowing that they will be taken care of most times without even asking. Try to imagine how that feels if you can. It feels safe, doesn't it?

The point is that if the best human parents can show compassion and reassurance to their children, surely you must realize that the Father of all fathers, whose words are pure and perfect truth, will do this and more for His children. You can trust His Word: He will be there for you while you walk the path with Him.

Thank You, Father, for reassuring us when we may have doubts.

Thank You for continuing to tell us about and show us Your support and loving mercy and grace.

Thank You for being the best Abba a child could ever have! Amen.

Psalm 13: I Will Sing unto the Lord because He Hath Dealt Bountifully with Me

> How long wilt thou forget me, O LORD? for ever? how long wilt thou hide thy face from me? How long shall I take counsel in my soul, having sorrow in my heart daily? how long shall mine enemy be exalted over me? Consider and hear me, O LORD my God: lighten mine eyes, lest I sleep the sleep of death; Lest mine enemy say, I have prevailed against him; and those that trouble me rejoice when I am moved. But I have trusted in thy mercy; my heart shall rejoice in thy salvation. I will sing unto the LORD, because he hath dealt bountifully with me.

In Psalm 13, verse 1, David sings, "How long wilt thou forget me, O LORD? for ever? how long wilt thou hide thy face from me?"

Before the Holy Spirit indwelt in humans, God came to His people from without through prayer, sacrifice, fasting, prophets, and supernatural events. Consequently, until Jesus, the Son of God, came onto the earth and sent down the Holy Spirit to dwell within us, the faithful of God carried a deep longing within their very being. Before Jesus and the Pentecost, man ached for God's love internally.

One of the major ways for the chosen people to communicate with God before we were presented with the Holy Spirit was through sacrifice. There are many examples of sacrifice that can be found throughout the Bible. Let us examine the biblical role of sacrifice. What did sacrifice accomplish and how in the Bible?

Study: The Role of Sacrifice

God required animal sacrifices in the Old Testament because there needed to be a way to demonstrate the severity of sin, the cost of rebellion against God, the death that sin brings, and the cost that must be paid to be redeemed. There is no doubt that a sacrifice for sin was necessary if people were to have any hope of eternal life. God established the necessity of the shedding of blood to cover sin.

Hebrews 9:22, "And almost all things are by the law purged with blood; and without shedding of blood is no remission."

In fact, God Himself performed the very first animal sacrifice to cover, temporarily, the sin of Adam and Eve when He slaughtered a beast to provide clothing for the two after the first sin.

Genesis 3:21, "Unto Adam also and to his wife did the LORD God make coats of skins, and clothed them."

Sacrifice was an act of atonement, a symbolic reckoning with God. The animals served as a kind of placeholder while people waited for the true Messiah to come and for the true sacrifice to be offered.

When finally, the Lord, once again, presented His own sacrifice in the body of His Son on the cross, He did so to make final atonement for sin, going back to the original sin of Adam and Eve. It could be imagined that the crucifixion of Jesus Christ on the cross worked in the following way to pay the price of sin: past, present, and future.

1. The human heart is the center of all pain and emotion.
2. The heart is the arbiter of blood.
3. Blood contains life force.
4. Sacrifice releases the life force.
5. Only by shedding His blood was Jesus able to release the full life force of God onto the world, which immediately began cleansing the world of all sin and allowed the Holy

Spirit to enter.
6. The blood of Christ was the pouring out of God Himself onto this world in a meaningful and tangible way. Anything less would have only been symbolic. God came to us through the blood of Jesus.

In that act, the Lord that lived without and dwelt among His people now became the Lord that dwelt inside His people through the Holy Spirit. This is our natural disposition as beings made in the image of God: to have access to Him from within. By following the right path, we can keep the flame of God burning brightly within us with all the fruits of the Spirit available. But the Lord will hide Himself within the spirit of the ungodly. Our spiritual environment is a very important factor in how powerful the Father displays Himself to us. Glory and praise to You. Amen.

Thank You, Lord, for giving us the opportunity to have You live within us. We ask that You help us in our holiness so that You may always burn brightly within our spirit.

Psalm 14: God Is in the Generation of the Righteous

> The fool hath said in his heart, There is no God. They are corrupt, they have done abominable works, there is none that doeth good. The LORD looked down from heaven upon the children of men, to see if there were any that did understand, and seek God. They are all gone aside, they are all together become filthy: there is none that doeth good, no, not one. Have all the workers of iniquity no knowledge? who eat up my people as they eat bread, and call not upon the LORD. There were they in great fear: for God is in the generation of the righteous. Ye have shamed the counsel of the poor, because the LORD is his refuge. Oh that the salvation of Israel came out of Zion! when the LORD bringeth back the captivity of his people, Jacob shall rejoice, and Israel shall be glad.

Psalm 14 reminds us that we live in an environment of ungodly men. So many of us do not seek God nor follow His ways.

Verse 1, "They are corrupt, they have done abominable works, there is none that doeth good."

Though made in the image of God, many of us have chosen not to seek Him out and, rather, to live outside the way of righteousness (aka, in sin). This is a fallback position for people who refuse to take responsibility for their lives. Sin is the easy way because it feeds upon the desires of our flesh. We give in and go for something we know may be bad for us in the long term for immediate satisfaction. Every person has been there, and most of us have failed to use good judgment at least once or twice in our lives. So, we know and understand the real effects of sin on our bodies and spirits (and many times our finances as well). These activities are a form of rejecting God, causing Him to move away.

Yet, the Lord lives in the generation of the righteous. As a group, we can call God closer through righteous living, praise, and worship. Community can act as the body itself by bringing God in closer, or we can do the opposite, push Him away by rejecting Him. Living amongst us or living away from us. It is our task as the children of God to always seek to bring the Lord nearer, for He is our refuge and a place of protection and refreshment away from the outside, ungodly world.

Where does God live within your world at this time?

Are you drawing Him closer, or do you tend to keep Him at arms' length or further away?

Hear our prayer, O Lord. A generation of good and godly men are being raised right now.

These evil times shall not prosper. We call You closer so that we may take refuge in Your loving Spirit. Thank You, Lord. All praise and honor to You. Amen.

Notes:

_____

_____

_____

_____

_____

_____

_____

Psalm 15: Who Shall Dwell in Thy Holy Hill?

LORD, who shall abide in thy tabernacle? who shall dwell in thy holy hill? He that walketh uprightly, and worketh righteousness, and speaketh the truth in his heart. He that backbiteth not with his tongue, nor doeth evil to his neighbour, nor taketh up a reproach against his neighbour. In whose eyes a vile person is condemned; but he honoureth them that fear the LORD. He that sweareth to his own hurt, and changeth not. He that putteth not put his money to usury, nor taketh reward against the innocent. He that doeth these things shall never be moved.

One of the definitions of "tabernacle" as defined by the Merriam-Webster Dictionary is:

- A house of worship, specifically, a large building or tent used for evangelistic services.
- An older and more archaic definition of "tabernacle" is: A dwelling place.

Both of these definitions seem to make sense for this psalm.

So…who shall abide in thy tabernacle? Who shall dwell in the holy hill? Let us consider what Psalm 15 indicates as an answer:

1. He that walketh upright.
2. Those who work righteously.
3. Those who speak the truth in their heart.
4. The ones who do not speak ill will nor gossip behind people's backs.
5. Those who do not do evil to their neighbor.
6. Those who do not argue with their neighbor.

7. Those who fear the LORD.

From that list, it seems that the righteous, upright, and good neighbors will be the ones who will be dwelling in the holy place.

Study: Fear of the Lord

But just what does it mean to "fear" the Lord? That is one of those terms that makes God sound a little scary. Is God frightening? Psalm 19:9 clarifies this term a bit, "The fear of the LORD is clean, enduring for ever: the judgments of the LORD are true and righteous altogether." So, this type of fear is clean, does not end, and is rooted in righteous judgment.

If we look at the Merriam-Webster Dictionary again, we come across this definition of fear that seems to fit the way it is used in Psalm 15 the most: "to have a reverential awe of." Another word that fits nicely into this category would be "piety," which is defined as a "reverence for God" (Dictionary.com). In other words, "Fear of the Lord," in the broadest sense of the term, means to "have a reverential awe of the Lord." Not scary at all.

Does God Hate?

But what about all the times in the Psalms and throughout the Bible when it states that God "hates" something? How can a loving and kind Father profess "hate" for something or someone?

It is true: God is love. When God is referring to something He "hates," it is that He cuts Himself off. So, when the Lord is referenced as "hating evil," it means removing Himself from those things that are evil, including people.

Since it is not possible for love (which is what God is) to hate—*they are mutually exclusive*—God cuts Himself off from the evil. This is why when it is referenced that the Lord hateth something like iniquity, it means He cuts Himself off from it and the doers of iniquity, which means He does not extend His grace, mercy, and protection toward them.

He will, however, always be available to bring them back into the fold. He will always forgive them up until the time of their death if they ask, have faith, and promise to repent their ways. *A door is locked at death.*

Hear our prayer: The wheat is growing once again in the fields. The weeds are being eradicated, and the fields are, once again, beginning to flourish. The Lord has heard His people, and He has shown us mercy and grace. He hateth us not. Thank You, my Lord. All praise and glory and honor to You!

Notes:

Psalm 16: Preserve Me, O God: For in Thee Do I Put My Trust

Preserve me, O God: for in thee do I put my trust. O my soul, thou hast said unto the LORD, Thou art my Lord: my goodness extendeth not to thee; But to the saints that are in the earth, and to the excellent, in whom is all my delight. Their sorrows shall be multiplied that hasten after another god: their drink offerings of blood will I not offer, nor take up their names into my lips. The LORD is the portion of mine inheritance and of my cup: thou maintainest my lot. The lines have fallen unto me in pleasant places; yea, I have a goodly heritage. I will bless the LORD, who hath given me counsel: my reins also instruct me in the night seasons. I have set the LORD always before me: because he is at my right hand, I shall not be moved. Therefore my heart is glad, and my glory rejoiceth: my flesh also shall rest in hope. For thou wilt not leave my soul in hell; neither wilt thou suffer thine Holy One to see corruption. Thou wilt shew me the path of life: in thy presence is fullness of joy; at thy right hand there are pleasures for evermore.

There is quite a lot going on in Psalm 16. On the surface, it appears to be another illustration of someone who is living a life of trust and faith in God. But there are many themes in this Psalm that continue throughout the book of Psalms.

1. My soul says, Thou art my God.
    a. Our souls know that God exists, and He is there for us on a personal level.
2. My soul is not capable of extending goodness to the Lord but to the saints who are on the earth and to the excellent, which is the delight of my soul.

      a. Because God is all goodness, any goodness we could ever offer to God would not be sufficient.
      b. Instead, our human souls delight when we offer goodness to those on the holy and righteous path, also known as the saints (or aspiring saints) on Earth.
      c. Understanding this is a sign of humility.
3. Because we know that those who hasten after another god shall see their sorrows multiply, when we trust in God:
      a. We will not take up what they offer.
      b. We will not put the names of their gods in our mouths.
4. Though there may be hardship, it falls on us in a pleasant place because we have a good inheritance in God.
      a. God offers to the people who love Him as an inheritance, a soft landing from the hardships of life.
5. The Lord blesses us with good counsel.
      a. The Lord instructs us even during our darkest times.
6. The Lord is at the right hand of those who trust in Him.
      a. Because we have always set the Lord before us.
      b. Therefore, we shall not be moved from our paths.
7. How to know when the Lord is at someone's right hand:
      a. Our heart is glad.
      b. We are rejoiceful.
      c. Our bodies find rest.
      d. We have hope.
      e. We will not be left in hell.
      f. God will not let us be given over to corruption.
      g. We are in the fullness of joy.
      h. There are endless pleasures.

When we dive into the meat of Psalm 16, we are given a wonderful laundry list of reasons why we should trust in God. Will every day be nothing but endless pleasure? Probably not, but God will be there to guide us out of hardship. Our definition of pleasure might even transform to become nearly the opposite of what we considered pleasurable before we gave God our trust.

Once we step onto the right path, God will be seeking to transform us into our most holy selves. The self that feels real joy and rest. The self that no longer seeks or finds pleasure in corruption or those activities that degrade our souls. With God at our right hand and through His grace, there will be a fullness of joy that overcomes us as He leads us to the final place where, indeed, there will be true pleasure evermore.

Trusting in God is a major theme in the Psalms, especially at the beginning of the book. It's as if by the power of the will of our Lord over the writers of the Psalms, He is laying out His offer of faith. "First, trust in Me and have faith, and all these good things will be for you."

So…why not take a chance? Trust in the Lord and begin to transform your life!

It will be so worth it.

Psalm 17: Keep Me on Your Path

Hear the right, O LORD, attend unto my cry, give ear unto my prayer, that goeth not out of feigned lips. Let my sentence come forth from thy presence; let thine eyes behold the things that are equal. Thou hast proved mine heart; thou hast visited me in the night; thou hast tried me, and shalt find nothing; I am purposed that my mouth shall not transgress. Concerning the works of men, by the word of thy lips I have kept me from the paths of the destroyer. Hold up my goings in thy paths, that my footsteps slip not. I have called upon thee, for thou wilt hear me, O God: incline thine ear unto me, and hear my speech. Shew thy marvellous lovingkindness, O thou that savest by thy right hand them which put their trust in thee from those that rise up against them. Keep me as the apple of the eye, hide me under the shadow of thy wings, From the wicked that oppress me, from my deadly enemies, who compass me about. They are enclosed in their own fat: with their mouth they speak proudly. They have now compassed us in our steps: they have set their eyes bowing down to the earth; Like as a lion that is greedy of his prey, and as if it were a young lion lurking in secret places. Arise, O LORD, disappoint him, cast him down: deliver my soul from the wicked, which is thy sword: From men which are thy hand, O LORD, from men of the world, which have their portion in this life, and whose belly thou fillest with thy hid treasure: they are full of children, and leave the rest of their substance to their babes. As for me, I will behold thy face in righteousness: I shall be satisfied, when I awake, with thy likeness.

Psalm 17 is a prayer that recognizes the Lord's path as one of a firm foundation and it is asking the Father to help keep the author from sliding off path.

Verse 5, "Hold up my goings in thy paths, that my footsteps slip not."

At the same time, this psalm is also asking our Father to protect us from the ones who pursue only the things of this world. These are the wicked who, like the lion pursuing their prey, compass the children of God to devour them in greed. But they will have their portion on Earth, which is fleeting. The love and protection of those who trust and glorify the Lord shall have everlasting gifts. Be not afraid and be present in His likeness.

Lord, keep my feet firmly on Your path as I make my way through this life. Your ways are filled with goodness and firm foundations. I will trust You to keep me on the path so that I may walk with You forever. Glory and honor to You, O Lord. Amen.

Notes:

___

___

___

___

___

___

___

___

___

Psalm 18: God Saves Us from Our Enemies

The LORD Is My Rock and My Fortress To the choirmaster. A Psalm of David, the servant of the LORD, who addressed the words of this song to the LORD on the day when the LORD delivered him from the hand of all his enemies, and from the hand of Saul. He said: I love you, O LORD, my strength. The LORD is my rock and my fortress and my deliverer, my God, my rock, in whom I take refuge, my shield, and the horn of my salvation, my stronghold. I call upon the LORD, who is worthy to be praised, and I am saved from my enemies. The cords of death encompassed me; the torrents of destruction assailed me; the cords of Sheol entangled me; the snares of death confronted me. In my distress I called upon the LORD; to my God I cried for help. From his temple he heard my voice, and my cry to him reached his ears. Then the earth reeled and rocked; the foundations also of the mountains trembled and quaked, because he was angry. Smoke went up from his nostrils, and devouring fire from his mouth; glowing coals flamed forth from him. He bowed the heavens and came down; thick darkness was under his feet. He rode on a cherub and flew; he came swiftly on the wings of the wind. He made darkness his covering, his canopy around him, thick clouds dark with water. Out of the brightness before him hailstones and coals of fire broke through his clouds. The LORD also thundered in the heavens, and the Most High uttered his voice, hailstones and coals of fire. And he sent out his arrows and scattered them; he flashed forth lightnings and routed them. Then the channels of the sea were seen, and the foundations of the world were laid bare at your rebuke, O LORD, at the blast of the breath of your nostrils. He sent from on high, he took me; he drew me out of many waters. He rescued me from my strong enemy and from those who hated me, for they were too mighty for me. They confronted me in the day of my calamity, but the LORD was my support. He brought me out into a broad place; he rescued me, because he delighted in me. The LORD dealt with me according to my righteousness; according to the cleanness of my hands he rewarded me. For I have kept the ways of the LORD, and have not wickedly departed from my God. For all his rulesc were before me, and his statutes I did not put away from me. I was blameless before him, and I kept myself from my guilt. So the LORD has rewarded me according to my righteousness, according to the cleanness of my hands in his sight. With the merciful you show yourself merciful; with the blameless man you show yourself blameless; with the purified you show yourself pure; and with the crooked you make yourself seem tortuous. For you save a humble people, but the haughty eyes you bring down. For it is you who light my lamp; the LORD my God lightens my darkness. For by you I can run against a troop, and by my God I can leap over a wall. This God—his way is perfect; the word of the LORD proves true; he is a shield for all those who take refuge in him. For who is God, but the LORD? And who is a rock, except our God?—the God who equipped me with strength and made my way blameless. He made my feet like the feet of a deer and set me secure on the heights. He trains my hands for war, so that my arms can bend a bow of bronze. You have given me the shield of your salvation, and your right hand supported me, and your gentleness made me great. You gave a wide place for my steps under me, and my feet did not slip. I pursued my enemies and overtook them, and did not turn back till they were consumed. I thrust them through, so that they were not able to rise; they fell under my feet. For you equipped me with strength for the battle; you made those who rise against me sink under me. You made my enemies turn their backs to me, and those who hated me I destroyed. They cried for help, but there was none to save; they cried to the LORD, but he did not answer them. I beat them fine as dust before the wind; I cast them out like the mire of the streets. You delivered me from strife with the people; you made me the head of the nations; people whom I had not known served me. As soon as they heard of me they obeyed me; foreigners came cringing to me. Foreigners lost heart and came trembling out of their fortresses. The LORD lives, and blessed be my rock, and exalted be the God of my salvation—the God who gave me vengeance and subdued peoples under me, who rescued me from my enemies; yes, you exalted me above those who rose against me; you delivered me from the man of violence. For this I will praise you, O LORD, among the nations, and sing to your name. Great salvation he brings to his king, and shows steadfast love to his anointed, to David and his offspring forever.

ESV

In Psalm 18, David walks us through the process of how God works to save us from those who do not wish us well in our lives. Here, David calls them his enemies. In many ways, David is presented as a prime example of a child of God and we can look to how God and David worked together as an example of how God will work in our own lives. We can imagine that God speaking through His servant David in the Psalms is speaking directly to us. This is how the Bible works as the living Word. So, what general things do we know about David?

1. David was wise in the sight of the Lord.
    a. "And David behaved himself wisely in all his ways; and the LORD was with him" (1 Samuel 18:14).
2. Saul was his enemy.
    a. Saul was chosen to be the first king of Israel.
    b. He recognized that God was with David, and it turned Saul into David's chief enemy.
    c. "And Saul was yet the more afraid of David; and Saul became David's enemy continually" (1 Samuel 18:29).

So, we can see that because Saul recognized God was with David, Saul committed to be the enemy of David. And such is the case in this life. The children who love God put their trust in Him, and with whom God dwells become the enemies of those who are afraid of the power of God. They would prefer that we are weak and not supported by God, even if they don't consciously realize it.

There are people in our lives, some whom we call friends and family, who may hide that they wish to harm us. There are others who do not live godly lives, who unwittingly harm us through their ungodly ways. In other words, not all enemies are like Saul to David and call themselves out as an enemy.

Because this is the case, it is up to us to be wise and to use discernment in who we choose to keep near us. This is a concept we should continuously renew within our lives.

So, according to Psalm 18, what does David do when he is presented with an enemy, and how does God respond?

1. *David calls upon the Lord to help him*: Verse 3 (ESV), "I call upon the LORD, who is worthy to be praised, and I am saved from my enemies."
2. *God hears his prayer*: Verse 6 (ESV), "In my distress I called upon the LORD; to my God I cried for help. From his temple he heard my voice, and my cry to him reached his ears."
3. God prepares the battlefield to defeat the enemy.

a. The earth shook.
   b. The fire of wrath came upon the earth.
   c. He compassed the enemies in a thunderous cloud.
   d. He secretly hid in a dark place.
4. *God strikes the enemies:* Verse 14 (ESV), "And he sent out his arrows and scattered them."
   a. Notice that it was God who ultimately brought down the enemy of David, not David himself.

David then considers why God chose to deliver him from his enemies. Indeed, God may not choose to help in this way for all who need deliverance or pray for help. However, David gives us a little insight into "why" God helped him.

1. Verse 21 (ESV), "For I have kept the ways of the LORD, and have not wickedly departed from my God."
2. And then again, in verse 24 (ESV), "So the LORD has rewarded me according to my righteousness, according to the cleanness of my hands in his sight."

According to David, God looked into David and saw that he was living right and his hands were clean in His sight, so David was rewarded for this. In God's judgment, David was compensated because he did not forget to follow God's ways, and he stayed away from his own immoral character. These are important things to remember when we are taking account of our own lives. We all have the potential to dive into the immoral side of our character and swim there. In fact, in our arrogance, it is easier for us to float through life finding selfish pleasure day to day, even though we know it may eventually hurt us. Living right is much harder and takes humility, diligence, and perseverance. And God knows that—He is well aware of human nature.

In the end, God delivers the ways and means to help David continue to find victory over his enemies by offering him certain graces to support him along the way:

1. The shield of salvation.

2. His right hand to hold David up.
3. His gentleness to make David great.
4. He enlarged David's steps so he would not slip.
5. He girded David with strength.
6. He subdued David's enemies.
7. He made David the head of the heathens.
8. He lifted David above those who rose up against him.
9. He delivered David from the violent man.
10. He gave great deliverance to David.

God knew David was going to need all those qualities to remain victorious and keep the enemies from holding power over him.

Though we might not be kings, God has a similar plan for us in our lives. You have enemies right now that you might not even know about that will need defeating. God will help and protect His children. And why does He offer this to those who love Him and follow His ways? As verse 19 (ESV) so wonderfully puts it, "He brought me out into a broad place; he rescued me, because he delighted in me."

God delights in us because He is our Father, and we are His children. The Lord delivers His faithful from their enemies. He lifts His children above their enemies and blesses us before them. The enemies of His children are avenged. His children are given salvation, and they sing praises and thanks to their Father while among the heathen (converting nations).

Zechariah 10:5, "And they shall be as mighty men, which tread down their enemies."

As children of God, we may be humble and meek, but we are reminded yet again that we are not weak. We are mighty through the power of our Lord. Therefore, I will give thanks unto Thee and sing praise unto His name among the unbelievers.

Praise God the Almighty and powerful friend of the righteous!

Thank You for Your help and support when we need it. Amen.

Psalm 19: O Lord, My Strength, and My Redeemer

The heavens declare the glory of God; and the firmament sheweth his handywork. Day unto day uttereth speech, and night unto night sheweth knowledge. There is no speech nor language, where their voice is not heard. Their line is gone out through all the earth, and their words to the end of the world. In them hath he set a tabernacle for the sun, Which is as a bridegroom coming out of his chamber, and rejoiceth as a strong man to run a race. His going forth is from the end of heaven, and his circuit unto the ends of it: and there is nothing hidden from the heat thereof. The law of the LORD is perfect, converting the soul: the testimony of the LORD is sure, making wise the simple. The statutes of the LORD are right, rejoicing the heart: the commandment of the LORD is pure, enlightening the eyes. The fear of the LORD is clean, enduring forever: the judgments of the LORD are true and righteous altogether. More to be desired are they than gold, yea, than much fine gold: sweeter also than honey and the honeycomb. Moreover by them is thy servant warned: and in keeping them there is great reward. Who can understand his errors? cleanse thou me from secret faults. Keep back thy servant also from presumptuous sins; let them not have dominion over me: then shall I be upright, and I shall be innocent from the great transgression. Let the words of my mouth, and the meditation of my heart, be acceptable in thy sight, O LORD, my strength, and my redeemer.

In many ways, Psalm 19 represents an evolution of the human spirit after a time of great trouble and in the aftermath of victory from God's hands. Sometimes, in our lives, we will be brought so low. The people around us will despise us, and all the filth of the world will seem to have taken us hostage. Maybe we are addicted to activities that we cannot let go of. Maybe a dream we had has blown up in our faces. Or we've hit a series of dead ends as we try to move forward. Our bank accounts are evaporating. Our hard work is coming to nothing. The people we live with abuse and demean us. Whatever the hardship, we find ourselves so desperate that we cry out to God, "Help me!"

And God hears us, and in His infinite compassion and mercy, He delivers us from our lowest point and begins to change our lives. He gets rid of all the people who are keeping us down. He hands us all the tools we need to stay out of the pit we just dragged ourselves out of, and for the first time in a long time, we begin to see the light and feel a glimmer of hope.

Psalm 19 is a prayer that comes from someone who has been given another chance.

When we find ourselves understanding how it was God and not ourselves that saved our lives, we begin to evolve and change. We become humbler, and we give more credit to God than we did before. We recognize that we don't ever want to feel that desperation again. So, we begin to understand what the "goodness of the Lord" means.

Psalm 19 exemplifies this understanding with a song of praise and by bearing witness to the goodness of the Lord:

1. The law of the Lord is perfect.
2. The law of the Lord is converting the seed.
3. The testimony of the Lord is pure.
4. The testimony of the Lord makes a simple person wise.
5. The statutes of the Lord are right.
6. The statutes of the Lord cause the heart to rejoice.

7. The commandment of the Lord is pure.
8. The commandment of the Lord is enlightening to our eyes.
9. The piety of the Lord is clean.
10. The piety of the Lord lasts forever.
11. The judgments of the Lord are true and righteous entirely.

This knowledge of God's goodness leads us to an understanding of our faults, and we begin to understand how the fear of the Lord guides us to be a better person for God's sake, not our own.

Verses 12–14 (emphasis added by the author),

> Who can understand his errors? cleanse thou me from secret faults. Keep back thy servant also from presumptuous sins; let them not have dominion over me: then shall I be upright, and I shall be innocent from the great transgression. *Let the words of my mouth, and the meditation of my heart, be acceptable in thy sight, O LORD, my strength, and my redeemer.*

This humble understanding that our Lord is our strength is an important and necessary step on the good path if we wish to continue making progress. Praise and glory to You, O Lord, Most Holy King.

"The gift of grace increases as the struggle increases" (St. Rosa of Lima).

Psalm 20: I Now Know That the Lord Saveth His Anointed

The LORD hear thee in the day of trouble; the name of the God of Jacob defend thee; Send thee help from the sanctuary, and strengthen thee out of Zion; Remember all thy offerings, and accept thy burnt sacrifice; Selah. Grant thee according to thine own heart, and fulfill all thy counsel. We will rejoice in thy salvation, and in the name of our God we will set up our banners: the LORD will fulfill all thy petitions. Now know I that the LORD saveth his anointed; he will hear him from his holy heaven with the saving strength of his right hand. Some trust in chariots, and some in horses: but we will remember the name of the LORD our God. They are brought down and fallen: but we are risen, and stand upright. Save, LORD: let the king hear us when we call

In Psalm 20, we see that after David's trials with his enemies and his subsequent victory over them by the hand of God, David comes to the firm conviction that our Lord saves His anointed.

Verse 6, "Now know I that the LORD saveth his anointed; he will hear him from his holy heaven with the saving strength of his right hand."

1. God hears His anointed from His holy heavenly place.
2. He gives salvation to those who trust Him.
3. God sets the anointed in a high place.
4. He sends help from the sanctuary.

Worksheet: How Has God Saved You? What Would You Like God to Save You From?

Contemplate those times when you know in your heart that the Lord saved you in a time of need or think deeply about what you need saving from in your life at this time and write your thoughts here.

_____
_____
_____
_____
_____
_____
_____
_____
_____
_____
_____
_____
_____
_____
_____

Thanks and praises for the day!

Psalm 21: The Lord Has Strength That *None* Can Overcome

{To the chief Musician, A Psalm of David.} The king shall joy in thy strength, O LORD; and in thy salvation how greatly shall he rejoice! Thou hast given him his heart's desire, and hast not withholden the request of his lips. Selah. For thou preventest him with the blessings of goodness: thou settest a crown of pure gold on his head. He asked life of thee, and thou gavest it him, even length of days for ever and ever. His glory is great in thy salvation: honour and majesty hast thou laid upon him. For thou hast made him most blessed for ever: thou hast made him exceedingly glad with thy countenance. For the king trusteth in the LORD, and through the mercy of the most High he shall not be moved. Thine hand shall find out all thine enemies: thy right hand shall find out those that hate thee. Thou shalt make them as a fiery oven in the time of thine anger: the LORD shall swallow them up in his wrath, and the fire shall devour them. Their fruit shall thou destroy from the earth, and their seed from among the children of men. For they intended evil against thee: they imagined a mischievous device, which they are not able to perform. Therefore shalt thou make them turn their back, when thou shalt make ready thine arrows upon thy strings against the face of them. Be thou exalted, LORD, in thine own strength: so will we sing and praise thy power.

Psalm 21:11, "For they intended evil against thee: they imagined a mischievous device, which they are not able to perform."

The Lord has strength that *none* can overcome.

One of the things that we learn in the Psalms is that our heavenly Father's will is always done and none can overcome what He desires to move forward. This includes destroying His enemies and the enemies of His children. As well as blessing His children with an inheritance that spans generations.

Study: Wrath

In Psalm 21, God's wrath is once again brought up. It's a common theme in the Bible, so perhaps it is a good time to explore the notion of "wrath," what part it plays in the Bible narrative, and how it ties into developing our faith.

According to the Merriam-Webster Dictionary, "wrath" is defined as:

Wrath, noun. (1) Strong vengeful anger or indignation. (2) Retributory punishment for an offense or a crime: divine chastisement.

Biblically, let's examine a few verses in which wrath is mentioned:

Deuteronomy 32:27,

> Were it not that I feared the wrath of the enemy, lest their adversaries should behave themselves strangely, and lest they should say, Our hand is high, and the LORD hath not done all this.

Fear not thy enemy. There is nothing that is done that the Lord has not allowed. Even the wrath of an enemy is the Lord's doing.

God will allow the enemy to gain a victory when it helps Him apply His judgment in the way that best serves Him and the souls of His children. So do not fear; God is always in control.

Proverbs 11:4, "Riches profit not in the day of wrath: but righteousness delivereth from death."

This verse is a reminder that we cannot buy ourselves a place *out of* the wrath of God nor purchase a place *into* eternal life.

Isaiah 54:8, "In a little wrath I hid my face from thee for a moment; but with everlasting kindness will I have mercy on thee, saith the LORD thy Redeemer."

The Lord is kind and merciful; His wrath shall not last for His faithful. There are times when God will allow harsh realities into our lives. Nowhere in the Bible does it say this life will be easy and free of hardship. But fear not; these times will not last forever for His faithful. God promises that hard times will end for those who love Him.

Matthew 3:7, "But when he [John the Baptist] saw many of the Pharisees and Sadducees come to his baptism, he said unto them, O generation of vipers, who hath warned you to flee from the wrath to come?" (See also Luke 3:7.)

Though the Lord knows our true intentions, He will lead even the evilest intentioned people unto the promise of redemption and away from His wrath. In the above verses, John the Baptist recognized this when he saw those who would accuse the Son of God come for their own baptism in fear of being judged harshly. God is merciful, and He will give even those who despise Him a chance to turn around and repent.

Ephesians 6:4, "And, ye fathers, provoke not your children to wrath: but bring them up in the nurture and admonition of the Lord."

This verse asks that we raise our children to follow the ways of the Lord, not the path of God's wrath and destruction.

When we understand that the wrath of God is a useful tool to separate His children from the enemies of God and to help strengthen our faith in Him through trials and hardship, we learn not to be afraid but to see His wrath as a foundation of His love and mercy.

Fear not, dear ones; God always has our back. We just need to have faith and trust in His goodness. Amen.

Psalm 22: David Speaks as the Messiah

{To the chief Musician upon Aijeleth Shahar, A Psalm of David.} My God, my God, why hast thou forsaken me? why art thou so far from helping me, and from the words of my roaring? O my God, I cry in the daytime, but thou hearest not; and in the night season, and am not silent. But thou art holy, O thou that inhabitest the praises of Israel. Our fathers trusted in thee: they trusted, and thou didst deliver them. They cried unto thee, and were delivered: they trusted in thee, and were not confounded. But I am a worm, and no man; a reproach of men, and despised of the people. All they that see me laugh me to scorn: they shoot out the lip, they shake the head, saying, He trusted on the LORD that he would deliver him: let him deliver him, seeing he delighted in him. But thou art he that took me out of the womb: thou didst make me hope when I was upon my mother's breasts. I was cast upon thee from the womb: thou art my God from my mother's belly. Be not far from me; for trouble is near; for there is none to help. Many bulls have compassed me: strong bulls of Bashan have beset me round. They gaped upon me with their mouths, as a raven and a roaring lion. I am poured out like water, and all my bones are out of joint: my heart is like wax; it is melted in the midst of my bowels. My strength is dried up like a potsherd; and my tongue cleaveth to my jaws; and thou hast brought me into the dust of death. For dogs have compassed me: the assembly of the wicked have enclosed me: they pierced my hands and my feet. I may tell all my bones: they look and stare upon me. They part my garments among them, and cast lots upon my vesture. But be not thou far from me, O LORD: O my strength, haste thee to help me. Deliver my soul

Nancy Johnston

from the sword; my darling from the power of the dog. Save me from the lion's mouth: for thou hast heard me from the horns of the unicorns. I will declare thy name unto my brethren: in the midst of the congregation will I praise thee. Ye that fear the LORD, praise him; all ye the seed of Jacob, glorify him; and fear him, all ye the seed of Israel. For he hath not despised nor abhorred the affliction of the afflicted; neither hath he hid his face from him; but when he cried unto him, he heard. My praise shall be of thee in the great congregation: I will pay my vows before them that fear him. The meek shall eat and be satisfied: they shall praise the LORD that seek him: your heart shall live forever. All the ends of the world shall remember and turn unto the LORD: and all the kindreds of the nations shall worship before thee. For the kingdom is the LORD'S: and he is the governor among the nations. All they that be fat upon earth shall eat and worship: all they that go down to the dust shall bow before him: and none can keep alive his own soul. A seed shall serve him; it shall be accounted to the Lord for a generation. They shall come, and shall declare his righteousness unto a people that shall be born, that he hath done this.

There are times in the Psalms when it is nearly impossible to see the verses as anything but prophetically speaking of Christ, the Messiah. This is one of them. When we examine Psalm 22 in this light, we can imagine the frame of mind of Jesus, by way of the words of David, as He made His way to the cross. In fact, Psalm 22 appears to expose the very heart of Jesus as He is heading toward persecution and the crucifix.

We can imagine as we read these verses that Jesus laments in a very human way that He is surrounded by ravenous enemies who mock and scorn Him. They laugh at Him for His trust in the Lord and mock, "Let the Lord help You now!"

Verse 8, " He trusted on the LORD that he would deliver him: let him deliver him, seeing he delighted in him."

We see Jesus (or rather David as Jesus) contemplate the Father's hand in His birth.

Verse 10, "I was cast upon thee from the womb: thou art my God from my mother's belly."

And at the time of His arrest, He recognizes that He is utterly alone, "for there is none to help."

The Pharisees and Romans compass about Him as ravens and as roaring lions. On this day, there is dread.

Verses 14–15,

> I am poured out like water, and all my bones are out of joint: my heart is like wax; it is melted in the midst of my bowels. My strength is dried up like a potsherd; and my tongue cleaveth to my jaws, and thou hast brought me into the dust of death.

The dogs of the devil pierced His hands and feet, and He was left naked for all to see in humiliation.

Verse 16, "For dogs have compassed me: the assembly of the wicked have enclosed me: they pierced my hands and my feet."

Verse 18, "They part my garments among them, and cast lots upon my vesture."

Finally, whereas Psalm 22 begins with this verse, "My God, my God, why hast thou forsaken me? why art thou so far from helping me, and from the words of my roaring?" Jesus fulfills this very psalm of David while taking His last few breaths on the cross, as witnessed by Matthew, His apostle.

Matthew 27:46, "And about the ninth hour Jesus cried with a loud voice, saying, Eli, Eli, lama sabachthani? that is to say, My God, my God, why hast thou forsaken me?"

In the end, however, the Father is never far from Him and offers Him strength in His day of sorrow. Both David and Jesus have declared the name of the Lord in the midst of the congregation and praised Him. It is a time to rejoice and praise the Lord because the vow of the Lord will be fulfilled, and Jesus paid the price. And then we will know that the kingdom is the Lord's, and He is the governor of all nations, and He sent His seed to serve Him. All will eventually bow down and declare His righteousness.

In the final verse of Psalm 22, David declares this about a future event:

Verse 31, "They shall come, and shall declare his righteousness unto a people that shall be born, that he hath done this."

Notes:

Psalm 23: The Lord Is My Shepherd

{A Psalm of David.} The LORD is my shepherd; I shall not want. He maketh me to lie down in green pastures: he leadeth me beside the still waters. He restoreth my soul: he leadeth me in the paths of righteousness for his name's sake. Yea, though I walk through the valley of the shadow of death, I will fear no evil: for thou art with me; thy rod and thy staff they comfort me. Thou preparest a table before me in the presence of mine enemies: thou anointest my head with oil; my cup runneth over. Surely goodness and mercy shall follow me all the days of my life: and I will dwell in the house of the LORD forever

The sentiments in Psalm 23 can be found in many ways throughout the Psalms. Life with the Lord is peaceful and joyful, even in the midst of turmoil and trouble. But it is interesting how this psalm follows the psalm that very clearly foreshadows the Messiah and His crucifixion and redemption. Christians throughout the world view Christ as a shepherd of men. Those of us who live a life in Christ know that Psalm 23 sums up what life with Christ is like. And yet, the Psalms were written centuries before Christ was born. We know David is describing the God of Abraham, David's own God. Could it be that the God of David and Jesus Christ are the same energy? The same Spirit? Let's look to the Bible for verses that talk about the Lord being shepherd-like:

The Lord is my shepherd.

Old Testament:

- He shall feed His flock like a shepherd; He will gather the lambs in His arms and keep them close (Isaiah 40:11).
- "Hear the word of the LORD, O ye nations, and declare it in the isles afar off, and say, He that scattered Israel will

gather him, and keep him, as a shepherd doth his flock" (Jeremiah 31:10).
- "For thus saith the Lord GOD; Behold, I, even I, will both search my sheep, and seek them out" (Ezekiel 34:11).
- I will feed them in good pasture upon the high mountains of Israel; I will feed my flock, and I will cause them to lie down (Ezekiel 34:14).
- "And ye my flock, the flock of my pasture, are men, and I am your God, saith the Lord GOD" (Ezekiel 34:31).

New Testament:

- "[Jesus said] I am the good shepherd: the good shepherd giveth his life for the sheep" (John 10:11).
- "What man of you, having a hundred sheep, if he lose one of them, doth not leave the ninety and nine in the wilderness, and go after that which is lost, until he find it?" (Luke 15:4).
- "For ye were sheep going astray; but are now returned unto the Shepherd and Bishop of your souls" (1 Peter 2:25).
- "For the Lamb which is in the midst of the throne shall feed them, and shall lead them unto living fountains of water: and God shall wipe away all tears from their eyes" (Revelation 7:17).
- "I am the door: by me if any man enter in, he shall be saved, and shall go in and out, and find pasture" (John 10:9).

I shall not want.

- And I will set up shepherds over them which shall feed them: and they shall thirst no more, no more dismay, they shall lack nothing (Jeremiah 23:4).
- "But my God shall supply all your needs according to his riches in glory by Jesus Christ" (Philippians 4:19).

He maketh me lie down in green pastures; He leadeth me besideth the "still waters."

- He shall lead them unto fountains of living water (Revelation 7:17).

He restoreth my soul.

- "For even hereunto were ye called: because Christ also suffered for us, leaving us an example, that ye should follow his steps …Who his own self bare our sins in his own body on the tree, that we, being dead to sins, should live unto righteousness: by whose stripes ye were healed" (1 Peter 2:21, 24).

As our shepherd, Christ, by dying on the cross, has restored our souls. He will lead us to His still waters and there, finally, we will begin to find rest.

Thank You, Lord—my most merciful and generous shepherd. Keep me, one of Your sheep, on the good path. Lead me to Your still waters. Restore my soul.

Psalm 24: Who Is the King of Glory?

The earth is the LORD'S, and the fulness thereof; the world, and they that dwell therein. For he hath founded it upon the seas, and established it upon the floods. Who shall ascend into the hill of the LORD? or who shall stand in his holy place? He that hath clean hands, and a pure heart; who hath not lifted up his soul unto vanity, nor sworn deceitfully. He shall receive the blessing from the LORD, and righteousness from the God of his salvation. This is the generation of them that seek him, that seek thy face, O Jacob. Selah. Lift up your heads, O ye gates; and be ye lift up, ye everlasting doors; and the King of glory shall come in. Who is this King of glory? The LORD strong and mighty, the LORD mighty in battle. Lift up your heads, O ye gates; even lift them up, ye everlasting doors; and the King of glory shall come in. Who is this King of glory? The LORD of hosts, he is the King of glory. Selah.

Coming off Psalm 22 and the images of the crucifixion, which was followed by Psalm 23 and the images of healing, restoration, and rest, we come to the third psalm, which appears to reference the glory of God at the gates of everlasting life. In keeping with the theme of prophetic verses of the Messiah, it is difficult not to see Psalm 24 as a foreshadowing of the resurrected Jesus Christ who comes into fullness of glory at the gates of heaven.

David asks:

"Who is the King of glory?"

Isaiah 62:2 (emphasis added by the author), "And the Gentiles shall see thy righteousness, and all kings thy glory: and thou shalt be called by a new name, *which the mouth of the LORD shall name.*"

Luke 1:30–31 (emphasis added by the author), "And the angel said unto her, Fear not, Mary: for thou hast found favour with God. And, behold, thou shalt conceive in thy womb, and bring forth a son, *and shalt call his name JESUS.*"

"Who shall ascend into the hill of the LORD? or who shall stand in his holy place?"

Verses 4–5,

> He that hath clean hands, and a pure heart; who hath not lifted up his soul unto vanity, nor sworn deceitfully. He shall receive the blessing from the LORD, and righteousness from the God of his salvation.

David then ends this psalm with images of the gates of heaven!

Verses 9–10, "Lift up your heads, O ye gates; even lift them up, ye everlasting doors; and the King of glory shall come in. Who is this King of glory? The LORD of hosts, he is the King of glory. Selah."

The King of glory enters the gates of heaven as the victorious general in a spiritual war that was waged by the enemies of God and finished off by the sacrifice of the Son of God on the cross.

> He was taken up; and a cloud received him out of their sight. …Two men stood by them [the apostles] in white apparel; Which also said, …why stand ye gazing up into heaven? this same Jesus, which is taken up from you into heaven, shall come in like manner as ye have seen him go into heaven."
>
> Acts 1:9–11

The return of the King. The glory of God is upon us. Amen.

Psalm 25: Shew Me Thy Ways, O Lord; Teach Me Thy Paths

Unto thee, O LORD, do I lift up my soul. O my God, I trust in thee: let me not be ashamed, let not mine enemies triumph over me. Yea, let none that wait on thee be ashamed: let them be ashamed which transgress without cause. Shew me thy ways, O LORD; teach me thy paths. Lead me in thy truth, and teach me: for thou art the God of my salvation; on thee do I wait all the day. Remember, O LORD, thy tender mercies and thy loving kindnesses; for they have been ever of old. Remember not the sins of my youth, nor my transgressions: according to thy mercy remember thou me for thy goodness' sake, O LORD. Good and upright is the LORD: therefore will he teach sinners in this way. The meek will guide in judgment: and the meek will he teach his way. All the paths of the LORD are mercy and truth unto such as keeping his covenant and his testimonies. For thy name's sake, O LORD, pardon mine iniquity; for it is great. What man is he that feareth the LORD? him shall he teach in the way that he shall choose. His soul shall dwell at ease; and his seed shall inherit the earth. The secret of the LORD is with them that fear him; and he will shew them his covenant. Mine eyes are ever toward the LORD; for he shall pluck my feet out of the net. Turn thee unto me, and have mercy upon me; for I am desolate and afflicted. The troubles of my heart are enlarged: O bring thou me out of my distresses. Look upon mine affliction and my pain; and forgive all my sins. Consider mine enemies; for they are many; and they hate me with cruel hatred. O keep my soul, and deliver me: let me not be ashamed; for I put my trust in thee. Let integrity and uprightness preserve me; for I wait on thee. Redeem Israel, O God, out of all his troubles.

Psalm 25 is a plea to gain instruction from the Lord to help us continue in an upright manner. We keep talking about paths in the Lord because this life we live is both a physical and spiritual journey. But none of us are above needing instruction to keep us on the right path, even David himself acknowledges this.

These are the qualities that David suggests make us more teachable in the Lord's ways. But because our journey is a lifelong pursuit, it is probable that most of us will not be entirely full of these qualities when we begin our journey nor may we perfect all of these things in our lifetimes. Nonetheless, it is good to know and work on the qualities that keep us teachable.

1. Be meek.
2. Fear the Lord.
3. Be patient.
4. Keep our eyes on the Lord.
5. Seek guidance.
6. Have integrity.
7. Search for truth.
8. Be upright.

In return, Psalm 25 reminds us that the Lord will teach us:

1. How to be led by His truth.
2. That He is the God of our salvation.
3. How to forget the shame of our transgressions.
4. That He is loving and kind.
5. That His ways are good and upright.
6. That His path is mercy and truth.
7. That we have the secret of the Lord within us.
8. That He will show us His covenant.
9. That He forgives our sins.
10. How He plucks our feet out of the net of sin.
11. That He brings us out of distress.

As we move forward on our good path, it is imperative that we remember that we must remain open to instruction from the Lord. The upright path of the Lord not only allows us to experience the fullness of God's goodness and reward, but it also keeps us safe from the harm of those who seek to destroy us.

Lord, we pray for the patience to persevere in right living in the midst of enemies who seek to destroy thy righteousness within ourselves. For Thou art our God, Thy Spirit is good, lead us unto and keep us on the path of Thy uprightness and mercy. Thank You, O Lord. Amen.

"Unto thee, O Lord, do I lift up my soul."

Psalm 26: Examine Me, O Lord

Judge me, O LORD; for I have walked in mine integrity: I have trusted also in the LORD; therefore I shall not slide. Examine me, O LORD, and prove me; try my reins and my heart. For thy lovingkindness is before mine eyes: and I have walked in thy truth. I have not sat with vain persons, nor will I go in with dissemblers. I have hated the congregation of evil doers; and will not sit with the wicked. I will wash mine hands in innocency: so will I compass thine altar, O LORD: That I may publish with the voice of thanksgiving, and tell of all thy wondrous works. LORD, I have loved the habitation of thy house, and the place where thine honor dwelleth. Gather not my soul with sinners, nor my life with bloody men: In whose hands is mischief, and their right hand is full of bribes. But as for me, I will walk in mine integrity: redeem me, and be merciful unto me. My foot standeth in an even place: in the congregations will I bless the LORD.

Moving on from the last psalm in which David pleas to the Lord to teach him His ways, in Psalm 26, David now asks the Lord to test his character and righteousness because he has strengthened his integrity, trusted in the truth of the Lord, and forsook the company of vain men and people who are dissemblers (liars).

Verses 1–2, "Judge me, O LORD; for I have walked in mine integrity: I have trusted also in the LORD; therefore I shall not slide. Examine me, O LORD, and prove me; try my reins and my heart."

It is so important that we remember that the Lord tests our faith and the strength of our character as we make our way through a life of trusting God. In many ways, He is our coach. He teaches us the foundations of faith and then puts us into situations that test our fortitude. Sometimes, we forget this when we find ourselves in particularly difficult times. It is easy for us to see our current distress as God's punishment or lack of love for us. And sometimes, when it is warranted, we may find ourselves being chastised for our transgressions. But let us not forget what we discussed earlier:

Isaiah 54:8, "In a little wrath I hid my face from thee for a moment; but with everlasting kindness will I have mercy on thee, saith the LORD thy Redeemer."

God's wrath is not lasting for His children, and it is used to strengthen our souls.

At the same time, sometimes life is just hard. And it is in these times that we can use our hardship to gain faith and trust in the Lord as we lean on Him to get us through. In Psalm 26, David asks that God challenge him so that he can prove to the Lord that he will not slide back and that his integrity will remain intact. No one is saying that any of this is easy. It takes a strong person to gain virtue during difficult times. We are fallible humans and often fail the tests the Lord throws our way. However, even in our failures, we can be tested by God and learn.

Right now would be an excellent time to reflect on those challenges in life that we have or continue to slide back from and to challenge ourselves to consider what we will do differently in the future.

Worksheet: Where Do I Slide Back in My Own Life, and What Can I Do about It?

_____
_____
_____
_____
_____
_____
_____
_____
_____
_____

At the time of writing this, my own list would look like:

1. There are still times that I find myself unwittingly listening to the music of artists who I suspect to be friends of the ways of the ungodly (satanic) world. It's insidious in our society.
2. I consume media sometimes with messages that are counter to the message of Christ. These messages promote fear and distrust and sow the seeds of division and chaos.
3. My mind fixes on material things from time to time, and I idolize purchasing merchandise rather than merely setting about to get the things I need. (Overconsumption.)
4. Occasionally, I miss going to church and confession if I am traveling. I believe that I lose ground because my regular prayer practice is interrupted.

(Praying for resolutions to make up for lost ground by sliding back because of these issues.)

Notes:

Psalm 27: The Lord Is the Strength of My Life

The LORD is my light and my salvation; whom shall I fear? the LORD is the strength of my life; of whom shall I be afraid? When the wicked, even my enemies and my foes, came upon me to eat up my flesh, they stumbled and fell. Though an host should encamp against me, my heart shall not fear: though war should rise against me, in this will I be confident. One thing have I desired of the LORD, that will I seek after; that I may dwell in the house of the LORD all the days of my life, to behold the beauty of the LORD, and to enquire in his temple. For in the time of trouble he shall hide me in his pavilion: in the secret of his tabernacle shall he hide me; he shall set me up upon a rock. And now shall my head be lifted up above mine enemies round about me: therefore will I offer in his tabernacle sacrifices of joy; I will sing, yea, I will sing praises unto the LORD. Hear, O LORD, when I cry with my voice: have mercy also upon me, and answer me. When thou saidst, Seek ye my face; my heart said unto thee, Thy face, LORD, will I seek. Hide not thy face far from me; put not thy servant away in anger: thou hast been my help; leave me not, neither forsake me, O God of my salvation. When my father and my mother forsake me, then the LORD will take me up. Teach me thy way, O LORD, and lead me in a plain path, because of mine enemies. Deliver me not over unto the will of mine enemies: for false witnesses are risen up against me, and such as breathe out cruelty. I had fainted, unless I had believed to see the goodness of the LORD in the land of the living. Wait on the LORD: be of good courage, and he shall strengthen thine heart: wait, I say, on the LORD.

Verse 1, "The LORD is my light and my salvation, whom should I fear? the LORD is the strength of my life; of whom shall I be afraid?"

Here, David praises the Lord for being His strength in life and the light of his salvation. Psalm 27 offers up the fruits of trusting the Lord and some of the ways in which the Lord protects and blesses His faithful children, even in the midst of those who seek to do them harm.

As faithful children of God, when we are tested in life and have waited on the Lord, there finally comes a time when we find ourselves on the other side of hardship and distress. This is when we can reflect and see where the power of the Lord worked in our lives to strengthen us and ultimately moved us into a position where we can once again flourish. This is very biblical. The Bible is the living Word of the Lord, so let us examine some verses within Scripture that reinforce the verses of Psalm 27 to feel comfort knowing that when we "wait on the LORD: be of good courage …he shall strengthen thine heart: wait, I say, on the LORD" (verse 14).

Contemplation: Strength through Faith

1. "For the LORD God is a sun and shield: the LORD will give grace and glory: no good thing will he withhold from them that walk uprightly" (Psalm 84:11).
2. The Lord shall be on for an everlasting light, and the days of mourning shall be ended (Isaiah 60:19–20).
3. "Behold, thou hast instructed many, and thou hast strengthened the weak hands" (Job 4:3).
4. "Rejoice not against me, O mine enemy: when I fall, I shall arise; when I sit in darkness, the LORD shall be a light unto me" (Micah 7:8).
5. "I will not be afraid of thousands of people who have set themselves around me" (Psalm 3:6) (paraphrased by the author).
    a. "He restoreth my soul: he leadeth me in the path of

righteousness" (Psalm 23:3).
    b. "He brought me up also out of a horrible pit out of the miry of clay and set my feet upon a rock and established my goings" (Psalm 40:2).
6. "Thus saith the LORD; Refrain thy voice from weeping, and thine eyes from tears: for thy work shall be rewarded, saith the LORD" (Jeremiah 31:16).
7. "That he would grant you, according to the riches of his glory, to be strengthened with might by his Spirit in the inner man" (Ephesians 3:16).
8. "I can do all things through Christ which strengtheneth me" (Philippians 4:13).
9. "But the God of all grace, who hath called us unto his eternal glory by Christ Jesus, after that ye have suffered a while, make you perfect, stablish, strengthen, settle you" (1 Peter 5:10).

The Lord will strengthen us if we wait on Him and His timing. This is a promise of God that can be found in many verses throughout the Bible. So, fear not as you go through difficult times; wait on the Lord, have faith, and be joyful in knowing that He is a good and merciful Father who is working out all things for your own good. He is the strength of your life.

Thank You, Lord, for helping me gain strength when I am at my weakest, for establishing my way forward on solid ground, and for having mercy on Your children during our darkest moments. With love, praise, glory, and honor to You, O Lord! Amen.

Notes:

_____
_____
_____
_____
_____

Psalm 28: Give unto Them According to Their Deeds

Unto thee will I cry, O LORD my rock; be not silent to me: lest, if thou be silent to me, I become like them that go down into the pit. Hear the voice of my supplications, when I cry unto thee, when I lift up my hands toward thy holy oracle. Draw me not away with the wicked, and with the workers of iniquity, which speak peace to their neighbours, but mischief is in their hearts. Give them according to their deeds, and according to the wickedness of their endeavours: give them after the work of their hands; render to them their desert. Because they regard not the works of the LORD, nor the operation of his hands, he shall destroy them, and not build them up. Blessed be the LORD, because he hath heard the voice of my supplications. The LORD is my strength and my shield; my heart trusts in him, and I am helped: therefore my heart greatly rejoiceth; and with my song I will praise him. The LORD is their strength, and he is the saving strength of his anointed. Save thy people, and bless thine inheritance: feed them also, and lift them up for ever.

Verse 1, "Unto thee will I cry, O LORD my rock; be not silent to me: lest, if thou be silent to me, I become like them that go down into the pit."

The first verse of Psalm 28 acknowledges that when the Lord turns away from someone and is silent to them, it is like what happens to those who go down into the pit or are on the lowly path. They are separated from God.

Recognizing this, David prays to the Lord in verse 3, "Draw me not away with the wicked, and with the workers of iniquity, which speak peace to their neighbours, but mischief is in their hearts."

One of the traits of those on the path of iniquity is that they are not authentic or truthful. They can appear to be peaceful out in front of people, but behind the scenes, they conspire mischief against them. They are duplicitous, fakes, and frauds. As such, David appeals to the Lord's just judgment:

Verse 4, "Give them according to their deeds, and according to the wickedness of their endeavours: give them after the work of their hands; render to them their desert."

In other words, David is asking that those who are wicked have wickedness befall them and banish them to the wilderness of the desert. The desert is a harsh and unyielding place to live.

However, David asks for the Lord's help to keep his own eyes on only that which is holy so he does not fall away with the wicked. David knows that when he surrounds himself with those who do not follow the Lord's path, he might eventually take up their wicked ways.

He implores, "The LORD is my strength and my shield" (verse 7).

Once again, we are confronted with the fact that those who do not observe and consider the way that God works will be destroyed and will not be built up. On the other hand, for those who observe the ways of the Lord and trust in Him (verse 7 continued), "[the] heart greatly rejoiceth; and with [our] song [we] will praise him."

At the end of the day, the Lord strengthens and protects His anointed and leaves those who do not hear Him to the elements and desert. It is as simple as that. Because this same message is offered up in various ways throughout the Psalms, it is wise that we should acknowledge it as important, and we should remember it when we are considering our faith.

Thank You, Lord, for being a fair and just judge. Help us to trust that in Your goodness, You will give according to our deeds. We pray that we shall continue to reap a good reward and that the wicked will be cast down and not built up. We pray that those who do not observe Your wonderful ways will repent and find You in their hearts. Amen.

Notes:

Psalm 29: Give unto the Lord Glory and Strength

Give unto the LORD, O ye mighty, give unto the LORD glory and strength. Give unto the LORD the glory due unto his name; worship the LORD in the beauty of holiness. The voice of the LORD is upon the waters: the God of glory thundereth: the LORD is upon many waters. The voice of the LORD is powerful; the voice of the LORD is full of majesty. The voice of the LORD breaketh the cedars; yea, the LORD breaketh the cedars of Lebanon. He maketh them also to skip like a calf; Lebanon and Sirion like a young unicorn. The voice of the LORD divideth the flames of fire. The voice of the LORD shaketh the wilderness; the LORD shaketh the wilderness of Kadesh. The voice of the LORD maketh the hinds calve, and discovereth the forests: and in his temple doth every one speak of his glory. The LORD sitteth upon the flood; yea, the LORD sitteth King for ever. The LORD will give strength unto his people; the LORD will bless his people with peace.

Psalm 29 creates a fantastic picture of how powerful the voice of God is and how we can see the power of His voice observed in nature. The voice of the Lord:

1. Is powerful.
2. Is full of majesty.
3. The glory of God thunders.
4. Moves the water.
5. Can break even the strongest of cedar trees.
6. Creates lightning (divides the flames of fire).
7. Blows wind through the wilderness so that it shakes.
8. Causes the deer and timid animals to become fearful and seek shelter.

So, because of this power—that we can observe for ourselves what it can create in the natural world—we should "give unto the LORD the glory due unto his name; worship the LORD in the beauty of holiness" (verse 2).

Because that same strength He shows us in nature will be given to His people.

Verse 11, "The LORD will give strength unto his people; the LORD will bless his people with peace."

The Lord shows us what He is capable of to make it easier for us to trust in Him. He is not the God of confusion, nor will He make us go through mental hoops to understand His ways. He shows us all the time how powerful He is—it is up to us to see it and believe and give glory unto Him, who is our strength. Amen.

Notes:

Psalm 30: O Lord My God, I Cried unto Thee, and Thou Hast Healed Me

I will extol thee, O LORD; for thou hast lifted me up, and hast not made my foes to rejoice over me. O LORD my God, I cried unto thee, and thou hast healed me. O LORD, thou hast brought up my soul from the grave: thou hast kept me alive, that I should not go down to the pit. Sing unto the LORD, O ye saints of his, and give thanks at the remembrance of his holiness. For his anger endureth but a moment; in his favour is life: weeping may endure for a night, but joy cometh in the morning. And in my prosperity I said, I shall never be moved. LORD, by thy favor thou hast made my mountain to stand strong: thou didst hide thy face, and I was troubled. I cried to thee, O LORD; and unto the LORD I made supplication. What profit is there in my blood, when I go down to the pit? Shall the dust praise thee? shall it declare thy truth? Hear, O LORD, and have mercy upon me: LORD, be thou my helper. Thou hast turned for me my mourning into dancing: thou hast put off my sackcloth, and girded me with gladness; To the end that my glory may sing praise to thee, and not be silent. O LORD my God, I will give thanks unto thee for ever.

In Psalm 30, David gives praise to the Lord that He has had mercy on him, has healed his soul, and saved him from the pit. The Lord kept the mountain of his troubles to stand strong so that in humility, he would have to trust and pray to the Lord to help him.

Verse 8, "I cried to thee, O LORD; and unto the LORD I made supplication."

In doing this, David recognizes that allowing his troubles to persist for a period was a favor from God because, in His time, God had mercy and saved David from falling into the pit and brought him back to joy and a firm foundation.

Verse 5, "For his anger endureth but a moment; in his favour is life: weeping may endure for a night, but joy cometh in the morning."

This is how God works. There is meaning in the waiting and in enduring hardship for a time. It is up to us to seek out and find the meaning. We are not called to be passive bystanders in our lives. When difficult times arise, it is good to recognize the potential for learning and growing in that season. What is God trying to teach us? What is our part in this painful period of our lives? How can we grow in virtue from this scenario?

Worksheet: Lessons Learned in the Waiting

Imagine your most difficult life experiences and try to recall any positive outcomes that may have arisen out of the hardship and how God may have had a hand in it.

_____

_____

_____

_____

_____

God gave the world David as an example of how the Lord works with His children and how we, in return, should work with God to form a communion of Spirit in faith with the Lord.

God is so very kind and merciful. He helps us grow and gives support in our waiting. Amen.

Psalm 31: Into Thine Hand, I Commit My Spirit

{To the chief Musician, a psalm of David.} In thee, O LORD, do I put my trust; let me never be ashamed: deliver me in thy righteousness. Bow down thine ear to me; deliver me speedily: be thou my strong rock, for an house of defense to save me. For thou art my rock and my fortress; therefore for thy name's sake lead me, and guide me. Pull me out of the net that they have laid privily for me: for thou art my strength. Into thine hand I commit my spirit: thou hast redeemed me, O LORD God of truth. I have hated those who regard lying vanities: but I trust in the LORD. I will be glad and rejoice in thy mercy: for thou hast considered my trouble; thou hast known my soul in adversities; And hast not shut me up into the hand of the enemy: thou hast set my feet in a large room. Have mercy upon me, O LORD, for I am in trouble: mine eye is consumed with grief, yea, my soul and my belly. For my life is spent with grief, and my years with sighing: my strength faileth because of mine iniquity, and my bones are consumed. I was a reproach among all mine enemies, I am forgotten as a dead man out of mind: I am like a broken vessel. For I have heard the slander of many: fear was on every side: while they took counsel together against me, they devised to take away my life. But I trusted in thee, O LORD: I said, Thou art my God. My times are in thy hand: deliver me from the hand of mine enemies, and from them that persecute me. Make thy face to shine upon thy servant: save me for thy mercies' sake. Let me not be ashamed, O LORD; for I have called upon thee: let the wicked be ashamed, and let them be silent in the grave. Let the lying lips be put to silence; which speak grievous things proudly and contemptuously against the righteous. Oh how great is thy goodness, which thou hast laid up for them that fear thee; which thou hast wrought for them that trust in thee before the sons of men! Thou shalt hide them in the secret of thy presence from the pride of man: thou shalt keep them secretly in a pavilion from the strife of tongues. Blessed be the LORD: for he hath shewed me his marvelous kindness in a strong city. For I said in my haste, I am cut off from before thine eyes: nevertheless thou heardest the voice of my supplications when I cried unto thee. O love the LORD, all ye his saints: for the LORD preserveth the faithful, and plentifully rewardeth the proud doer. Be of good courage, and he shall strengthen your heart, all ye that hope in the LORD.

In Psalm 31, David does not attribute the goodness in his life to his own doing. David recognizes that he is a sinful man with human grief. It is only through the Lord that we are strengthened and given hope. God *is* the hope—not anything that we can imagine or possess on Earth. When we commit our spirit to God and have hope, He will strengthen our hearts to continue trusting in Him and to have faith that He will not forget us.

Verse 24, "Be of good courage, and he shall strengthen your heart, all ye that hope in the LORD."

Because hope is such an important element of faith, now would be a good time to examine what hope is both in definition and what some examples of it are in the Bible.

Study: Hope

Dictionary definition:

Hope: noun.

- The feeling that what is wanted can be had or that events will turn out for the best:
  - "I had high hopes of passing the exam."
- A particular instance of this feeling: the hope of winning.
- A feeling of trust.

Verb (used with object), hoped, hoping.

- To look forward to with desire and reasonable confidence.
- To believe, desire, or trust:
  - "I hope that my work will be satisfactory."

Similar:

- Aspiration, desire, wish, expectation, dream of.
- Ambition, aim, plan.
- Anticipate, be hopeful of, hope against hope for.

Examples of hope in the Bible:

Old Testament

1. "For there is hope of a tree, if it be cut down, that it will sprout again, and that the tender branch thereof will not cease" (Job 14:7).
2. "For thou art my hope, O Lord GOD: thou art my trust from my youth" (Psalm 71:5).
3. "Hope deferred maketh the heart sick: but when the desire cometh, it is a tree of life" (Proverbs 13:12).
4. "Blessed is the man that trusteth in the LORD, and whose hope the LORD is" (Jeremiah 17:7).
5. "For to him that is joined to all the living there is hope: for a living dog is better than a dead lion" (Ecclesiastes 9:4).

6. "It is good that a man should both hope and quietly wait for the salvation of the LORD" (Lamentations 3:26).

New Testament

1. "Therefore did my heart rejoice, and my tongue was glad; moreover also my flesh shall rest in hope" (Acts 2:26).
2. "And not only so, but we glory in tribulations also: knowing that tribulation worketh patience; And patience, experience; and experience, hope" (Romans 5:3–4).
3. "Beareth all things, believeth all things, hopeth all things, endureth all things" (1 Corinthians 13:7).
4. "For we through the Spirit wait for the hope of righteousness by faith" (Galatians 5:5).
5. "According to my earnest expectation and my hope, that in nothing I shall be ashamed, but that with all boldness, as always, so now also Christ shall be magnified in my body, whether it be by life, or by death" (Philippians 1:20).
6. "Now our Lord Jesus Christ himself, and God, even our Father, which has loved us, and hath given us everlasting consolation and good hope through grace" (2 Thessalonians 2:16).

We are given hope through the grace of God, who is the living hope of the world. Even in our darkest hours, our patient endurance and trust in the Lord serve to increase the grace of hope for a joyful future. The Lord is all good things. He will not let us down. Amen.

"In all things, pray, hope and don't worry" (St. Padre Pio).

Psalm 32: I Acknowledge My Sin unto Thee

Blessed is he whose transgression is forgiven, whose sin is covered. Blessed is the man unto whom the LORD imputeth not iniquity, and in whose spirit there is no guile. When I kept silence, my bones waxed old through my roaring all the day long. For day and night thy hand was heavy upon me: my moisture is turned into the drought of summer. Selah. I acknowledged my sin unto thee, and mine iniquity have I not hid. I said, I will confess my transgressions unto the LORD; and thou forgavest the iniquity of my sin. Selah. For this shall every one that is godly pray unto thee in a time when thou mayest be found: surely in the floods of great waters they shall not come nigh unto him. Thou art my hiding place; thou shalt preserve me from trouble; thou shalt compass me about with songs of deliverance. Selah. I will instruct thee and teach thee in the way which thou shalt go: I will guide thee with mine eye. Be ye not as the horse, or as the mule, which have no understanding: whose mouth must be held in with bit and bridle, lest they come near unto thee. Many sorrows shall be to the wicked: but he that trusteth in the LORD, mercy shall compass him about. Be glad in the LORD, and rejoice, ye righteous: and shout for joy, all ye that are upright in heart.

With more than a little foreshadowing of the Beatitudes of the New Testament, David acknowledges the qualities of the righteous who are blessed in the Lord in Psalm 32.

Verse 1, "Blessed is he whose transgression is forgiven, whose sin is covered."

Verse 2, "Blessed is the man unto whom the Lord imputeth not iniquity, and in whose spirit there is no guile." (Guile: deceit, treachery, dishonesty.)

Yet, at the same time, we are presented with the outcome of those who live a life filled with iniquity.

Verse 10, "Many sorrows shall be to the wicked."

Now would be a good time to look further into the concept of iniquity and how righteousness differs. They are such large themes not only within the Psalms but throughout the Bible.

Study: Iniquity

(Also known as wicked, unrighteous, sinful.)

Iniquity Definition: Immoral or grossly unfair behavior.

Iniquity

- Grossly unfair.
- Win/lose.
- Selfish to extreme.
- Self-serving.
- Manipulative (taker).
- Pleasure-heavy/at the expense of responsibility.
- Doing things that are outside moral codes.
- Moral codes are simply codes that set boundaries around behaviors that go against the benefit of individuals co-existing in society (i.e., murder).

Righteousness

- Fair-minded.
- Win/win.
- Equitable.
- Good of all.
- Servant (giver).
- Pleasure-balanced/with responsibility.
- Doing things that uphold morals codes to an extent that society benefits from such behavior (i.e., being honest).

Thank You for this wisdom, Lord. There is none that is all righteous and it is good for us to contemplate ways in which our behavior is sinful and to ask forgiveness when we make mistakes in life. It is also good to be able to recognize those around us who are living on the sinful path so that we may pray for them and not be caught up in their ways. Thank You, Lord, for helping us discern iniquity from righteousness as we make our way further into faith.

Verse 11, "Be glad in the LORD, and rejoice, ye righteous; and shout for joy, all ye that are upright in heart." Amen.

Notes:

_____

_____

_____

_____

_____

_____

_____

_____

_____

_____

_____

_____

_____

_____

_____

_____

_____

Psalm 33: Sing unto Him a New Song

Rejoice in the LORD, O ye righteous: for praise is comely for the upright. Praise the LORD with harp: sing unto him with the psaltery and an instrument of ten strings. Sing unto him a new song; play skilfully with a loud noise. For the word of the LORD is right; and all his works are done in truth. He loveth righteousness and judgment: the earth is full of the goodness of the LORD. By the word of the LORD were the heavens made; and all the host of them by the breath of his mouth. He gathereth the waters of the sea together as an heap: he layeth up the depth in storehouses. Let all the earth fear the LORD: let all the inhabitants of the world stand in awe of him. For he spake, and it was done; he commanded, and it stood fast. The LORD bringeth the counsel of the heathen to nought: he maketh the devices of the people of none effect. The counsel of the LORD standeth for ever, the thoughts of his heart to all generations. Blessed is the nation whose God is the LORD; and the people whom he hath chosen for his own inheritance. The LORD looketh from heaven; he beholdeth all the sons of men. From the place of his habitation he looketh upon all the inhabitants of the earth. He fashioneth their hearts alike; he considereth all their works. There is no king saved by the multitude of an host: a mighty man is not delivered by much strength. An horse is a vain thing for safety: neither shall he deliver any by his great strength. Behold, the eye of the LORD is upon them that fear him, upon them that hope in his mercy; To deliver their soul from death, and to keep them alive in famine. Our soul waiteth for the LORD: he is our help and our shield. For our heart shall rejoice in him, because we have trusted in his holy name. Let thy mercy, O LORD, be upon us, according as we hope in thee.

Psalm 33 reminds us that when we have reverential fear in the Lord and trust in Him, our life becomes new. We see the Lord in all things and begin to understand that there is nothing that is not overseen by the Lord. This is our new song! Whereas before, in our vanity, we may have been blind to His presence in all things, our eyes become open to the ways the Lord moves within our lives.

Verses 4–5 (emphasis added by the author), "For the word of the LORD is right; and all His works are done in *truth*. He loveth righteousness and judgment: the earth is full of the goodness of the LORD."

Like a veil that is lifted, as our faith increases, we cannot help but acknowledge that our lives are permeated with the Lord's will. Perhaps, before we moved fully onto the path of trusting in the Lord, we imagined that we were fully in control of every moment of our lives. We told ourselves that it was up to us to protect ourselves and provide all our sustenance. Once the veil is lifted and our eyes opened, it becomes apparent that the Lord has been with us every step of the way. Psalm 33 reminds us of this reality.

Verses 13–15,

> The LORD looketh from heaven; he beholdeth all the sons of men. From the place of his habitation he looketh upon all the inhabitants of the earth. He fashioneth their hearts alike; he considereth all their works.

He is watching us, and He is our help and our shield. It is important to read the words and believe them, for this is the truth. There are no vain promises that come from the mouth of the Lord or His prophets. A life with the Lord is a wonderful adventure, and the more we lean into His will alone, the greater our lives become.

Verses 21–22, "For our heart shall rejoice in him, because we have trusted in his holy name. Let thy mercy, O LORD, be upon us, according as we hope in thee."

The old song of our lives was worry, anxiety, and feeling alone.

There was little hope. But this new song is peaceful. It sings of the goodness of God and praises His mercy in our lives. It is filled with hope and joy!

Verse 18, "Behold, the eye of the LORD is upon them that fear him, upon them that hope in his mercy."

Thanks and praise and glory to You, O Lord, master of our lives. King of compassion and our hope for eternal life! We sing our new song to You and pray that You receive it! Amen.

Psalm 34: The Lord Redeemeth the Soul of His Servants

I will bless the LORD at all times: his praise shall continually be in my mouth. My soul shall make her boast in the LORD: the humble shall hear thereof, and be glad. O magnify the LORD with me, and let us exalt his name together. I sought the LORD, and he heard me, and delivered me from all my fears. They looked unto him, and were lightened: and their faces were not ashamed. This poor man cried, and the LORD heard him, and saved him out of all his troubles. The angel of the LORD encampeth round about them that fear him, and delivereth them. O taste and see that the LORD is good: blessed is the man that trusteth in him. O fear the LORD, ye his saints: for there is no want to them that fear him. The young lions do lack, and suffer hunger: but they that seek the LORD shall not want any good thing. Come, ye children, hearken unto me: I will teach you the fear of the LORD. What man is he that desireth life, and loveth many days, that he may see good? Keep thy tongue from evil, and thy lips from speaking guile. Depart from evil, and do good; seek peace, and pursue it. The eyes of the LORD are upon the righteous, and his ears are open unto their cry. The face of the LORD is against them that do evil, to cut off the remembrance of them from the earth. The righteous cry, and the LORD heareth, and delivereth them out of all their troubles. The LORD is nigh unto them that are of a broken heart; and saveth such as be of a contrite spirit. Many are the afflictions of the righteous: but the LORD delivereth him out of them all. He keepeth all his bones: not one of them is broken. Evil shall slay the wicked: and they that hate the righteous shall be desolate. The LORD redeemeth the soul of his servants: and none of them that trust in him shall be desolate.

Verse 4, "I sought the LORD, and he heard me, and delivered me from all my fears."

Psalm 34 is clearly a Psalm that explores the concept of God's ability to redeem those who have fallen away from His path or even those who are ignorant that the path even exists.

Redemption is such a big concept within the Bible and one of the core traits of the living God. He is our redeemer. It's one of those words that we all just assume that we know what it means when we read or hear it. But when we look at the concept of "redeem," we can see that it encompasses so many layers. To look at "redemption" with new eyes, now would be a very good time to study what it truly means.

Study: Redemption

Psalm 34:22, "The LORD redeemeth the soul of his servants: and none of them that trust in him shall be desolate."

According to the Merriam-Webster Dictionary, "redeem" is a verb with several significant implications, and "redemption" is the act or process of being or having been "redeemed." In a very general way, "redeem" means "to set free from confinement or danger." In fact, one of the most famous of all Gospel verses breaks this down nicely.

John 8:32, "And ye shall know the truth, and the truth shall make you free."

In other words, the truth is redemptive. It sets us free from the confinement and danger inherent in deception.

Let us now look a little deeper into the notion of redemption and then strengthen our understanding with a few Bible verses that illustrate each concept.

Ways to consider the verb "redeem" are as follows:

1. To rescue: implies freeing from imminent danger by prompt or vigorous action.
   a. Daniel 6:27, "He delivereth and rescueth, and he worketh signs and wonders in heaven and in earth, who hath delivered Daniel from the power of the lions."
   b. Psalm 35:17, "Lord, how long wilt thou look on? rescue my soul from their destructions, my darling from the lions."
2. To deliver: implies release, usually of a person from confinement, temptation, slavery, or suffering.
   a. Exodus 18:10, "And Jethro said, Blessed be the LORD, who hath delivered you out of the hand of the Egyptians, and out of the hand of Pharaoh, who hath delivered the people from under the hand of the Egyptians."
   b. Matthew 6:13, "And lead us not into temptation, but deliver us from evil: For thine is the kingdom, and the power, and the glory, for ever. Amen."
3. To redeem: implies releasing from bondage or penalties by giving what is demanded or necessary (i.e., the sacrifice was given to redeem the sins of the person).
   a. Job 19:25, "For I know that my redeemer liveth, and that he shall stand at the latter day upon the earth."
   b. Galatians 3:13–14, "Christ hath redeemed us from the curse of the law, being made a curse for us: for it is written, Cursed is every one that hangeth on a tree: That the blessing of Abraham might come on the Gentiles through Jesus Christ; that we might receive the promise of the Spirit through faith."
4. To ransom: specifically applies to buying out of captivity.
   a. Proverbs 21:18, "The wicked shall be a ransom for the righteous, and the transgressor for the upright."
   b. Isaiah 35:10, "And the ransomed of the LORD shall return, and come to Zion with songs and everlasting

joy upon their heads: they shall obtain joy and gladness, and sorrow and sighing shall flee away."
5. To reclaim/recover: suggests a bringing back to a former state or condition of someone or something abandoned or debased.
   a. Isaiah 11:11, "And it shall come to pass in that day, that the Lord shall set his hand again the second time to recover [reclaim] the remnant of his people, which shall be left, from Assyria, and from Egypt, and from Pathros, and from Cush, and from Elam, and from Shinar, and from Hamath, and from the islands of the sea."
6. To save: may replace any of the foregoing terms; it may further imply a preserving or maintaining for usefulness or continued existence.
   a. Deuteronomy 20:4, "For the LORD your God is he that goeth with you, to fight for you against your enemies, to save you."
   b. Luke 19:10, "For the Son of man is come to seek and to save that which was lost."
   c. John 3:16–17, "For God so loved the world, that he gave his only begotten Son, that whosoever believeth in him should not perish, but have everlasting life. For God sent not his Son into the world to condemn the world; but that the world through him might be saved."

As we can see, the concept of redemption in all its many forms is embedded within the Psalms we are studying as well as throughout the entire Bible's Old and New Testaments. A case could be made that the Bible itself is a collection of books specifically about how God has redeemed His children over and over since the beginning of time and how His redemption leads to everlasting life in heaven with Him. Let us give thanks to our great redeemer!

Are you ready for the most holy one to begin or continue to redeem you and your life?

Psalm 35: Lord, How Long Wilt Thou Look On?

Plead my cause, O LORD, with them that strive with me: fight against them that fight against me. Take hold of shield and buckler, and stand up for mine help. Draw out also the spear, and stop the way against them that persecute me: say unto my soul, I am thy salvation. Let them be confounded and put to shame that seek after my soul: let them be turned back and brought to confusion that devise my hurt. Let them be as chaff before the wind: and let the angel of the LORD chase them. Let their way be dark and slippery: and let the angel of the LORD persecute them. For without cause have they hid for me their net in a pit, which without cause they have digged for my soul. Let destruction come upon him at unawares; and let his net that he hath hid catch himself: into that very destruction let him fall. And my soul shall be joyful in the LORD: it shall rejoice in his salvation. All my bones shall say, LORD, who is like unto thee, which deliverest the poor from him that is too strong for him, yea, the poor and the needy from him that spoileth him? False witnesses did rise up; they laid to my charge things that I knew not. They rewarded me evil for good to the spoiling of my soul. But as for me, when they were sick, my clothing was sackcloth: I humbled my soul with fasting; and my prayer returned into mine own bosom. I behaved myself as though he had been my friend or brother: I bowed down heavily, as one that mourneth for his mother. But in mine adversity they rejoiced, and gathered themselves together: yea, the abjects gathered themselves together against me, and I knew it not; they did tear me, and ceased not:

With hypocritical mockers in feasts, they gnashed upon me with their teeth. Lord, how long wilt thou look on? rescue my soul from their destructions, my darling from the lions. I will give thee thanks in the great congregation: I will praise thee among much people. Let not them that are mine enemies wrongfully rejoice over me: neither let them wink with the eye that hate me without a cause. For they speak not peace: but they devise deceitful matters against them that are quiet in the land. Yea, they opened their mouth wide against me, and said, Aha, aha, our eye hath seen it. This thou hast seen, O LORD: keep not silence: O Lord, be not far from me. Stir up thyself, and awake to my judgment, even unto my cause, my God and my Lord. Judge me, O LORD my God, according to thy righteousness; and let them not rejoice over me. Let them not say in their hearts, Ah, so would we have it: let them not say, We have swallowed him up. Let them be ashamed and brought to confusion together that rejoice at mine hurt: let them be clothed with shame and dishonour that magnify themselves against me. Let them shout for joy, and be glad, that favour my righteous cause: yea, let them say continually, Let the LORD be magnified, which hath pleasure in the prosperity of his servant. And my tongue shall speak of thy righteousness and of thy praise all the day long.

In human fashion, David cries out to the Lord to take revenge on those who wish to cause him harm. He asks the Lord to give the harm back to those people and to judge them accordingly.

Verse 8, "Let destruction come upon him at unawares; and let his net that he hath hid catch himself: into that very destruction let him fall."

Psalm 35 addresses the fact that we need to lean on the Father to make right and good the evil others may have toward us. "Vengeance is mine, says the Lord." Though we may be in the middle of distress at the hands of others, we must pray and continue to do the ways of God and be patient while the injustice pursues us. It is not up to us to seek revenge.

Verse 17, "Lord, how long wilt thou look on? rescue my soul from their destructions, my darling from the lions."

The Lord will make all things right. Like David in this Psalm, we are to pray, ask for help (which the Lord is already aware of what is needed), and be patient. Psalm 35 reminds us that we must have faith that what we ask will come to be in the way God desires the outcome. During the waiting, we should sing praise to the Lord. In fact, we should give Him thanks in community so that others may witness our faith.

Verse 18, "I will give thee thanks in the great congregation: I will praise thee among much people."

Give Him thanks and glory, for according to the Scriptures, when you ask, sing thanks, and praise for it is done. Thank You, O Lord! Amen.

"Thank God ahead of time" (Blessed Solanus Casey).

Psalm 36: O Continue Thy Lovingkindness unto Them That Know Thee

The transgression of the wicked saith within my heart, that there is no fear of God before his eyes. For he flattereth himself in his own eyes, until his iniquity be found to be hateful. The words of his mouth are iniquity and deceit: he hath left off to be wise, and to do good. He deviseth mischief upon his bed; he setteth himself in a way that is not good; he abhorreth not evil. Thy mercy, O LORD, is in the heavens; and thy faithfulness reacheth unto the clouds. Thy righteousness is like the great mountains; thy judgments are a great deep: O LORD, thou preservest man and beast. How excellent is thy lovingkindness, O God! therefore the children of men put their trust under the shadow of thy wings. They shall be abundantly satisfied with the fatness of thy house; and thou shalt make them drink of the river of thy pleasures. For with thee is the fountain of life: in thy light shall we see light. O continue thy lovingkindness unto them that know thee; and thy righteousness to the upright in heart. Let not the foot of pride come against me, and let not the hand of the wicked remove me. There are the workers of iniquity fallen: they are cast down, and shall not be able to rise.

The Lord is merciful, faithful, wise and gives lovingkindness to His children, but to the wicked, they shall be cast down and not be able to rise. Again, Psalm 36 illustrates the ways of wickedness versus the ways of righteousness and reminds us of the very different outcomes for each lifestyle. Let us examine further the characteristics of the wicked and the righteous, consider these ways, and pray for the courage to stay on course on the good path.

The wicked:

1. Do evil because they do not fear the Lord.
2. Flatters himself until it becomes hateful.
3. He speaks about things that are grossly unfair and deceitful.
4. No longer tries to be wise and do good.
5. Devises mischief.
6. Sets himself up to do no good.
7. Does not abhor evil.

The righteous:

1. Has judgments that are great deep.
2. Trusts the Lord.
3. Will be satisfied with the abundance of thy house.
4. Shall drink of the rivers of pleasure.
5. With the Lord, they shall be in the fountain of life.
6. Shall be in the light and see light.
7. Shall have the loving kindness of the Lord continue onto them.

The Psalms continue to bring up the differences between the wicked and the righteous because to know and understand how each way differs is to understand how to keep the traits of one way and to forgo the ways of the other. In His lovingkindness, the Lord seeks continuously to edify the behavior of His children, for we live in a world surrounded by wickedness, and it is quite easy to fall back to that condition. Try to remember that the Lord's ways are always for the love of His children—all of them. We can never fall too far while we live so that the Lord will not be able to lift us out of the pit and put us on the righteous path.

Worksheet: Where Are You Today?

Let's check in and take an accounting of how God is working in our lives right now and examine those areas where we may be resisting His hand in our lives:

Increased good behavior:

_____

_____

_____

_____

Poor behavior I am resisting to change:

_____

_____

_____

_____

Thank You, Lord, for always helping us to stay on the path as we make our way through this life. We know that sometimes it is difficult, but when we follow Your ways, You will be merciful and loving, and in that, we will be given the strength to move forward toward eternal life with You.

Help us to gracefully acknowledge those areas where we need change instead of resisting Your loving prompts to better our lives.

Psalm 37: The Lord Shall Give Thee the Desires of Thine Heart

Fret not thyself because of evildoers, neither be thou envious against the workers of iniquity. For they shall soon be cut down like the grass, and wither as the green herb. Trust in the LORD, and do good; so shalt thou dwell in the land, and verily thou shalt be fed. Delight thyself also in the LORD; and he shall give thee the desires of thine heart. Commit thy way unto the LORD; trust also in him; and he shall bring it to pass. And he shall bring forth thy righteousness as the light, and thy judgment as the noonday. Rest in the LORD, and wait patiently for him: fret not thyself because of him who prospereth in his way, because of the man who bringeth wicked devices to pass. Cease from anger, and forsake wrath: fret not thyself in any wise to do evil. For evildoers shall be cut off: but those that wait upon the LORD, they shall inherit the earth. For yet a little while, and the wicked shall not be: yea, thou shalt diligently consider his place, and it shall not be. But the meek shall inherit the earth; and shall delight themselves in the abundance of peace. The wicked plotteth against the just, and gnasheth upon him with his teeth. The Lord shall laugh at him: for he seeth that his day is coming. The wicked have drawn out the sword, and have bent their bow, to cast down the poor and needy, and to slay such as be of upright conversation. Their sword shall enter into their own heart, and their bows shall be broken. A little that a righteous man hath is better than the riches of many wicked. For the arms of the wicked shall be broken: but the LORD upholdeth the righteous. The LORD knoweth the days of the upright: and their inheritance shall be for ever. They shall not be ashamed in the evil time: and in the days of famine they shall be satisfied. But the wicked shall perish, and the enemies of the LORD shall be as the fat of lambs: they shall consume; into smoke shall they consume away. The wicked borroweth, and payeth not again: but the righteous sheweth mercy, and giveth. For such as be blessed of him shall inherit the earth; and they that be cursed of him shall be cut off. The steps of a good man are ordered by the LORD: and he delighteth in his way. Though he fall, he shall not be utterly cast down: for the LORD upholdeth him with his hand. I have been young, and now am old; yet have I not seen the righteous forsaken, nor his seed begging bread. He is ever merciful, and lendeth; and his seed is blessed. Depart from evil, and do good; and dwell for evermore. For the LORD loveth judgment, and forsaketh not his saints; they are preserved for ever: but the seed of the wicked shall be cut off. The righteous shall inherit the land, and dwell therein for ever. The mouth of the righteous speaketh wisdom, and his tongue talketh of judgment. The law of his God is in his heart; none of his steps shall slide. The wicked watcheth the righteous, and seeketh to slay him. The LORD will not leave him in his hand, nor condemn him when he is judged. Wait on the LORD, and keep his way, and he shall exalt thee to inherit the land: when the wicked are cut off, thou shalt see it. I have seen the wicked in great power, and spreading himself like a green bay tree. Yet he passed away, and, lo, he was not: yea, I sought him, but he could not be found. Mark the perfect man, and behold the upright: for the end of that man is peace. But the transgressors shall be destroyed together: the end of the wicked shall be cut off. But the salvation of the righteous is of the LORD: he is their strength in the time of trouble. And the LORD shall help them, and deliver them: he shall deliver them from the wicked, and save them, because they trust in him.

In Psalm 37, David speaks about the many ways that God will reward the faithfulness of His righteous children. In the New Testament, Acts 13:22 describes David as, "[and God said] I have found David the son of Jesse, a man after mine own heart, which shall fulfil all my will."

So, we see that one of the roles of David, the author of many psalms, is to fulfill all the will of God. One can imagine that by having a heart that is similar to the heart of God, David is particularly sensitive to the ways of God, including the way in which He engages with His children. Psalm 37 lists some of the ways God's will is fulfilled toward those who trust in Him and do good (aka His children):

1. We will be fed.
2. He shall give us the desires of our hearts.
3. He will make our righteousness shine as a light.
4. Our good judgment will illuminate.
5. Those who wait on the Lord shall inherit the earth.
6. The meek shall inherit the earth.
7. The meek shall delight in an abundance of peace.
8. Our little wealth will be found to be better than the riches of many wicked.
9. We will be supported by the Lord.
10. Our inheritance will be forever.
11. We will not be shamed in times of evil.
12. We will be fed in times of famine.
13. Our lives will be ordered by the Lord.
14. The Lord will delight in our ways.
15. Our lineage will be blessed and continue over time.
16. The law of God is in our hearts.
17. The Lord is our strength in times of trouble.
18. We will not be condemned in His judgment.
19. At our end, there will be peace.
20. The Lord will deliver us and save us.

All of these things will be in our lives because we have had faith and trusted in the Lord and by doing so, we have continued to walk His path. In return, He offers us all these wonderful rewards. However, on the other hand, "Fret not thyself because of evildoers, neither be thou envious against the workers of iniquity. For they shall soon be cut down like the grass, and wither as the green herb" (verses 1–2).

This is a common theme throughout the Psalms and within the Bible as a whole: there is a reward for the faithful who have chosen the good path, but those who choose an evil path have no future and will perish.

In fact, as Psalm 37 reminds us, the faithful shouldn't even be afraid of evildoers. The only requirement is to "trust in the Lord and do good," and the Lord will be our strength in times of trouble. Isn't God so good to His faithful?

Let us rejoice and give thanks to the Lord, our most merciful and loving Father. For Your heart is generous, and You will protect us from the evil of each and every day. Thank You, Abba! Amen.

Psalm 38: For I Will Declare Mine Iniquity; I Will Be Sorry for My Sin

O LORD, rebuke me not in thy wrath: neither chasten me in thy hot displeasure. For thine arrows stick fast in me, and thy hand presseth me sore. There is no soundness in my flesh because of thine anger; neither is there any rest in my bones because of my sin. For mine iniquities are gone over mine head: as an heavy burden they are too heavy for me. My wounds stink and are corrupt because of my foolishness. I am troubled; I am bowed down greatly; I go mourning all the day long. For my loins are filled with a loathsome disease: and there is no soundness in my flesh. I am feeble and sore broken: I have roared by reason of the disquietness of my heart. Lord, all my desire is before thee; and my groaning is not hid from thee. My heart panteth, my strength faileth me: as for the light of mine eyes, it also is gone from me. My lovers and my friends stand aloof from my sore; and my kinsmen stand afar off. They also that seek after my life lay snares for me: and they that seek my hurt speak mischievous things, and imagine deceits all the day long. But I, as a deaf man, heard not; and I was as a dumb man that openeth not his mouth. Thus I was as a man that heareth not, and in whose mouth are no reproofs. For in thee, O LORD, do I hope: thou wilt hear, O Lord my God. For I said, Hear me, lest otherwise they should rejoice over me: when my foot slippeth, they magnify themselves against me. For I am ready to halt, and my sorrow is continually before me. For I will declare mine iniquity; I will be sorry for my sin. But mine enemies are lively, and they are strong: and they that hate me wrongfully are multiplied. They also that render evil for good are mine adversaries; because I follow the thing that good is. Forsake me not, O LORD: O my God, be not far from me. Make haste to help me, O Lord my salvation.

While crying out to the Lord for help in Psalm 38, David is remembering his sinful life and iniquitous behavior, and he is remorseful and sick to his bones.

Verses 5–6, "My wounds stink and are corrupt because of my foolishness. I am troubled; I am bowed down greatly; I go mourning all the day long."

His friends, family, and loved ones keep their distance, and his enemies try to trip him up so they can rejoice in his foolishness. In his remorse, David can feel the wrath of God bearing down on him as he feels the pains of his sins. He asks the Lord for help in his day of distress and confesses his own treachery.

Verse 18, "For I will declare mine iniquity; I will be sorry for my sin."

There are times in all our lives when we feel the burden of our own sinful behaviors. We know when we have done wrong in the sight of the Lord (whether we admit it or not), and it grieves us down to the very core of our being. Like David, we can fall to our knees in pain and cry out, "I am feeble and sore broken: I have roared by reason of the disquietness of my heart" (verse 8).

During these difficult times, we become consumed with the memories of the things we have done in our lives that not only hurt us and others but have offended our creator and, perhaps, in extreme cases, cut us off from His love. Even those of us who deny the very existence of God will be tortured by memories of bad behavior. A conscience was designed to cause us pain in the face of our iniquity. Psalm 38 is a cathartic outpouring of grief for sin and a humbling of self in the face of God's mercy.

Verses 21–22, "Forsake me not, O LORD: O my God, be not far

from me. Make haste to help me, O Lord my salvation."

The Lord creates the desire for His will so that we may feel deficient without it. This is how we follow His ways and stay on path. He creates desolation so we will hunger for Him, and in coming back from desolation, we edify anew our manner of living in ever-mounting higher holiness.

Contemplation: An Interesting and Enlightening Exercise

It is recommended to read Psalm 38 while imagining that Jesus Christ is speaking as He prepares for the cross. Perhaps these were thoughts He had while He prayed in preparation for the crucifixion. Though He was without the burden of sin, Jesus took on the sins of all and felt the full weight of sorrow and pain of His people, which Psalm 38 only begins to illustrate.

Though Jesus was the salvation, in His flesh, He was human like David. In His pain, did Jesus cry out, "But mine enemies are lively, and they are strong: and they that hate me wrongfully are multiplied" (verse 19), while He prayed in the garden on His last free day? Imagine Jesus crying out to the Lord in His time of loneliness and trouble, "Forsake Me not, O Lord, My Father. Be not far from Me. Make haste to help Me, Abba!"

This is the way of the saint. No pain, no gain, in Christ-like fashion.

Psalm 39: Verily Every Man at His Best State Is Altogether Vanity

I said, I will take heed to my ways, that I sin not with my tongue: I will keep my mouth with a bridle, while the wicked is before me. I was dumb with silence, I held my peace, even from good; and my sorrow was stirred. My heart was hot within me, while I was musing the fire burned: then spake I with my tongue, LORD, make me to know mine end, and the measure of my days, what it is; that I may know how frail I am. Behold, thou hast made my days as an handbreadth; and mine age is as nothing before thee: verily every man at his best state is altogether vanity. Selah. Surely every man walketh in a vain shew: surely they are disquieted in vain: he heapeth up riches, and knoweth not who shall gather them. And now, Lord, what wait I for? my hope is in thee. Deliver me from all my transgressions: make me not the reproach of the foolish. I was dumb, I opened not my mouth; because thou didst it. Remove thy stroke away from me: I am consumed by the blow of thine hand. When thou with rebukes dost correct man for iniquity, thou makest his beauty to consume away like a moth: surely every man is vanity. Selah. Hear my prayer, O LORD, and give ear unto my cry; hold not thy peace at my tears: for I am a stranger with thee, and a sojourner, as all my fathers were. O spare me, that I may recover strength, before I go hence, and be no more.

Psalm 39 reminds us that even at our best, people are self-centered and vain. There are times when the Psalms seem like nothing more than a rebuke of the character of man, but this is not the way we are meant to perceive our humanity. It is wise for us to recognize that even in our most righteous and holiest behavior, our flesh is still consumed with self. It is how we were made, and this will never change. In fact, being an entirely selfless and humble person is not within the construct of our being. We cannot even begin to understand what it feels like to be completely unaware of self. God is well aware of all our shortcomings, and He still loves us despite them.

Knowing this frees us to put our trust in God, who is all things good and whose love is genuinely pure. God's mercy is here to show us that we cannot be fully righteous and good but that it is through our Father that we are improved and given the strength to stay on the path to eternal life. We need God to sustain life. It is in our humble understanding that when we do God's will—which is an act of humility—we get closer to being like Him. He who is life.

We cannot do it on our own. So relax. Do not be anxious. Trust the Lord and lean into Him, and our lives will change for the best. Have faith. God is with you throughout it all. He is so very good and kind to us.

Thank You, Father, for standing by us even in our imperfect state. Amen.

Don't you feel better knowing that all the burden of life does not rest on your shoulders alone?

Psalm 40: And He Put a New Song in My Mouth

I waited patiently for the LORD; and he inclined unto me, and heard my cry. He brought me up also out of an horrible pit, out of the miry clay, and set my feet upon a rock, and established my goings. And he hath put a new song in my mouth, even praise unto our God: many shall see it, and fear, and shall trust in the LORD. Blessed is that man that maketh the LORD his trust, and respecteth not the proud, nor such as turn aside to lies. Many, O LORD my God, are thy wonderful works which thou hast done, and thy thoughts which are to us-ward: they cannot be reckoned up in order unto thee: if I would declare and speak of them, they are more than can be numbered. Sacrifice and offering thou didst not desire; mine ears hast thou opened: burnt offering and sin offering hast thou not required. Then said I, Lo, I come: in the volume of the book it is written of me, I delight to do thy will, O my God: yea, thy law is within my heart. I have preached righteousness in the great congregation: lo, I have not refrained my lips, O LORD, thou knowest. I have not hid thy righteousness within my heart; I have declared thy faithfulness and thy salvation: I have not concealed thy lovingkindness and thy truth from the great congregation. Withhold not thou thy tender mercies from me, O LORD: let thy lovingkindness and thy truth continually preserve me. For innumerable evils have compassed me about: mine iniquities have taken hold upon me, so that I am not able to look up; they are more than the hairs of mine head: therefore my heart faileth me. Be pleased, O LORD, to deliver me: O LORD, make haste to help me. Let them be ashamed and confounded together that seek after my soul to destroy it; let them be driven backward and put to shame that wish me evil. Let them be desolate for a reward of their shame that say unto me, Aha, aha. Let all those that seek thee rejoice and be glad in thee: let such as love thy salvation say continually, The LORD be magnified. But I am poor and needy; yet the Lord thinketh upon me: thou art my help and my deliverer; make no tarrying, O my God.

In Psalm 40, David is proclaiming that the Lord took him off his path of treachery, placed him on a rock, and established for him a new way of going. The Lord put into David's mouth a new song that is filled with praises of God that will result in many converts to trust God.

Verse 8, "I delight to do thy will, O my God: yea, thy law is within my heart."

Once again, David asks that the Lord keep those that wish evil upon him to stay away. He asks the Lord to avenge him against the wicked doers and to deliver him from evil and keep him in salvation. The new song of Psalm 40 did not require David to turn to the traditional ways of sacrifice and burnt offerings to open his ears to God's will and make atonement for his sins.

Verse 6, "Sacrifice and offering thou didst not desire; mine ears hast thou opened: burnt offering and sin offering hast thou not required."

David's ears were opened to the fact that songs of praise, glory, and honor to the Lord carry the same weight as the old song of sacrifice at the altar. This new song is a powerful substitute for animal sacrifice for the atonement of sins. This would have been a radical, transformative thought in David's time. Psalm 40 recognizes that this new song of praise for all the congregation, which will be on the lips of David, is an act of redemption for him and his people.

Verses 16–17, "Let all those that seek thee rejoice and be glad in thee: let such as love thy salvation say continually, The LORD be magnified …[for] thou art my help and my deliverer; make no tarrying, O my God."

Song is so important to the soul of the faithful. Not only is it joyful and entertaining, but it acts as a way deeper into salvation as we make our way down the path to eternal life.

It is good for us to sing songs of praise to the Lord!

Psalm 41: Thou Upholdest Me in Mine Integrity

Blessed is he that considereth the poor: the LORD will deliver him in time of trouble. The LORD will preserve him, and keep him alive; and he shall be blessed upon the earth: and thou wilt not deliver him unto the will of his enemies. The LORD will strengthen him upon the bed of languishing: thou wilt make all his bed in his sickness. I said, LORD, be merciful unto me: heal my soul; for I have sinned against thee. Mine enemies speak evil of me, When shall he die, and his name perish? And if he come to see me, he speaketh vanity: his heart gathereth iniquity to itself; when he goeth abroad, he telleth it. All that hate me whisper together against me: against me do they devise my hurt. An evil disease, say they, cleaveth fast unto him: and now that he lieth he shall rise up no more. Yea, mine own familiar friend, in whom I trusted, which did eat of my bread, hath lifted up his heel against me. But thou, O LORD, be merciful unto me, and raise me up, that I may requite them. By this I know that thou favourest me, because mine enemy doth not triumph over me. And as for me, thou upholdest me in mine integrity, and settest me before thy face for ever. Blessed be the LORD God of Israel from everlasting, and to everlasting. Amen, and Amen.

In Psalm 41, we, once again, see David lamenting that he is surrounded by those who wish him harm and hate him. Even those who have eaten with him have fled during his time of trouble. Such is the transient nature of man: here today, gone tomorrow. But the Lord is steadfast and will preserve, strengthen, and be merciful to those who consider the poor and disadvantaged. In other words, those who do not perceive themselves to be above even the lowliest of people will be favored and blessed.

One of the ways that David knows he is blessed by the Lord is that his enemies have not triumphed over him. Another way David recognizes that the Lord is with him is that even amid the evil surrounding him, his integrity has remained intact. He continues to uphold the ways of God.

So many times, when we are around discord and wickedness, we can become a part of it. For instance, gossiping with co-workers or taking drugs with friends. But when we have faith and have made it clear to God that we wish to walk His right path, God will give us strength to stay within our integrity and not go along with the whims of the world. Make no mistake, the Lord will make very clear those blessings that He has bestowed upon us. It is up to us to practice seeing the evidence of His favor—the fruits of faith—by cultivating discernment in our lives.

In order to begin to cultivate discernment or to strengthen our already existing discerning spirit, let us contemplate and begin listing those things that God has made clear is a gift of faith and blessing in our lives. There are no wrong answers here. Just write down anything that comes to mind. Feel free to add and edit as you see fit.

Worksheet: Cultivating Discernment

List of blessings in my life that God has made clear came from Him:

_____
_____
_____
_____
_____
_____
_____
_____
_____
_____
_____
_____

Consider this: God is the author of free will. Outside the just laws of society, if a circumstance, situation, request, decision, guidepost, voice, or directive is issued in such a way that does *not* allow for free participation but, instead, issues or implies a penalty for non-compliance, then it is *not* authorized by God. God does not force His will on His children. In the same way that God allows us to freely choose Him, we must always be aware of the choices we make that affect our lives. While cultivating our discernment, it is important that we pay attention to how we hear the will of God and how we recognize what He has gifted us.

Throughout the Bible, God is referred to as a meek and gentle yet powerful Father. Discernment soon recognizes these characteristics in our listening.

Notes:

Psalm 42: I Shall Praise God; He Is the Health of My Countenance

As the hart panteth after the water brooks, so panteth my soul after thee, O God. My soul thirsteth for God, for the living God: when shall I come and appear before God? My tears have been my meat day and night, while they continually say unto me, Where is thy God? When I remember these things, I pour out my soul in me: for I had gone with the multitude, I went with them to the house of God, with the voice of joy and praise, with a multitude that kept holyday. Why art thou cast down, O my soul? and why art thou disquieted in me? hope thou in God: for I shall yet praise him for the help of his countenance. O my God, my soul is cast down within me: therefore will I remember thee from the land of Jordan, and of the Hermonites, from the hill Mizar. Deep calleth unto deep at the noise of thy waterspouts: all thy waves and thy billows are gone over me. Yet the LORD will command his lovingkindness in the daytime, and in the night his song shall be with me, and my prayer unto the God of my life. I will say unto God my rock, Why hast thou forgotten me? why go I mourning because of the oppression of the enemy? As with a sword in my bones, mine enemies reproach me; while they say daily unto me, Where is thy God? Why art thou cast down, O my soul? and why art thou disquieted within me? hope thou in God: for I shall yet praise him, who is the health of my countenance, and my God.

Psalm 42 speaks about how when God is felt to be close to us, we can feel it in our health. Our faces and mannerisms look and feel more alive and joyful. However, when we cannot feel God's presence near us, our soul feels cast down, and there are feelings of sadness and lack.

Verses 2–3, "My soul thirsteth for God, for the living God: when shall I come and appear before God? My tears have been my meat day and night, while they continually say unto me, Where is thy God?"

In other words, during the periods when we feel like we are waiting for God to draw near to us, our souls thirst for Him. There is a sadness within us during these times that we feel abandoned by God. It would be easy to say that we feel this way out of personal loneliness or feelings of rejection. Maybe we are feeling sorry for ourselves? Psalm 42 is here to remind us that our thirst for God has nothing to do with anything we are capable of doing. This thirst is a gift.

Verse 5 (paraphrased by the author), "Hope thou in God with the voice of joy, praise Him for help of His countenance."

Verse 11, "Hope thou in God: for I shall praise him, who is the health of my countenance, and my God."

Or consider this:

Psalm 63:1, "My flesh longeth for thee in a dry and thirsty land, where no water is."

Also, later on in the Bible, we see this in the Gospel:

John 7:37, "Jesus stood and cried, …If any man thirsts, let him come unto me, and drink."

We thirst for God because He created us to thirst for Him.

When God is near us, we feel health and joy despite what we are going through, and when He is far from us, we feel a sadness that thirsts for God, whether we know, believe, or understand how this works. God *is* the health of our countenance. But there is more to countenance than just what we can visualize about our state of health and mind. Let's take a brief closer look at *countenance* and explore this concept further.

Study: Countenance

1. A person's face or facial expression.
2. Support.
3. Admit as acceptable, endorsement, endure, appearance, assistance, blessing.

How God is the health of our countenance:

1. The goodness of His support.
2. His healthy support.
3. Abundance of blessing.
4. Good fruits of faith.
5. Positive issuance or making His good way known to us.

Bible References

God gives us peace:

Numbers 6:26, "The LORD lift up his countenance upon thee, and give thee peace."

The light of God's countenance:

Psalm 4:6, "There be many that say, Who will shew us any good? LORD, lift thou up the light of thy countenance upon us."

God's blessing:

Psalm 21:6, "For thou hast made him most blessed for ever: thou hast made him exceeding glad with thy countenance."

A disquieted countenance when we feel God has departed from us:

> And Samuel said to Saul, Why hast thou disquieted me, to bring me up? And Saul answered, I am sore distressed; for the Philistines make war against me, and God is departed from me, and answereth me no more,

neither by prophets, nor by dreams: therefore I have called thee, that thou mayest make known unto me what I shall do.

1 Samuel 28:15

The Lord, in His divine wisdom and love for us, created us to thirst for Him. When we find Him, our hearts are filled with joy and supernatural peace. He alone is the health of our countenance, and without Him, we are filled with the thirst of loneliness and sadness that surpasses all understanding. With Him, we will be exceedingly glad, and it will show in the way we present ourselves.

Thank You for Your lovingkindness in our lives and for showing us Your goodness and glory. We ask You to keep us in faith. Praise to You, our Most High God and Father. Amen.

Psalm 43: O Deliver Me from the Deceitful and Unjust Man

> Judge me, O God, and plead my cause against an ungodly nation: O deliver me from the deceitful and unjust man. For thou art the God of my strength: why dost thou cast me off? why go I mourning because of the oppression of the enemy? O send out thy light and thy truth: let them lead me; let them bring me unto thy holy hill, and to thy tabernacles. Then will I go unto the altar of God, unto God my exceeding joy: yea, upon the harp will I praise thee, O God my God. Why art thou cast down, O my soul? and why art thou disquieted within me? hope in God: for I shall yet praise him, who is the health of my countenance, and my God.

Again, we see the author of Psalm 43 being disquieted within his soul for feeling that God has cast Him off. This time, the author is asking to be delivered from the deceitful and unjust man, for he is feeling oppressed by him. As a result, his countenance is sad and depressed.

So many times in life, we can take on the temperament of those people who are near to us. If we find ourselves in the company of liars and those who seek to do harm to us or others, the weight of their intentions can create oppression within our being. Imagine knowing that a person you spend time with is a known liar and has created discord within others' lives. In your deepest heart, you know that it will be only a matter of time before this person does the same to you. Does this make you feel free to trust that person? Or do you feel the need to continuously edit your behavior so you won't give them a reason to harm you? Perhaps some of your tactics to put off their harm include lying to them or causing them harm before they harm you. It can become a vicious cycle, causing more and more oppression.

Who we spend time with is so important to how we end up living our lives. Any time you are unable to be fully open and honest with a person, this creates oppression in the will. The will does not feel comfortable not acting in its truest nature, which is always troublesome for us.

So, what does the author of Psalm 43 do to overcome his oppression? He prays to God. He sings songs of praise. He asks God to draw near. Whereas those who are oppressed or who seek to oppress when near are unhealthy to be around, God is the health of our countenance.

When we commit to being near to Him in our lives, we begin to take on His countenance, which is goodness, loving, and merciful. Our lives are then conformed to joy and gladness, which begins the process of delivering us from those who bring about oppression. When we have hope, we hold joy and gladness in our hearts and experience freedom within our souls.

Through this, we learn to resist those things, people, and situations that generate feelings of oppression and discord within, and we begin to create physical, mental, and spiritual health within our lives. Doesn't that sound wonderful? Thank You, Abba, Father!

Stay near to God, and your life will become the healthiest it's ever been. Count on it, and keep the faith.

Psalm 44: My Confusion Is Continually Before Me

We have heard with our ears, O God, our fathers have told us, what work thou didst in their days, in the times of old. How thou didst drive out the heathen with thy hand, and plantedst them; how thou didst afflict the people, and cast them out. For they got not the land in possession by their own sword, neither did their own arm save them: but thy right hand, and thine arm, and the light of thy countenance, because thou hadst a favour unto them. Thou art my King, O God: command deliverances for Jacob. Through thee will we push down our enemies: through thy name will we tread them under that rise up against us. For I will not trust in my bow, neither shall my sword save me. But thou hast saved us from our enemies, and hast put them to shame that hated us. In God we boast all the day long, and praise thy name for ever. Selah. But thou hast cast off, and put us to shame; and goest not forth with our armies. Thou makest us to turn back from the enemy: and they which hate us spoil for themselves. Thou hast given us like sheep appointed for meat; and hast scattered us among the heathen. Thou sellest thy people for nought, and dost not increase thy wealth by their price. Thou makest us a reproach to our neighbours, a scorn and a derision to them that are round about us. Thou makest us a byword among the heathen, a shaking of the head among the people. My confusion is continually before me, and the shame of my face hath covered me, For the voice of him that reproacheth and blasphemeth; by reason of the enemy and avenger. All this is come upon us; yet have we not forgotten thee, neither have we dealt falsely in thy covenant. Our heart is not turned back, neither have our steps declined from thy way; Though thou hast sore broken us in the place of dragons, and covered us with the shadow of death. If we have forgotten the name of our God, or stretched out our hands to a strange god; Shall not God search this out? for he knoweth the secrets of the heart. Yea, for thy sake are we killed all the day long; we are counted as sheep for the slaughter. Awake, why sleepest thou, O Lord? arise, cast us not off for ever. Wherefore hidest thou thy face, and forgettest our affliction and our oppression? For our soul is bowed down to the dust: our belly cleaveth unto the earth. Arise for our help, and redeem us for thy mercies' sake.

In Psalm 44, we find David and the chosen people situated in the middle of a nation that despises them and which is overrun with the ungodly and blasphemous. David laments that in the days of the old times, the Lord saved the chosen by casting out the heathen and those who sought to slaughter them. Yet now, David and the children of God find themselves immersed in a society that despises them and their God, but the Lord has left them on their own.

Verse 22, "For thy sake are we killed all the day long; we are counted as sheep for the slaughter."

It is getting bad for the people of David out in the streets of their nation.

Verse 23, "Awake, why sleepest thou, O Lord? arise, cast us not off for ever."

One of the reasons David is confused by the working of God in this time is that the people are not bending to the will of the heathen nation, but they have continued to deal within the covenant they have with God.

Verse 8, "In God we boast all the day long, and praise thy name for ever. Selah."

So why does it seem that God is not listening to their pleas for help? After all, they are doing everything they should, they believe, and still, their city is overrun by those who hate them. Why is God not having mercy on them in their day of trouble?

This is where faith comes in and how patience is a good fruit of faith. Nowhere in the Bible does it say that God, the creator of the universe, will do the will of man no matter how much we pray. Prayer is a way to communicate with God and offer our desires, but it is foolish to think that God will bend His will to men. Even in times of deep despair and persecution, at the end of the day, all is done that reflects the will of God.

So, yes, as a child of God, it is right to continue to be righteous in the face of hard times. It is right to sing praise and pray to the Father amid death threats and smear campaigns. Faith comes from knowing and accepting that God is good and merciful even when everything around us seems to be failing. True faith is not for the faint of heart. True faith cultivates strength, perseverance, patience, courage, and those virtues that help us make it through the tough times because there are going to be times in our lives that are harder than anything we think we are capable of living through. And believe it or not, our hard times are just as much in the will of God as those times when everything seems to be going well.

It may not seem like it when there is nothing but chaos and failure in our lives, but the will of God is always merciful and just in the end. Upon reflection, we will see how God's grace helped us through our trials and we were made stronger in countenance and faith. Praise God Almighty, King of the universe.

While studying this psalm, I heard this message, which I will pass on to you, dear reader.

"For nothing happens that the Lord does not allow, and everything happens at its appointed time. You, My daughter and sister, have not the strength nor the will to change that. Rest easy knowing that your days are in My will."

This, too, shall pass, and better times are ahead. Have faith. Thank You, Lord!

Psalm 45: When We Enter the King's Palace

My heart is inditing a good matter: I speak of the things which I have made touching the king: my tongue is the pen of a ready writer. Thou art fairer than the children of men: grace is poured into thy lips: therefore God hath blessed thee for ever. Gird thy sword upon thy thigh, O most mighty, with thy glory and thy majesty. And in thy majesty ride prosperously because of truth and meekness and righteousness; and thy right hand shall teach thee terrible things. Thine arrows are sharp in the heart of the king's enemies; whereby the people fall under thee. Thy throne, O God, is for ever and ever: the sceptre of thy kingdom is a right sceptre. Thou lovest righteousness, and hatest wickedness: therefore God, thy God, hath anointed thee with the oil of gladness above thy fellows. All thy garments smell of myrrh, and aloes, and cassia, out of the ivory palaces, whereby they have made thee glad. Kings' daughters were among thy honourable women: upon thy right hand did stand the queen in gold of Ophir. Hearken, O daughter, and consider, and incline thine ear; forget also thine own people, and thy father's house; So shall the king greatly desire thy beauty: for he is thy Lord; and worship thou him. And the daughter of Tyre shall be there with a gift; even the rich among the people shall intreat thy favour. The king's daughter is all glorious within: her clothing is of wrought gold. She shall be brought unto the king in raiment of needlework: the virgins her companions that follow her shall be brought unto thee. With gladness and rejoicing shall they be brought: they shall enter into the king's palace. Instead of thy fathers shall be thy children, whom thou mayest make princes in all the earth. I will make thy name to be remembered in all generations: therefore shall the people praise thee for ever and ever.

The people of God are being compared to a daughter of the king, and, in many ways, Psalm 45 asks us to understand how it will be when His faithful enter the kingdom of God. We must not forget that we are the children of God, who is King. Though humility is a good and necessary character trait for us to cultivate, David is reminding us who we are and that our Father is above all the kings and princes of this world.

Let us consider the royal spectacle of those who shall meet God at His palace when our time comes to enter into eternity. Psalm 45 uses the illustration of a daughter to exemplify the spirit of God's faithful children walking into the kingdom.

1. She is fairer than the children of this world.
2. She speaks with grace.
3. She has been blessed by her King forever.
4. Her prosperity comes from her truth, meekness, and righteousness.
5. She has been anointed with gladness above the worldly.
6. Her garments shall smell of myrrh, aloes, and cassia, which are exotic scents.
7. At the right hand of God, the queen shall stand, dressed in the finest gold.
8. The daughter is honorable.
9. The King will delight in the beauty of His daughter.
10. The daughter shall bring a gift for the King to entreat His favor.
11. She shall be glorious within.
12. She shall be dressed in a majestic garment of gold and needlework.
13. With joy and gladness, she shall enter into the King's palace.

14. All shall praise the King forever and ever.

What an amazing occasion that will be! As the King of heaven welcomes His child into paradise, the spiritual being takes on the magnificence of a prince or princess whose rightful inheritance is to lay claim to a place in the King's palace. It sounds as if it will be a joyful gathering of friends and family in the opulence of the one who is the King of kings.

But the secret is that we can have this now!

So many of us, deep in our hearts, think that there is no way that God our Father could ever love us. We imagine ourselves to be unworthy of the type of love that is spoken of in places of worship or what we read in the Bible. We read that God so loved us that He sacrificed His only Son, Jesus, so that we may be redeemed of our sins and worthy to take a place in heaven alongside Him. It sounds like a nice story, and we want to believe it, but we just can't seem to accept that we are the worthy ones if we are honest with ourselves. They must be talking about someone else, right? There have been things that we have done that have offended the Father, who just wants to love us. We might have neglected Him or downright rejected Him, and there is no way, no matter what this book or any other book tells us, that we are truly forgiven and loved. If you have ever felt this way, do not worry; you are not alone. But let us look at a story:

Imagine that you are living in poverty. Your clothes are dirty. You don't have regular access to bathing. Every day, you sit outside the walls of the King's palace and beg for money so you can buy yourself a meal or an article of clothing. In your poverty, you feel invisible and unwanted and less than human, and many times, the people outside the palace shout degrading words to you or tell you to go away. You really are at a low place in the humiliation that you feel. Sometimes, you wish you were dead. You cry out in pain for someone to help you.

Then, one day, the door to the palace opens, and the Prince is standing at the entrance. He sees you sitting there in your misery. But instead of punishing you for sitting outside the palace, He gets excited to see you.

"My brother (or sister)," He says and takes you in His arms and hugs you. "Come into My home. Father will be so glad to see you."

In your amazement and confusion, you follow Him into the palace. *Father?* you think to yourself. *Is He talking to me?*

With great compassion in His eyes, He sees the pain you have been in, and He begins to help you clean up. He draws you a bath and lays out His finest garments for you to wear. He feeds you and gives you water to give you health. When you are finished getting ready, He brings you into the sitting room, where the Father immediately recognizes you and rushes over to embrace you.

It turns out that you are one of the King's children, and the whole time you were living in poverty, He was hoping every day that you would return to Him. And now, here you are in the palace, dressed in fine garments, eating the finest foods, and enjoying life with the King—who happens to be your Father. Where before your soul was filled with the pain and disillusion of poverty and you didn't know where you were going to sleep from one day to the next, your soul is now calm and safe, knowing that you are a child of the King, living in the refuge of the palace, and finally, after all these years, you have rest.

This is not just any story. This is the story of faith. Have faith and trust in God, and even while you walk this earth, you can lay claim to your inheritance as a child of God. Keep on the good path and stay in the will of God, and not only will your earthly life be filled with goodness and support, but at the end of it all, your spirit will live for eternity in the palace of the King in heaven. That's how this story ends. There really is happiness ever after.

Psalm 45 is here to remind us of our royal lineage and all that it means to be a child of the King of the universe. Sometimes, we need to be reminded that we are so much more than what the world tells us who we are. Thank You, Lord. Our good Father and King of kings. Amen.

We are the children of the Almighty and everlasting God. Let that bring you comfort when you doubt yourself and your worthiness as you move forward in faith.

Psalm 46: God Is Our Refuge and Strength, a Very Present Help in Trouble

God is our refuge and strength, a very present help in trouble. Therefore will not we fear, though the earth be removed, and though the mountains be carried into the midst of the sea; Though the waters thereof roar and be troubled, though the mountains shake with the swelling thereof. Selah. There is a river, the streams whereof shall make glad the city of God, the holy place of the tabernacles of the most High. God is in the midst of her; she shall not be moved: God shall help her, and that right early. The heathen raged, the kingdoms were moved: he uttered his voice, the earth melted. The LORD of hosts is with us; the God of Jacob is our refuge. Selah. Come, behold the works of the LORD, what desolations he hath made in the earth. He maketh wars to cease unto the end of the earth; he breaketh the bow, and cutteth the spear in sunder; he burneth the chariot in the fire. Be still, and know that I am God: I will be exalted among the heathen, I will be exalted in the earth. The LORD of hosts is with us; the God of Jacob is our refuge. Selah.

A refuge is an area set aside from alteration from the outside. For instance, the National Bird Refuge is a place where birds can go and be reassured that their habitation will not be corrupted. In this same way, the Lord sets aside a space for us where we can feel safe and be uncorrupted by the world, especially during difficult times.

A refuge is also very much needed in times of war. Psalm 46 seems to correlate the refuge of God as a place available during very turbulent times when "the heathen raged, the kingdoms were moved: he uttered his voice, the earth melted. [But] the Lord of hosts is with us; the God of Jacob is our refuge. Selah" (verses 6–7).

It is interesting to note that whenever God is referred to as the "God of hosts," it is meant to illustrate that He is the Lord of armies. He fights for us and supports His children on the day of their battle. This can refer to an earthly battle where a person is fighting a person, but also the spiritual battle between the powers of evil and the powers of good. During these times, the Lord is our refuge, and we are the refugees whom He supports and shelters from the battles we fight, with others and internally. And like the sanctuary of the National Bird Refuge, in His shelter He keeps us from the corruption of the outside world.

Whereas the battles waged by the ungodly can create bitterness and vengeance, within the refuge of God, we are able to maintain our sanctity and strength of character. The wars we fight do not alter us to conform to the world but help us become stronger in our faith and conviction.

The Lord is our refuge, for He is a strong and merciful Lord, the general of all battles. Amen.

Psalm 47: For the LORD Most High Is Terrible; He Is a Great King over All the Earth

{To the chief Musician, A Psalm for the sons of Korah.} O clap your hands, all ye people; shout unto God with the voice of triumph. For the LORD most high is terrible; he is a great King over all the earth. He shall subdue the people under us, and the nations under our feet. He shall choose our inheritance for us, the excellency of Jacob whom he loved. Selah. God is gone up with a shout, the LORD with the sound of a trumpet. Sing praises to God, sing praises: sing praises unto our King, sing praises. For God is the King of all the earth: sing ye praises with understanding. God reigneth over the heathen: God sitteth upon the throne of his holiness. The princes of the people are gathered together, even the people of the God of Abraham: for the shields of the earth belong unto God: he is greatly exalted.

In many places in the Bible, we see the Lord being referred to as terrible. In fact, in Psalm 47, not only is God called "terrible," but immediately after, he is called "great."

Verse 2, "For the LORD most high is terrible; he is a great King over all the earth."

How can this be? In our modern understanding, being terrible is a negative thing. If we say that the food was terrible, it means that it was beyond bad. It was terrible. It is doubtful that the Bible's use of terrible to refer to God means the same as how we tend to use it in our time, so let's examine this concept for a few moments.

Study: God Is Terrible; What Does It Mean?

Perhaps getting a definition of "terrible" can begin to open our understanding.

Terrible: adjective.

1. Distressing; severe:
   a. A terrible winter.
2. Extremely bad; horrible:
   a. Terrible coffee; a terrible movie.
3. Exciting terror, awe, or great fear; dreadful; awful.
4. Formidably great:
   a. A terrible responsibility.

Okay, it is starting to make sense, but what does the Bible have to say about our "terrible" God?

1. Deuteronomy 7:21, "Thou shalt not be affrighted at them: for the LORD thy God is among you, a mighty God and terrible."
2. Nehemiah 1:5, "And said, I beseech thee, O LORD God of heaven, the great and terrible God, that keepeth covenant and mercy for them that love him and observe his commandments."
3. Job 37:22, "Fair weather cometh out of the north: with God is terrible majesty."
4. Psalm 66:5, "Come and see the works of God: he is terrible in his doing toward the children of men."
5. Psalm 99:3, "Let them praise thy great and terrible name; for it is holy."
6. Zephaniah 2:11, "The LORD will be terrible unto them: for he will famish all the gods of the earth; and men shall worship him, every one from his place, even all the isles of the heathen."
7. Jeremiah 20:11, "But the LORD is with me as a mighty terrible one: therefore my persecutors shall stumble, and they shall not prevail: they shall be greatly ashamed; for

they shall not prosper: their everlasting confusion shall never be forgotten."
8. Joel 2:31, "The sun shall be turned into darkness, and the moon into blood, before the great and terrible day of the LORD come."

The picture that is forming about our God is that not only is He good and filled with lovingkindness, but He is a terrible God as well. We are reminded that our Most High God is capable of being extreme. It's not always in the middle with God. In fact, famously, He despises lukewarm.

Revelation 3:16, "So then because thou art lukewarm, and neither cold nor hot, I will spue thee out of my mouth."

In the same way that the Lord is extreme in His truth, for He cannot lie, His justice is extreme. There are no plea bargains with God once He has come down on judgment with us.

Our God is a terrible God to the iniquities and wicked. He will destroy His enemies and is a master strategist who will never lose. He is terrible to those who blaspheme Him and speak evil onto Him. He is mighty and powerful, yet, at the same time, produces great fear in those who hate Him. But to His children who trust Him, *reverentially* fear Him, and obey His laws, He will never forsake them and will have mercy for them. For His Love is extreme as well.

In the fire of His wrath, God made hell and all that it possesses. Never doubt the strong arm of justice that He provides. As fiercely as He loves His children, when one is cut off at death, the desolation He provides is extreme. This is why we must try to save as many souls as we can. Our Lord weeps for the fate of any souls that are lost. It is a terrible finality, and He knows this.

Praise be to the Most High Father, for You *are* terrible and great in Thy love and just judgment! Hallelujah!

Psalm 48: The City of the Great King

> Great is the LORD, and greatly to be praised in the city of our God, in the mountain of his holiness. Beautiful for situation, the joy of the whole earth, is mount Zion, on the sides of the north, the city of the great King. God is known in her palaces for a refuge. For, lo, the kings were assembled, they passed by together. They saw it, and so they marvelled; they were troubled, and hasted away. Fear took hold upon them there, and pain, as of a woman in travail. Thou breakest the ships of Tarshish with an east wind. As we have heard, so have we seen in the city of the LORD of hosts, in the city of our God: God will establish it for ever. Selah. We have thought of thy lovingkindness, O God, in the midst of thy temple. According to thy name, O God, so is thy praise unto the ends of the earth: thy right hand is full of righteousness. Let mount Zion rejoice, let the daughters of Judah be glad, because of thy judgments. Walk about Zion, and go round about her: tell the towers thereof. Mark ye well her bulwarks, consider her palaces; that ye may tell it to the generation following. For this God is our God for ever and ever: he will be our guide even unto death

It is interesting how the Psalms frequently use David as a reflection of God Himself. It makes sense when we learn that God compared Himself to David and proclaimed that he would fulfill the will of God. As a reminder,

> And when he [God] had removed him, he raised up unto them David to be their king; to whom also he gave testimony, and said, I have found David the son of Jesse, a man after mine own heart, which shall fulfil all my will.
>
> Acts 13:22

So, now we see Psalm 48 talk about the city of the great King.

Verse 2, "Beautiful for situation, the joy of the whole earth, is mount Zion, on the sides of the north, the city of the great King."

Can we assume this psalm is talking about the city of David, another term for "Old" Jerusalem, and is located on Ophel Hill, near Mount Zion, and at the bottom of the Southern slope of Mount Moriah?

Matthew 5:34–35, "Neither by heaven; for it is God's throne: Nor by the earth; for it is his footstool: neither by Jerusalem; for it is the city of the great King."

So, we see that even 1000 years after King David reigned, in the time of Matthew, an apostle of Jesus, Jerusalem was referred to as the city of the great King. However, at the same time, Psalm 48 makes it clear that this is the city of our God.

Verse 1, "Great is the LORD, and greatly to be praised in the city of our God, in the mountain of his holiness."

So, we see that Jerusalem is referred to as both the city of our God and the city of the great King. Isn't that interesting? Perhaps this psalm is prophesying about a King to come?

Matthew 27:11, "And Jesus stood before the governor: and the governor asked him, saying, Art thou the King of the Jews? And Jesus said unto him, Thou sayest."

What is even more interesting is that God created the earth, and on the earth, He made a city for Himself, which is Jerusalem. This city was established in the earlier days as the city of David, who was a mighty king whom God saw as a man after His own heart and who became the father of the chosen people on Earth for all generations.

God came down from His throne in heaven and was incarnated as Jesus Christ, a human man in the flesh. Mary, the mother of Jesus, was born in the line of David.

In human form, He came to Jerusalem, which is the city He created as a place for His temple so He could be worshiped. Unfortunately, not only was the Lord not recognized inside His own temple, but He was also rejected by His own city.

Jesus, who is God, came down to the earth to save us from our flesh. God knows the inherent filth within our flesh yet it is also our flesh that is in a similar image to Him. God looks like us. We look like God. Jesus is proof of this, for He is the face of God. Human beings are at once filled with the sin and stench of Earth by way of Satan as well as the majesty and Spirit of God Himself. In our finest form, human beings are magnificent and masterpieces of God the creator. And in faith, we are shepherded through life with Him at our right hand, and Psalm 48 reminds us of this.

Verse 14, "For this God is our God for ever and ever: he will be our guide even unto death."

Satan tries to keep us from this knowledge by continually beating us down so that we think we are filth and unworthy. He is like a toxic partner who fears us finding our true, beautiful worth and gaining the courage to leave his bondage. God is worthiness and freedom, and once in His fold, we mount higher and higher and can leave the bonds of the devil behind confidently and permanently.

Thank You, Father, for being the King in our lives and giving us support to stay on Your path. Amen.

Psalm 49: Man That Is in Honour, and Understandeth Not, Is Like the Beasts That Perish

Hear this, all ye people; give ear, all ye inhabitants of the world: Both low and high, rich and poor, together. My mouth shall speak of wisdom; and the meditation of my heart shall be of understanding. I will incline mine ear to a parable: I will open my dark saying upon the harp. Wherefore should I fear in the days of evil, when the iniquity of my heels shall compass me about? They that trust in their wealth, and boast themselves in the multitude of their riches; None of them can by any means redeem his brother, nor give to God a ransom for him: (For the redemption of their soul is precious, and it ceaseth for ever:) That he should still live for ever, and not see corruption. For he seeth that wise men die, likewise the fool and the brutish person perish, and leave their wealth to others. Their inward thought is, that their houses shall continue for ever, and their dwelling places to all generations; they call their lands after their own names. Nevertheless man being in honour abideth not: he is like the beasts that perish. This their way is their folly: yet their posterity approve their sayings. Selah. Like sheep they are laid in the grave; death shall feed on them; and the upright shall have dominion over them in the morning; and their beauty shall consume in the grave from their dwelling. But God will redeem my soul from the power of the grave: for he shall receive me. Selah. Be not thou afraid when one is made rich, when the glory of his house is increased; For when he dieth he shall carry nothing away: his glory shall not descend after him. Though while he lived he blessed his soul: and men will praise thee, when thou doest well to thyself. He shall go to the generation of his fathers; they shall never see light. Man that is in honour, and understandeth not, is like the beasts that perish.

Verses 1, 3, "Hear this, all ye people; give ear, all ye inhabitants of the world …My mouth shall speak of wisdom; and the meditation of my heart shall be of understanding."

This psalm is presented as if by someone who has wisdom because they have lived through something and, in meditating, has come to an understanding of the issue. In essence, Psalm 49 explains that having great fortune and honor in life will not guarantee the redemption of a soul.

Verses 6–7, "They that trust in their wealth, and boast themselves in the multitude of their riches; None of them can by any means redeem his brother, nor give to God a ransom for him."

In other words, riches cannot buy salvation. In fact, Psalm 49 indicates the exact opposite: those who gain power, honor, and wealth while they are in the flesh but who do not follow and trust in the Lord shall perish.

Verses 12–13, "Nevertheless man being in honour abideth not: he is like the beasts that perish. This their way is their folly: yet their posterity approve their sayings. Selah."

Those who live in iniquity and are praised here on Earth are like the beasts that perish and shall not see the light. They will go to the generations of their fathers, which is darkness, and their beauty shall be consumed in the grave. It is not enough to have riches; one must have faith in God and follow the path that pleases the Father.

Verses 14–15,

> Like sheep they are laid in the grave; death shall feed on them; and the upright shall have dominion over them in the morning; and their beauty shall consume in the

grave from their dwelling. But God will redeem my soul from the power of the grave: for he shall receive me [His children rich and poor but humble in stature]. Selah.

It is the riches we gain from the grace of God through humility, prayer, faith, and upright living that are everlasting and not anything we could ever earn here on Earth. In other words, riches are no indication that we are honorable. The lowest among us may very well be more honorable in God's sight than the richest person on Earth. Thank You for this wisdom, O Lord our redeemer. Amen.

God is not interested in what we have. He wants our beautiful and humble hearts to trust in Him.

Psalm 50: Our God Shall Come, and Shall Not Keep Silence

{A Psalm of Asaph.} The mighty God, even the LORD, hath spoken, and called the earth from the rising of the sun unto the going down thereof. Out of Zion, the perfection of beauty, God hath shined. Our God shall come, and shall not keep silence: a fire shall devour before him, and it shall be very tempestuous round about him. He shall call to the heavens from above, and to the earth, that he may judge his people. Gather my saints together unto me; those that have made a covenant with me by sacrifice. And the heavens shall declare his righteousness: for God is judge himself. Selah. Hear, O my people, and I will speak; O Israel, and I will testify against thee: I am God, even thy God. I will not reprove thee for thy sacrifices or thy burnt offerings, to have been continually before me. I will take no bullock out of thy house, nor he goats out of thy folds. For every beast of the forest is mine, and the cattle upon a thousand hills. I know all the fowls of the mountains: and the wild beasts of the field are mine. If I were hungry, I would not tell thee: for the world is mine, and the fulness thereof. Will I eat the flesh of bulls, or drink the blood of goats? Offer unto God thanksgiving; and pay thy vows unto the most High: And call upon me in the day of trouble: I will deliver thee, and thou shalt glorify me. But unto the wicked God saith, What hast thou to do to declare my statutes, or that thou shouldest take my covenant in thy mouth? Seeing thou hatest instruction, and castest my words behind thee. When thou sawest a thief, then thou consentedst with him, and hast been partaker with adulterers. Thou givest thy mouth to evil, and thy tongue frameth deceit. Thou sittest and speakest against thy brother; thou slanderest thine own mother's son. These things hast thou done, and I kept silence; thou thoughtest that I was altogether such an one as thyself: but I will reprove thee, and set them in order before thine eyes. Now consider this, ye that forget God, lest I tear you in pieces, and there be none to deliver. Whoso offereth praise glorifieth me: and to him that ordereth his conversation aright will I shew the salvation of God.

Asaph was a Levite who was commissioned to sing to Yahweh in the temple before King David. Psalm 50 paints a picture of how it will be when God comes down from the heavens and judges the people. On that day, we shall see that:

1. God shall not keep silent.
2. A fire shall devour everything before Him.
3. It shall be tempestuous around Him.
4. He shall call to the heavens from above.
5. To the earth, He shall call so that He may judge His people.
6. He will gather His saints unto Him, those that made a covenant with Him by sacrifice.
7. The heavens will declare His righteousness.
8. God will be the judge Himself.

As we can see, on the day that God comes, it will be evident that He has come down from heaven and is in the process of declaring His judgment upon the people. Not only will He come down with a fire before Him which devours all that is in its way, but there will be a mighty storm surrounding Him. In other words, it will be clear He has arrived.

One of the first things He will do is separate the people into camps: first, those who made a sacrificial covenant with Him whom He calls saints, and second, those whom He recognizes as the wicked. To the wicked, whom He has seen hates instruction and disregards His words, He will not accept their sacrificial offerings as a token of covenant and repentance. Psalm 50 gives a good list of why God will not accept them:

1. They consented with thieves.
2. They partook with adulterers.
3. They spoke evil words.
4. They lied in words and actions.
5. They speak and sit against their own family.
6. They slander their own brothers and mothers.

Those who forget God in their ways and daily lives will be torn to pieces (there's that terrible God again) and not delivered. But to those who praise and glorify God and who live in goodness, He shall offer salvation.

Is it a time for celebration, knowing that there are people throughout history and even until today that will be "torn to pieces" on the day of their judgment? No, this is not something anyone—especially children of God—should ever gain happiness from because it is celebrating a terrible and eternal misery for those who are judged harshly. Psalm 50 is a warning for everyone. It asks us to find a way out of our own wicked behaviors by recognizing them and seeking to change lest our day of judgment end in that terrible way.

Worksheet: How Is Your Life Going Right Now?

Consider Psalm 50: Are there areas in your life that resemble the way of the saints and will be rewarded?

_____

_____

_____

_____

_____

Are there areas of your life that resemble those who will receive harsh punishment? Be honest.

_____

_____

_____

_____

_____

Let us pray.

Dear Holy Father, we pray that all people, including ourselves, find their way onto Your most holy and merciful path. Give us the strength to overcome our own faults and the bravery to help others overcome theirs as we come onto Your good path. We ask for Your compassion as we sometimes stumble through life and pray for Your gentle instruction to help us back on path.

May we all join You one day in heaven. Thank You, our most holy and compassionate Father. Amen.

Psalm 51: Restore unto Me the Joy of Thy Salvation

{To the chief Musician, A Psalm of David, when Nathan the prophet came unto him, after he had gone in to Bathsheba.} Have mercy upon me, O God, according to thy lovingkindness: according unto the multitude of thy tender mercies blot out my transgressions. Wash me throughly from mine iniquity, and cleanse me from my sin. For I acknowledge my transgressions: and my sin is ever before me. Against thee, thee only, have I sinned, and done this evil in thy sight: that thou mightest be justified when thou speakest, and be clear when thou judgest. Behold, I was shapen in iniquity; and in sin did my mother conceive me. Behold, thou desirest truth in the inward parts: and in the hidden part thou shalt make me to know wisdom. Purge me with hyssop*, and I shall be clean: wash me, and I shall be whiter than snow. Make me to hear joy and gladness; that the bones which thou hast broken may rejoice. Hide thy face from my sins, and blot out all mine iniquities. Create in me a clean heart, O God; and renew a right spirit within me. Cast me not away from thy presence; and take not thy holy spirit from me. Restore unto me the joy of thy salvation; and uphold me with thy free spirit. Then will I teach transgressors thy ways; and sinners shall be converted unto thee. Deliver me from bloodguiltiness, O God, thou God of my salvation: and my tongue shall sing aloud of thy righteousness. O Lord, open thou my lips; and my mouth shall shew forth thy praise. For thou desirest not sacrifice; else would I give it: thou delightest not in burnt offering. The sacrifices of God are a broken spirit: a broken and a contrite heart, O God, thou wilt

> not despise. Do good in thy good pleasure unto Zion: build thou the walls of Jerusalem. Then shalt thou be pleased with the sacrifices of righteousness, with burnt offering and whole burnt offering: then shall they offer bullocks upon thine altar.

In Psalm 51, David prays that God may purge him of his transgressions so he may be restored in the sight of God. This is a psalm of a contrite heart, asking for another chance to be cleansed of sin.

David recognizes a very important fact about all of us: we were born into sin by no fault of ourselves. This is our natural disposition even before we were born.

Verse 5, "I was shapen in iniquity; and in sin did my mother conceive me."

The first step to solving a problem is recognizing that a problem exists, and this is the core problem of humanity: even at the moment of conception, we are bound to sin. This is such an important concept to understand as we make our way in faith. When we understand this, we can approach God with a humble heart.

Verses 1–3,

> Have mercy upon me, O God, according to thy lovingkindness: according unto the multitude of thy tender mercies blot out my transgressions. Wash me throughly from mine iniquity, and cleanse me from my sin. For I acknowledge my transgressions: and my sin is ever before me.

It is only through God that we can truly cleanse our sin because our sinful nature has no idea that, first, it is sinful, and second, that sin is something to be cleansed. It would be like asking a lump of clay to not be a lump of clay but to be a vase. The lump of clay has no idea what a vase is—but the sculpture does. If we do not know and listen to God and His ways, we will always be like a lump of clay born in sin instead of a child of God with a royal inheritance—which is what God, in His lovingkindness, is seeking for all of us.

It is said by some in this world, that it is easier for humans to be good than to be wicked, but this is the opposite of truth. The natural path of man is to pursue sinful endeavors. There are the laws of God that explain the worst of sinful behaviors such as adultery, murder, lying, or honoring false idols, but within us, we have foreknowledge that these behaviors are evil because most people will feel guilt or distress of conscience over doing these things.

However, even those things that in themselves are not necessarily bad behaviors in moderation, we take them to sinful levels through a lack of discipline like greed, gluttony, or laziness. Without the purposeful intervention of will, the natural inclination of man is to continue feeding himself with pleasure long after the behavior has ceased to be pleasurable. We've all been there. We can break our hearts through these behaviors, especially when the foundation of our lives comes crashing down like they frequently do when built on sin.

The sacrifice of restraint in these instances, with the help of God, is seen positively in the sight of the Father. And Psalm 51 reminds us of this.

Verse 17, "The sacrifices of God are a broken spirit: a broken and a contrite heart, O God, thou wilt not despise."

At the end of the day, it comes back to our humility, where we can once again come into a greater communion with the Lord.

When we look at Psalm 51, we can see that the steps of one who comes back to full communion and service with the Most High are as follows:

1. Our sin is thoroughly judged before God.
2. We are forgiven.
3. Our souls are cleansed of sin.
4. Our hearts are filled with the flames of the Holy Spirit.

5. We seek service to one another rather than only ourselves.
6. We worship and praise the Lord for His kindness and mercy.
7. Our souls are restored in fellowship with God.
8. This is not about self but about the blessing of Zion (aka the kingdom of God).

Amen.

*Hyssop: a shrub with which the blood and water of purification were applied.

Psalm 52: I Will Wait on Thy Name; for It Is Good before Thy Saints

Why boastest thou thyself in mischief, O mighty man? the goodness of God endureth continually. Thy tongue deviseth mischiefs; like a sharp rasor, working deceitfully. Thou lovest evil more than good; and lying rather than to speak righteousness. Selah. Thou lovest all devouring words, O thou deceitful tongue. God shall likewise destroy thee for ever, he shall take thee away, and pluck thee out of thy dwelling place, and root thee out of the land of the living. Selah. The righteous also shall see, and fear, and shall laugh at him: Lo, this is the man that made not God his strength; but trusted in the abundance of his riches, and strengthened himself in his wickedness. But I am like a green olive tree in the house of God: I trust in the mercy of God for ever and ever. I will praise thee for ever, because thou hast done it: and I will wait on thy name; for it is good before thy saints.

In Psalm 52, David laments the treachery and lying tongue of Saul, who was his adversary. It appears that Saul has been boasting of his mighty power, but David reminds Saul that God is good and endures forever.

On the other hand, Saul:

1. Devises mischief.
2. Works deceitfully.
3. Loves evil more than good.
4. Speaks about the ruin and destruction of David.
5. Has not made God his strength.
6. Has put his trust in his riches over God.
7. Has become more and more wicked.

Because of all these things, David foretells that the power of God will strike Saul down and bring him out of the land of the living. Whereas Saul will be plucked out of the land, David is one of the green olive trees that is growing, healthy, and fully rooted in the house of the Lord. David knows God is merciful, and he trusts in His mercy forever. Therefore, David will wait for the Lord to overthrow Saul because he knows this will be the eventual result. God is good to His saints.

The wicked are despised, but the children of God are given mercy. David has been around long enough to know that God protects and supports His faithful, and he trusts in God's mercy for His children over those who continue to have wicked ways.

The deeper our faith, the more we recognize and know that this is what God does: He shows up for His people and gains victory for us. Thank You, Lord!

Notes:

Psalm 53: The Fool Hath Said in His Heart, There Is No God

> The fool hath said in his heart, There is no God. Corrupt are they, and have done abominable iniquity: there is none that doeth good. God looked down from heaven upon the children of men, to see if there were any that did understand, that did seek God. Every one of them is gone back: they are altogether become filthy; there is none that doeth good, no, not one. Have the workers of iniquity no knowledge? who eat up my people as they eat bread: they have not called upon God. There were they in great fear, where no fear was: for God hath scattered the bones of him that encampeth against thee: thou hast put them to shame, because God hath despised them. Oh that the salvation of Israel were come out of Zion! When God bringeth back the captivity of his people, Jacob shall rejoice, and Israel shall be glad.

In Psalm 53, David laments that it makes one foolish to think that there is not a God. And those who do not regard God become corrupt, extremely unjust, and don't even try to do good.

Verses 2–3,

> God looked down from heaven upon the children of men, to see if there were any that did understand, that did seek God. Every one of them is gone back: they are altogether become filthy; there is none that doeth good, no, not one.

God looked down from heaven to see if there were any people who sought Him and did good, but He could not find one person. In His mercy, God wonders if it is because the people lack information about Him.

Verse 4, "Have the workers of iniquity no knowledge?"

He is talking about the ungodly who have idols and sacrifice to these earthly gods—even sacrificing the people of God to the altars of these strange gods. Could they also be eating the flesh of the children of God in their wickedness?

Verse 4 (continued), "Who eat up my people as they eat bread: they have not called upon God."

Because they do not call upon Him but continue in their immoral and corrupt ways, God has put them to shame and despised them.

David is distraught by what he sees going on around him and wonders when God will save His people from captivity. In the end, he has hope in God and knows that someday, He will put Israel back together.

Interestingly, centuries later, was it Psalm 53 that Paul seemed to reference when speaking to the Romans in a letter after the Son of God, Jesus Christ, was crucified and risen from the dead in an act of redemption for the sins of all people?

> For I would not, brethren, that ye should be ignorant of this mystery, lest ye should be wise in your own conceits; that blindness in part is happened to Israel, until the fulness of the Gentiles be come in. And so all Israel shall be saved: as it is written, There shall come out of Sion the Deliverer, and shall turn away ungodliness from Jacob: For this is my covenant unto them, when I shall take away their sins.
>
> Romans 11:25–27

Paul is saying that a certain blindness was created in the people of Israel that will be broken after God allows the fullness of all Gentiles to come into His covenant. And as it was written, a deliverer will come out of Zion, and then all will be saved and have their sins redeemed. It seems that the prophecy of Psalm 53 was fulfilled.

Psalm 53:6, "Oh that the salvation of Israel were come out of Zion! When God bringeth back the captivity of his people, Jacob shall rejoice, and Israel shall be glad."

Ultimately, Psalm 53 speaks about living within a corrupt world and how, even amid mass corruption, God will always find a way to protect His people and save them from the oppression of iniquity. There are times when that seems impossible because everywhere we look, criminals and those who reject the law seem to rule the day. But one day, the corrupt will be ruined, and then those who have continued to follow the ways of God and trust in Him will rejoice and be glad. Thank You, Lord. You are our Savior, redeemer, and protector. Amen.

The tides will turn as they have always done, and the people of God will find themselves saved, and they will flourish. Have hope!

Psalm 54: Behold, God Is Mine Helper

{To the chief Musician on Neginoth, Maschil, A Psalm of David, when the Ziphims came and said to Saul, Doth not David hide himself with us?} Save me, O God, by thy name, and judge me by thy strength. Hear my prayer, O God; give ear to the words of my mouth. For strangers are risen up against me, and oppressors seek after my soul: they have not set God before them. Selah. Behold, God is mine helper: the Lord is with them that uphold my soul. He shall reward evil unto mine enemies: cut them off in thy truth. I will freely sacrifice unto thee: I will praise thy name, O LORD; for it is good. For he hath delivered me out of all trouble: and mine eye hath seen his desire upon mine enemies.

In Psalm 54, David is expressing his troubles to the Lord. There are people who surround him who wish him harm. However, because David has seen the power of God in action, he knows that it is just a matter of time before his enemies are ruined and he is saved. Because of this, in the end, David sings a song of praise to God, for He hath delivered him out of all trouble. In his faith, he knows God will help him through the day of his trouble and save him.

Right now, you may be going through similar travails as David. Perhaps there are people in your life who have been hurting you emotionally, physically, or spiritually. Or maybe you are in a situation where there are two paths you could take, and you don't know what to do. Whatever your current situation, how do you need God to help you right now?

Worksheet: Help Me, O Lord!

Take a few moments to write down those needs you have at this moment and ask God to help you through them. Then, have faith that He will help you in a way that is according to His will—which is always seeking your best interests.

_____

_____

_____

_____

_____

_____

_____

_____

_____

_____

_____

_____

_____

_____

_____

The love of God is always seeking the highest good for His children, even in times of trouble.

Psalm 55: For It Was Not an Enemy That Reproached Me

Give ear to my prayer, O God; and hide not thyself from my supplication. Attend unto me, and hear me: I mourn in my complaint, and make a noise; Because of the voice of the enemy, because of the oppression of the wicked: for they cast iniquity upon me, and in wrath they hate me. My heart is sore pained within me: and the terrors of death are fallen upon me. Fearfulness and trembling are come upon me, and horror hath overwhelmed me. And I said, Oh that I had wings like a dove! for then would I fly away, and be at rest. Lo, then would I wander far off, and remain in the wilderness. Selah. I would hasten my escape from the windy storm and tempest. Destroy, O Lord, and divide their tongues: for I have seen violence and strife in the city. Day and night they go about it upon the walls thereof: mischief also and sorrow are in the midst of it. Wickedness is in the midst thereof: deceit and guile depart not from her streets. For it was not an enemy that reproached me; then I could have borne it: neither was it he that hated me that did magnify himself against me; then I would have hid myself from him: But it was thou, a man mine equal, my guide, and mine acquaintance. We took sweet counsel together, and walked unto the house of God in company. Let death seize upon them, and let them go down quick into hell: for wickedness is in their dwellings, and among them. As for me, I will call upon God; and the LORD shall save me. Evening, and morning, and at noon, will I pray, and cry aloud: and he shall hear my voice. He hath delivered my soul in peace from the battle that was against me: for there were many with me. God shall hear, and afflict them, even he that

> abideth of old. Selah. Because they have no changes, therefore they fear not God. He hath put forth his hands against such as be at peace with him: he hath broken his covenant. The words of his mouth were smoother than butter, but war was in his heart: his words were softer than oil, yet were they drawn swords. Cast thy burden upon the LORD, and he shall sustain thee: he shall never suffer the righteous to be moved. But thou, O God, shalt bring them down into the pit of destruction: bloody and deceitful men shall not live out half their days; but I will trust in thee.

As we make our way through the Psalms, we notice that David offers many prayers to God about his enemies and how they surround him and wish harm upon him and his people. Sometimes, his enemies are the adversaries of his kingdom, and other times, they are the godless who have taken over his city and nation. In Psalm 55, however, David is talking about a person whom he called a friend and with whom he took counsel and prayed.

Verses 12–14,

> For it was not an enemy that reproached me; then I could have borne it: neither was it he that hated me that did magnify himself against me; then I would have hid myself from him: But it was thou, a man mine equal, my guide, and mine acquaintance. We took sweet counsel together, and walked unto the house of God in company.

David is lamenting about being betrayed by someone close to him. Being betrayed by an enemy is a difficult thing but easy to imagine because it is expected. That is what people who hate us tend to do. But to be betrayed by someone whom we call a friend and whom we have spoken to in confidence about our lives? It is like having a sword pierce our hearts.

It is difficult not to see Psalm 55 as an illumination of the mind of Jesus after being betrayed by His apostle Judas in the garden. We can imagine the terrible pain that would have been brought to His heart, even though He had foreknowledge that it would happen.

Matthew 26:47, "And while [Jesus] yet spake, lo, Judas, one of the twelve, came, and with him a great multitude with swords and staves, from the chief priests and elders of the people." (Judas was with the very ones who wished Jesus harm.)

Does this psalm give an opening into the heart of Jesus as He lamented in jail after Judas gave Him up to those who wished to condemn Him?

Centuries after David lived and wrote the Psalms, the apostle Paul speaks of David and the Psalms in reference to the betrayal of Jesus by Judas as a fulfillment of the Scriptures.

Acts 1:16, "Men and brethren, this scripture must needs have been fulfilled, which the Holy Ghost by the mouth of David spake before concerning Judas, which was guide to them that took Jesus."

As with David, Jesus was not betrayed by the people who did not know Him and who would be His enemy, but by one with whom He had prayed and walked together in the house of the Lord. Could not Jesus Himself have spoken this same psalm while He languished in a jail cell waiting to be put to death?

Verses 4–6,

> My heart is sore pained within me: and the terrors of death are fallen upon me. Fearfulness and trembling are come upon me, and horror hath overwhelmed me. And I said, Oh that I had wings like a dove! for then would I fly away, and be at rest.

The most bitter of all fruits is to be abandoned and tormented by those we call friends. When we set ourselves on the good path, trust the Lord with our lives, and seek to do the will of God, we become His friends in faith. Even when our hearts are in the right place, we, too, can act in ways that betray the will of God in our daily lives, either willfully or out of disregard. That is why it is always good to examine our hearts to see where we are in our daily lives.

Worksheet: How Do I Betray the Will of God in My Daily Life?

To get you started, here is an example of how I betray the will of God in my own life:

1. I use my free will to bend my way and not in the way God wills me.
   a. Distractions.
   b. Lack of time (excuse).
   c. Temptations.
2. When I don't give the good word in circumstances that would call for it.
   a. I don't always give credit to God in a public forum.
   b. I don't always tell the good news of Christ to those who need to hear it.
3. I can spend more time thinking of the material world than praying.
   a. I focus on what I need rather than what I can do and give thanks to God.

Now, spend a few moments thinking about and writing down how you may betray the will of God in your own daily life:

_____
_____
_____
_____
_____

O Lord, I will try to do better and be more mindful of Your will as I live my daily life. It is not my intention to betray Your goodwill for me and to hurt You. I love You. Amen.

Nancy Johnston

Psalm 56: In God Have I Put My Trust: I Will Not Be Afraid What Man Can Do unto Me

{To the chief Musician upon Jonathelemrechokim, Michtam of David, when the Philistines took him in Gath.} Be merciful unto me, O God: for man would swallow me up; he fighting daily oppresseth me. Mine enemies would daily swallow me up: for they be many that fight against me, O thou most High. What time I am afraid, I will trust in thee. In God I will praise his word, in God I have put my trust; I will not fear what flesh can do unto me. Every day they wrest my words: all their thoughts are against me for evil. They gather themselves together, they hide themselves, they mark my steps, when they wait for my soul. Shall they escape by iniquity? in thine anger cast down the people, O God. Thou tellest my wanderings: put thou my tears into thy bottle: are they not in thy book? When I cry unto thee, then shall mine enemies turn back: this I know; for God is for me. In God will I praise his word: in the LORD will I praise his word. In God have I put my trust: I will not be afraid what man can do unto me. Thy vows are upon me, O God: I will render praises unto thee. For thou hast delivered my soul from death: wilt not thou deliver my feet from falling, that I may walk before God in the light of the living?

When we choose to walk in faith and seek to live an upright life pleasing to God, many times, we find ourselves at odds with this world. There may be times when, like David, everywhere we look, there is fighting, and it feels like we are going to be swallowed up by those who hate us and wish us harm.

Verses 5–6, "Every day they wrest my words: all their thoughts are against me for evil. They gather themselves together, they hide themselves, they mark my steps, when they wait for my soul."

As we grow in faith, we learn not to take any of this personally because, unfortunately, this is the way of the world at its very core. There is a reason for the saying "cold, cruel world" because that is how the world works, especially in particularly godless times. Without trust in God and His ways, we have no moral compass. The "cold, cruel world" comes from souls flailing without purpose and fully engaged in lives of vainglory—which is just a fancy word for selfishness and self-glory. As a result, human connection is reduced to transaction and manipulation. A "what can you do for me" mentality permeates society.

As a child of God, this attitude is the antithesis of how we are trying to live our lives. Our trust in the Lord commits us to lives of service and love of humanity. We seek to uphold the laws that God created to keep society in harmony with our true spiritual and godly nature. Without God, we fall back on the nature of our flesh, which is pure selfishness. Because these two camps live lives counter to each other, there are bound to be clashes between the godless and those who walk with God. It is inevitable.

When we understand this, it becomes easier for us to willfully disengage from the world and its ways and to seek only the ways that please God because it is there where we find true peace and rest. Psalm 56 recognizes that by staying close to God, we can walk freely and not fear what this world brings.

Verses 10–12,

> In God will I praise his word: in the LORD will I praise his word. In God have I put my trust: I will not be afraid what man can do unto me. Thy vows are upon me, O God: I will render praises unto thee.

One of the things that the Psalms emphasize over and over is that God will deliver us from evil, and He will keep us on the path to everlasting life. Let us remember that and give praise, for He is a good and mighty Father. Amen.

(For additional contemplation on living our lives for God and what to expect, now would be a good time to go back and read the Psalm 33 chapter in this book again.)

Psalm 57: In the Shadow of Thy Wings Will I Make My Refuge

{To the chief Musician, Altaschith, Michtam of David, when he fled from Saul in the cave.} Be merciful unto me, O God, be merciful unto me: for my soul trusteth in thee: yea, in the shadow of thy wings will I make my refuge, until these calamities be overpast. I will cry unto God most high; unto God that performeth all things for me. He shall send from heaven, and save me from the reproach of him that would swallow me up. Selah. God shall send forth his mercy and his truth. My soul is among lions: and I lie even among them that are set on fire, even the sons of men, whose teeth are spears and arrows, and their tongue a sharp sword. Be thou exalted, O God, above the heavens; let thy glory be above all the earth. They have prepared a net for my steps; my soul is bowed down: they have digged a pit before me, into the midst whereof they are fallen themselves. Selah. My heart is fixed, O God, my heart is fixed: I will sing and give praise. Awake up, my glory; awake, psaltery and harp: I myself will awake early. I will praise thee, O Lord, among the people: I will sing unto thee among the nations. For thy mercy is great unto the heavens, and thy truth unto the clouds. Be thou exalted, O God, above the heavens: let thy glory be above all the earth.

When hard times come, and they will come, make no mistake, we can take refuge in the Lord to protect us until the season passes. The Lord's loving protection is being compared to being in the shadow of His wings in Psalm 57. It is as if the Lord, in His wondrous ways, shields us from the brunt and harshest burden of difficult times by hiding us under the shadow of His wings.

It is interesting how the Bible frequently refers to God's shadow. In Psalm 57, His shadow becomes a refuge from the calamities of life. As we learned in Psalm 46, the refuge of the Lord is a space where we can feel safe and be uncorrupted by the world, especially during difficult times. So, the shadow of God's wings creates this place of incorruptible rest from the harshness of life.

In Lamentations, we see that God's shadow creates an atmosphere that allows the people of God to go unnoticed amid their prosecutors.

> Our persecutors are swifter than the eagles of the heaven: they pursued us upon the mountains, they laid wait for us in the wilderness. The breath of our nostrils, the anointed of the LORD, was taken in their pits, of whom we said, Under his shadow we shall live among the heathen.
>
> Lamentations 4:19–20

The shadow of God envelopes His people rendering them invisible in front of those who worship strange gods and idols. In this invisibility, they shall not be disturbed or, worse, oppressed and sacrificed. This is one of the ways of God's mercy.

In the book of Jonah, the shadow of God is expressed as an actual, perceived shadow that the Lord sends down to him to help him in his time of need.

Jonah 4:6, "And the LORD God prepared a gourd, and made it to come up over Jonah, that it might be a shadow over his head, to deliver him from his grief. So Jonah was exceeding glad of the gourd."

However, in the very next verse, we find out that the shadow of the gourd was temporary.

Jonah 4:7, "But God prepared a worm when the morning rose the next day, and it smote the gourd that it withered."

It's almost as if God was presenting a physical manifestation of a shadow to protect Jonah as a lesson that the shadow of God is very real. Though most of us will not be graced with a miracle such as the gourd of Jonah, the spirit of the shadow of God does show up in times of trouble, and it is not just a metaphor. God, in His infinite mercy, sends His shadow as a refuge when we need protection or when He wishes to hide us in plain sight of our enemies.

Thank You, Lord! You are so very good to Your children. You are our shadow and our shield. We praise You and give You glory! Amen.

Psalm 58: A Man Shall Say, Verily, There Is a Reward for the Righteous

{To the chief Musician, Altaschith, Michtam of David.} Do ye indeed speak righteousness, O congregation? do ye judge uprightly, O ye sons of men? Yea, in heart ye work wickedness; ye weigh the violence of your hands in the earth. The wicked are estranged from the womb: they go astray as soon as they be born, speaking lies. Their poison is like the poison of a serpent: they are like the deaf adder that stoppeth her ear; Which will not hearken to the voice of charmers, charming never so wisely. Break their teeth, O God, in their mouth: break out the great teeth of the young lions, O LORD. Let them melt away as waters which run continually: when he bendeth his bow to shoot his arrows, let them be as cut in pieces. As a snail which melteth, let every one of them pass away: like the untimely birth of a woman, that they may not see the sun. Before your pots can feel the thorns, he shall take them away as with a whirlwind, both living, and in his wrath. The righteous shall rejoice when he seeth the vengeance: he shall wash his feet in the blood of the wicked. So that a man shall say, Verily there is a reward for the righteous: verily he is a God that judgeth in the earth.

On the surface, Psalm 58 is another psalm that speaks of the justice of the supreme judge, our Lord. It outlines further ways and means of wickedness and expresses how God judges those who live evil lives. The author implores God to offer swift judgment and harsh penalties.

Verses 6–7,

> Break their teeth, O God, in their mouth: break out the great teeth of the young lions, O LORD. Let them melt away as waters which run continually: when he bendeth his bow to shoot his arrows, let them be as cut in pieces.

In other words, show no mercy toward those people who prowl about the earth, speaking words that poison and charm their victims.

Verses 4–5, "Their poison is like the poison of a serpent: they are like the deaf adder that stoppeth her ear; Which will not hearken to the voice of charmers, charming never so wisely."

In fact, the beginning of Psalm 58 suggests that there are those who are set upon a wicked path from the womb and are liars from the moment of their birth.

Verse 3, "The wicked are estranged from the womb: they go astray as soon as they be born, speaking lies."

It is interesting that this psalm brings up the point that evil people can be set on the wrong path from birth, and we can see this through the lying words they speak. It would be beneficial for us to examine a little closer the concept of words and how our words determine the course of our lives over time.

Contemplation: How Words Are Life

"The words that I speak unto you, they are spirit, and they are life" (John 6:63).

Although the apostle John was referring to a quote from Jesus in the Gospel, essentially, Christ is saying that words are spirit and life. In fact, the Bible, which is, at its essence, the book of life, is frequently called the "Good Word." Words are important.

In Psalm 58, we see that in verse 3, "The wicked are estranged from the womb: they go astray as soon as they be born, speaking lies." In the wicked, the words are lies, which then means that the spirit and life of the wicked is a lie. However, to those who are keeping on the good path, "Verily there is a reward for the righteous" (verse 11). The life and spirit of the right living is just reward. The people on the upright path say, "There is a reward for the righteous," and it becomes the reality of their lives. Though we are not God, and we should never hope to be at His level of perfection and might, God Himself spoke creation into being. Our creator brought about life through His words.

Jesus was not lying or being dramatic when He said, "The words that I speak unto you …are spirit, and they are life." He was stating a fact.

Therein lies the difference between the wicked and right living: one is living a life of lies, and the other is living a life of reward. It could not be any plainer.

Furthermore, the spirit and life of God are love, the truth, and the way. It is the duty of the right living to give ourselves as a living sacrifice over to the will and way of God. We should strive to sacrifice our will to do His work. This is the fulfillment of what it means to be human. The most simple and difficult thing to do. God gives us life to use our freewill to serve Him. This is what it means to serve God by yielding to His will. To give God to the world. To give love, and truth, and His way to the world.

This is serving God. This is being *fully* in our intended humanity and is the ultimate life of the saint, which is what someone who is sanctified in holiness is called and what you are becoming through your faith and trust in God and through the spirit and life of your words.

"And we have known and believed the love that God hath to us. God is love; and he that dwelleth in love dwelleth in God, and God in him" (1 John 4:16).

Psalm 59: God Is My Defence, and the God of My Mercy

Deliver me from mine enemies, O my God: defend me from them that rise up against me. Deliver me from the workers of iniquity, and save me from bloody men. For, lo, they lie in wait for my soul: the mighty are gathered against me; not for my transgression, nor for my sin, O LORD. They run and prepare themselves without my fault: awake to help me, and behold. Thou therefore, O LORD God of hosts, the God of Israel, awake to visit all the heathen: be not merciful to any wicked transgressors. Selah. They return at evening: they make a noise like a dog, and go round about the city. Behold, they belch out with their mouth: swords are in their lips: for who, say they, doth hear? But thou, O LORD, shalt laugh at them; thou shalt have all the heathen in derision. Because of his strength will I wait upon thee: for God is my defence. The God of my mercy shall prevent me: God shall let me see my desire upon mine enemies. Slay them not, lest my people forget: scatter them by thy power; and bring them down, O Lord our shield. For the sin of their mouth and the words of their lips let them even be taken in their pride: and for cursing and lying which they speak. Consume them in wrath, consume them, that they may not be: and let them know that God ruleth in Jacob unto the ends of the earth. Selah. And at evening let them return; and let them make a noise like a dog, and go round about the city. Let them wander up and down for meat, and grudge if they be not satisfied. But I will sing of thy power; yea, I will sing aloud of thy mercy in the morning: for thou hast been my defence and refuge in the day of my trouble. Unto thee, O my strength, will I sing: for God is my defence, and the God of my mercy.

In Psalm 59, David is speaking about those who wish harm to him, not because he is guilty of wrongdoing but because he is innocent.

Verse 3, "For, lo, they lie in wait for my soul: the mighty are gathered against me; not for my transgression, nor for my sin, O LORD."

Many of the loathsome acts of the wicked people who surround David and seek to destroy him come from their mouths. The picture that is painted is of a group of blowhard fools who are determined to rise against him.

Consider these characteristics:

1. They go around the city, making a noise like a dog.
2. They belch out with their mouths.
3. Swords are in their lips.
4. They speak curses.
5. They lie.

David cries out to the Lord to see the transgressions, particularly of their mouths.

Verse 12, "For the sin of their mouth and the words of their lips let them even be taken in their pride."

However, David is determined to wait on the Lord to take care of the troublemakers who prowl around at night and in the shadows, barking like dogs.

Verses 9–10, "Because of his strength will I wait upon thee … The God of my mercy shall prevent me: God shall let me see my desire upon mine enemies."

This is faith. David knows and has no doubt that God will take his prayers into consideration and, in His will, will make sure David's enemies are punished. However, David does offer up a suggestion for retribution, which he feels would be fitting considering that, in their pride, they have barked like dogs roundabout in the streets.

Verses 14–15, "And at evening let them return; and let them make a noise like a dog, and go round about the city. Let them wander up and down for meat, and grudge if they be not satisfied."

In other words, let their barking become hunger and dissatisfaction. It is not difficult to imagine the type of men David is up against. Psalm 59 does a wonderful job of illustrating what is happening around him, and though David imagines the fate he would like to see befall his enemies, "Consume them in wrath, consume them, that they may not be" (verse 13), he vows to let God take care of the situation. By a sheer act of will, David defers to his most merciful God to handle things and will sing Him praise instead while he waits.

Verses 16–17,

> But I will sing of thy power; yea, I will sing aloud of thy mercy in the morning: for thou hast been my defence and refuge in the day of my trouble. Unto thee, O my strength, will I sing: for God is my defence, and the God of my mercy.

Though we may want our enemies to be torn up in the streets and to look for meat and not find it, and we may want them consumed in God's wrath and live lives of perpetual dissatisfaction, it is wise to wait on the judgment and punishment of the Lord. He is the just and Almighty judge. In the meantime, we will sing Your praises, O Lord. Glory and praise and honor to You!

Notes:

_____

_____

_____

_____

_____

Psalm 60: Give Us Help from Trouble: For Vain Is the Help of Man

> O God, thou hast cast us off, thou hast scattered us, thou hast been displeased; O turn thyself to us again. Thou hast made the earth to tremble; thou hast broken it: heal the breaches thereof; for it shaketh. Thou hast shewed thy people hard things: thou hast made us to drink the wine of astonishment. Thou hast given a banner to them that fear thee, that it may be displayed because of the truth. Selah. That thy beloved may be delivered; save with thy right hand, and hear me. God hath spoken in his holiness; I will rejoice, I will divide Shechem, and mete out the valley of Succoth. Gilead is mine, and Manasseh is mine; Ephraim also is the strength of mine head; Judah is my lawgiver; Moab is my washpot; over Edom will I cast out my shoe: Philistia, triumph thou because of me. Who will bring me into the strong city? who will lead me into Edom? Wilt not thou, O God, which hadst cast us off? and thou, O God, which didst not go out with our armies? Give us help from trouble: for vain is the help of man. Through God we shall do valiantly: for he it is that shall tread down our enemies.

At its core, Psalm 60 reminds us that seeking help from God is more wise than seeking help from people. Even when we perceive that it is God who has abandoned us and cast us off, we are better off seeking the help of God in our distress.

Verses 3, 5, "Thou hast shewed thy people hard things: thou hast made us to drink the wine of astonishment. …That thy beloved may be delivered; save with thy right hand, and hear me."

The author of this psalm recognizes that everything that comes into our lives is allowed by God; therefore, He is the one we should pray to for deliverance in our times of trouble.

There are going to be many times in our lives when situations are not going to go the way we would like them. Perhaps we encounter a truly traumatic event in life that leads us into deep despair. Or maybe we don't get the promotion we were seeking. There will be times when our bank accounts will dry up and cause anxiety, or a natural calamity will cause expensive repairs on our homes. Maybe we encounter a person who gains our trust only to end up stealing from us or hurting us. Whatever life throws our way, it has been allowed by God for a reason—to strengthen our faith.

A lot of times, our first instinct is to seek help from others in these circumstances. We ask for loans, seek counseling, or distract ourselves with entertainment. And this is very understandable because, as a person, we want to feel relief from our circumstances in a tangible way. Merely praying to God for help, we think, feels somewhat like a form of illusion.

As we grow in faith, however, using prayer as a regular habit and living upright lives, we begin to see how the Lord moves through our lives, offering a more permanent form of relief called peace of mind. He becomes our refuge during our distresses and opens us up to true healing. We find ourselves moved to take actions that affect our situations in powerfully positive ways, and things come our way out of the blue that end up being the very thing we needed.

When we rely entirely on man for help, including ourselves, things will get done, but compared to the full healing of the Lord, it will look like we put a bandage on a gaping wound.

When we trust in the Lord for our help, we've got the master problem-solver working with us.

Verses 11–12, "Give us help from trouble: for vain is the help of man. Through God we shall do valiantly."

God gives us the courage to persist in His will and to fully overcome, whereas the help of man is rooted in vanity and selfish motives, which can cloud our judgment and cause us to overlook certain circumstances. Consider Psalm 118:8, "It is better to trust in the LORD than to put confidence in man." Amen.

Remember: Seek God first in all things, and your life will be so much better.

Psalm 61: Hear My Cry, O God; Attend unto My Prayer

Hear my cry, O God; attend unto my prayer. From the end of the earth will I cry unto thee, when my heart is overwhelmed: lead me to the rock that is higher than I. For thou hast been a shelter for me, and a strong tower from the enemy. I will abide in thy tabernacle for ever: I will trust in the covert of thy wings. Selah. For thou, O God, hast heard my vows: thou hast given me the heritage of those that fear thy name. Thou wilt prolong the king's life: and his years as many generations. He shall abide before God for ever: O prepare mercy and truth, which may preserve him. So will I sing praise unto thy name for ever, that I may daily perform my vows.

As we make our way through the Psalms, we begin to recognize the poetic language of the words and phrases that can, at times, generate images and thoughts for us to contemplate. On the surface, many of the Psalms seem to be speaking to a similar list of issues, such as righteous living, patience, ungodly life, trusting in God, and other issues that help us understand the complexities of faith. While this is very true, as we delve deeper into the body of each psalm, we see that the Psalms can present like part of an outline, with each psalm focusing on an attribute of our faith that gives us further understanding.

Psalm 61 is an excellent example of how this works. It is easy to assume that this psalm is David, once again, praying to God for help. He implores God to attend to his prayer as he cries out, "From the end of the earth will I cry unto thee" (verse 2).

But the meat of Psalm 61 is deeper than that. It is a psalm that offers us a clear look into how God works when we pray to Him.

In many ways, it is a litany of the way God attends to us when we pray to Him in our time of trouble. Let us examine these ways.

Study: Ways That God Attends to Us When He Hears Our Prayers for Help

1. He leads us to a sturdy place that is higher than man.
   a. God will never lead us to shaky ground; His foundations are always firm.
2. He gives us shelter.
   a. He protects us from the storms of life.
3. He becomes a strong tower against our enemies.
   a. He is our fortress.
4. He is a tabernacle where we can abide.
   a. He is a dwelling place in which we can live.
5. He gives us the cover of His wings.
   a. His protection is as gentle as a feather but as secure as the wings of the strongest bird.
6. He gives us the heritage due to those who reverentially fear His name.
   a. Those who vow to glorify God are entitled to His royal heritage.
7. He will prolong our lives in remembrance of the many generations that follow us.
   a. We will last longer than the days of our lives through the memory of the generations that follow us.

In the last psalm, Psalm 60, we were reminded that even when God allows hardship into our lives, it is better for us to pray to Him for help than to seek the help of another person. Psalm 61 breaks that down further by showing us how God will attend to us when we cry out in prayer for help.

A lot of times, people misunderstand how God communicates. It is common for people, in general, to think that God offers riddles or some other mysterious way to communicate. But this is the opposite of the truth.

"For God is not the author of confusion, but of peace, as in all churches of the saints" (1 Corinthians 14:33).

The language of God is clear. He is not the author of confusion, nor does He want to be misunderstood. The Bible is here for us to learn the ways of God so that we may know Him and be at peace. Psalm 61 gives clarity about how God shows up when we are in trouble. For God is the truth, and the truth is always clear and without a speck of confusion.

Thank You, O Lord, for giving us Your Word so that we may grow to understand You and Your ways clearly and concisely. We ask to do Your will in our everyday life, and even in our darkest times, we will turn to You for help. You are our shelter and our refuge. Thanks and praise to You, Almighty Father, creator of heaven and Earth! Amen.

Help reveal Yourself to us more deeply so we can attain the type of faith that will not doubt but will always trust in You.

Psalm 62: For Thou Renderest to Every Man According to His Work

Truly my soul waiteth upon God: from him cometh my salvation. He only is my rock and my salvation; he is my defence; I shall not be greatly moved. How long will ye imagine mischief against a man? ye shall be slain all of you: as a bowing wall shall ye be, and as a tottering fence. They only consult to cast him down from his excellency: they delight in lies: they bless with their mouth, but they curse inwardly. Selah. My soul, wait thou only upon God; for my expectation is from him. He only is my rock and my salvation: he is my defence; I shall not be moved. In God is my salvation and my glory: the rock of my strength, and my refuge, is in God. Trust in him at all times; ye people, pour out your heart before him: God is a refuge for us. Selah. Surely men of low degree are vanity, and men of high degree are a lie: to be laid in the balance, they are altogether lighter than vanity. Trust not in oppression, and become not vain in robbery: if riches increase, set not your heart upon them. God hath spoken once; twice have I heard this; that power belongeth unto God. Also unto thee, O Lord, belongeth mercy: for thou renderest to every man according to his work.

Psalm 62 makes it very clear that no matter what our station in life, God has the power. What we choose to do within our lives, God will see, and He will give both mercy as well as our rendered reward or punishment.

Verse 10, "Trust not in oppression, and become not vain in robbery: if riches increase, set not your heart upon them."

The soul of man can imagine power where there is none. The slave owner who cruelly treats and oppresses his slaves imagines that he has a type of supreme power by having control over his captives, even unto whether a person lives or dies. Criminals frequently feel the rush of power when committing their crimes, and after, when they count their spoils, they vainly think their corrupt wealth makes them more important than they truly are.

Every day, we see people who have amassed wealth, even by legal means, give the air of being important or powerful purely because they have acquired riches, but this, too, is pure vanity. Psalm 62 advises strongly against equating wealth with power because, at the end of the day, only God has the power, and He will one day render judgment, and in the twinkling of an eye, everything can be taken away.

Verse 12, "Also unto thee, O Lord, belongeth mercy: for thou renderest to every man according to his work."

Instead, it is better to be humble and recognize the power that the Lord has to do all things. When we begin to see that everything that happens is in the will of God and He is the only true power, we learn to be patient. As David reminds us, "God hath spoken once; twice have I heard this; that power belongeth unto God" (verse 11).

The world would love for us to imagine that we are our own supreme being and that in self and only self is the power of our lives. As children of God, we see things very differently. We understand that it is through humbling ourselves and seeking to do the will of God that we open ourselves to true power, for nothing is impossible with God.

Worksheet: Examination of Where I Imagine I Am Powerful

Now would be an excellent time to consider those areas in our lives where we imagine being or feeling like we have power. Is it in a job, having wealth, or overseeing a family? Whatever ways you feel that you have power, list here.

_____

_____

_____

_____

_____

_____

_____

Now, consider what it is about those situations that cause you to anchor onto feeling powerful.

_____

_____

_____

_____

_____

_____

_____

_____

_____

_____

Finally, what would it take for you to lose this sense of power in these areas of your life?

_____

_____

_____

_____

_____

_____

_____

None of this is to judge ourselves but to recognize areas where we may need to reconsider our conceptions of power and how it works within our own lives.

A mindset of self-power eventually becomes a burden on us as we imagine the weight of the world resting entirely on our shoulders. When we can finally hand over every situation into the hands of the Father, not only do we lose the burden of "power," we begin to rest easy in knowing that the true power of God is working in our lives. This is when life begins to get fun.

You can trust God to perform miracles in your life!

Psalm 63: My Flesh Longeth for Thee in a Dry and Thirsty Land

O God, thou art my God; early will I seek thee: my soul thirsteth for thee, my flesh longeth for thee in a dry and thirsty land, where no water is; To see thy power and thy glory, so as I have seen thee in the sanctuary. Because thy lovingkindness is better than life, my lips shall praise thee. Thus will I bless thee while I live: I will lift up my hands in thy name. My soul shall be satisfied as with marrow and fatness; and my mouth shall praise thee with joyful lips: When I remember thee upon my bed, and meditate on thee in the night watches. Because thou hast been my help, therefore in the shadow of thy wings will I rejoice. My soul followeth hard after thee: thy right hand upholdeth me. But those that seek my soul, to destroy it, shall go into the lower parts of the earth. They shall fall by the sword: they shall be a portion for foxes. But the king shall rejoice in God; every one that sweareth by him shall glory: but the mouth of them that speak lies shall be stopped.

When we have faith and praise God, we satisfy a yearning within us that thirsts for His presence. At our core, people are made in the image of God and need to connect with Him. He is our living water and will satisfy our thirst and hunger.

In Psalm 63:1, David compares this earth to a desert, "A dry and thirsty land, where no water is." Without water, there is no life. And like water, without the Lord, we continually thirst for His presence whether we know it or not. Without God, we will never truly, fully be satisfied. And like water, without the living waters of our Father, we will eventually die. But with God, our thirst will be quenched, and we will find life everlasting.

Let us look at the significance of the living water of God that Psalm 63 refers to and where we see it throughout the Bible.

Study: The Living Water

Throughout the Bible, we see God and Jesus, the Son of God, being compared to water and the living water. Let us consider a few of those verses from both the Old Testament and the New Testament.

Old Testament

1. Jeremiah 2:13, "For my people have committed two evils; they have forsaken me the fountain of living waters, and hewed them out cisterns, broken cisterns, that can hold no water." The people of Jeremiah have committed two sins:
   a. They have abandoned God, the fountain of living waters.
   b. They have turned the temple of their bodies into vessels that cannot hold the presence of God through their evil ways.
2. Again, in Jeremiah 17:13, we see God being compared to a "fountain of living waters." "O LORD, the hope of Israel, all that forsake thee shall be ashamed, and they that depart from me shall be written in the earth, because they have forsaken the LORD, the fountain of living waters."
   a. In this passage, those who choose to live apart from the Lord, the fountain of living waters, will end up being ashamed.
3. Isaiah 44:3, "For I will pour water upon him that is thirsty, and floods upon the dry ground: I will pour my spirit upon thy seed, and my blessing upon thine offspring."
   a. The Lord will pour His water upon those who thirst for Him.
   b. The Lord will water the seed of His faithful and will bless their children.

i. The living water of God can grow families and give blessings.
4. Isaiah 58:11, "And the LORD shall guide thee continually, and satisfy thy soul in drought, and make fat thy bones: and thou shalt be like a watered garden, and like a spring of water, whose waters fail not."
   a. The guidance of God satisfies the soul.
   b. The guidance of God feeds us.
   c. The guidance of God is like water in the garden of our soul, which will never fail.
5. Isaiah 41:17–18, "When the poor and needy seek water, and there is none, and their tongue faileth for thirst, I the LORD will hear them, I the God of Israel will not forsake them."
   a. The Lord will never abandon the poor and needy when they seek His water; He will hear them and always quench their thirst.
   b. Notice that "the poor and needy" can refer to those who need material help as well as those of us who need spiritual help.

The New Testament

1. John 4:10–11, 13–14, "Jesus answered and said unto her, If thou knewest the gift of God, and who it is that saith to thee, Give me to drink; thou wouldest have asked of him, and he would have given thee living water. The woman saith unto him, Sir, thou hast nothing to draw with, and the well is deep: from whence then hast thou that living water? …Jesus answered and said unto her, Whosoever drinketh of this water shall thirst again: But whosoever drinketh of the water that I shall give him shall never thirst; but the water that I shall give him shall be in him a well of water springing up into everlasting life."
   a. These verses give excellent illustration of what the living water of God is, and Jesus offers up a very clear

idea of what is meant by living water. It is a well of water that God gives us that springs up into everlasting life.
2. And where does this living water originate? Revelation 22:1, "And he shewed me a pure river of water of life, clear as crystal, proceeding out of the throne of God and of the Lamb."
   a. The living water originates with God and flows from Him, as well as from the Lamb of God, who is Jesus Christ.
3. Revelation 21:6, "And he said unto me, It is done. I am Alpha and Omega, the beginning and the end. I will give unto him that is athirst of the fountain of the water of life freely."
   a. To anyone who thirsts for His water, it will be given freely to him.
   b. The living water of God is a gift; just ask to receive it, and it will be done.

Let us end our discussion of this with Psalm 63:3–5,

> Because thy lovingkindness is better than life, my lips shall praise thee. Thus will I bless thee while I live: I will lift up my hands in thy name. My soul shall be satisfied as with marrow and fatness; and my mouth shall praise thee with joyful lips.

Our God is the living water. He is lovingkindness, and He is most worthy of praise.

Psalm 64: O God, Preserve My Life from Fear of the Enemy

> Hear my voice, O God, in my prayer: preserve my life from fear of the enemy. Hide me from the secret counsel of the wicked; from the insurrection of the workers of iniquity: Who whet their tongue like a sword, and bend their bows to shoot their arrows, even bitter words: That they may shoot in secret at the perfect: suddenly do they shoot at him, and fear not. They encourage themselves in an evil matter: they commune of laying snares privily; they say, Who shall see them? They search out iniquities; they accomplish a diligent search: both the inward thought of every one of them, and the heart, is deep. But God shall shoot at them with an arrow; suddenly shall they be wounded. So they shall make their own tongue to fall upon themselves: all that see them shall flee away. And all men shall fear, and shall declare the work of God; for they shall wisely consider of his doing. The righteous shall be glad in the LORD, and shall trust in him; and all the upright in heart shall glory.

It is difficult not to notice that those who wish to commit crimes against innocent people are everywhere. Stories of everything from petty crimes to conspiracy to commit murder and worse seem to plague the news and social media outlets. Many of us ask for protection from crimes committed against us in our daily prayers. We feel it is necessary. This is not a new phenomenon. Crime has been an affliction on the earth since the dawn of time—even in King David's time, and he addresses it in Psalm 64.

God has a plan that deals with crime and criminals that is illuminated in Psalm 64 by showing us the path the Lord takes when dealing with the criminals in our midst.

Let us examine one of the core messages of Psalm 64.

Righteous people avoid crime by:

1. Asking God to hide them from the secret counsel of the wicked.
2. Asking God to hide them from the insurrection of the workers of iniquity.
3. Declaring the works of God.
4. Wisely considering God's ways.
5. Maintaining their upright heart.
6. Trusting in the Lord.

But the workers of iniquity:

1. Shoot out bitter words like arrows.
2. Plan, in secret, the perfect assassination, and don't fear getting caught.
3. Encourage themselves in evil matters.
4. Conspire together privately to lay snares and traps.
5. Do not fear because they do not think their evil matters will be seen.
6. Their inward thoughts diligently search out different ways to be wicked.

In the end, God shall:

1. Shoot at the workers of iniquity with an arrow (direct hit), and suddenly, they shall be wounded (physically, materially, financially, etc.).
2. See that the snares and traps the iniquitous conspire for others will fall upon themselves.
3. Cause others to see the wicked snare into their own traps and flee from them.
4. When the wicked fail, all will see and fear God and declare His ways.

In other words, what the wicked plan and do in the shadows, God will correct in the full light of day. Thank You, most blessed, loving

Father. Your ways are always just.

Have faith and patience that God sees all and hears our prayers.

Psalm 65: Blessed Is the Man Whom Thou Choosest

Praise waiteth for thee, O God, in Sion: and unto thee shall the vow be performed. O thou that hearest prayer, unto thee shall all flesh come. Iniquities prevail against me: as for our transgressions, thou shalt purge them away. Blessed is the man whom thou choosest, and causest to approach unto thee, that he may dwell in thy courts: we shall be satisfied with the goodness of thy house, even of thy holy temple. By terrible things in righteousness wilt thou answer us, O God of our salvation; who art the confidence of all the ends of the earth, and of them that are afar off upon the sea: Which by his strength setteth fast the mountains; being girded with power: Which stilleth the noise of the seas, the noise of their waves, and the tumult of the people. They also that dwell in the uttermost parts are afraid at thy tokens: thou makest the outgoings of the morning and evening to rejoice. Thou visitest the earth, and waterest it: thou greatly enrichest it with the river of God, which is full of water: thou preparest them corn, when thou hast so provided for it. Thou waterest the ridges thereof abundantly: thou settlest the furrows thereof: thou makest it soft with showers: thou blessest the springing thereof. Thou crownest the year with thy goodness; and thy paths drop fatness. They drop upon the pastures of the wilderness: and the little hills rejoice on every side. The pastures are clothed with flocks; the valleys also are covered over with corn; they shout for joy, they also sing.

Our Father is not a passive entity that sits around waiting for people to approach Him. In fact, the Lord actively searches the hearts and souls of men and women for signs that they are seeking Him, and He will make Himself known to them.

Deuteronomy 4:29, "But if from thence thou shalt seek the LORD thy God, thou shalt find him, if thou seek him with all thy heart and with all thy soul."

He is always searching for those who wish to know Him and to understand His ways. We see an earlier reference to this in Psalm 14.

Psalm 14:2, "The LORD looked down from heaven upon the children of men, to see if there were any that did understand, and seek God."

Psalm 65 gives us more information about this process. Not only does the Lord search for those who are calling Him or who are seeking to know Him, but He chooses those who do and causes them to approach Him. The first part of verse 4 explains this, "Blessed is the man whom thou choosest, and causest to approach unto thee, that he may dwell in thy courts."

As we grow in faith, we begin to understand that everything that happens is in the will of God. In the case of Psalm 65, we see that the will of God Himself is searching, seeking, and causing people to come to Him and begin their faith journey. By searching the hearts and souls of people, He has an intimate understanding of all of us and in which direction our free will is drawing us at any moment. When we draw near to God through our own will, He connects His will to ours and begins to draw us into His spiritual holy palace where we may then dwell in faith and be satisfied. Verse 4 continues, "We shall be satisfied with the goodness of thy house, even of thy holy temple."

If you have found yourself seeking ways to understand God, or even if you are just curious, you have begun to be drawn toward the holy dwelling place of God through His will. Imagine you are a light plug, and you are unplugged and in search of an outlet. God sees your desire and presents the outlet to you in a place you can see. Once you plug into that source, you find that you are finally satisfied. Your light plug has found its source of power, which is God.

Have you ever felt fully satisfied? If not, then you know the frustration of not having peace of mind and a lack of wholeness in the moment. Perhaps your life is filled with anxiety and worry. Psalm 65 explains to us that when our will connects with the will of God, not only will we be satisfied with the goodness of God, but we are blessed.

This world would like for us to think that dwelling in the house of the Lord is nearly impossible to achieve. We are told to think we are unworthy, and some of us even scoff at the idea that God cares about us. *God has better things to do than care about my whims*, we may think.

Psalm 65 is here to remind us that not only does God care, but He is also always searching our hearts and available every time we seek Him out. Ours is a very present God who wants nothing more than to receive us in faith and to bless us.

Verse 9, "Thou visitest the earth, and waterest it: thou greatly enrichest it with the river of God, which is full of water: thou preparest them corn, when thou hast so provided for it."

Truly, God is active with His children. He is not resting on His throne, waiting for us to die. He seeks us during our lives on Earth and is always ready to receive us with open arms.

Thank You, our good and loving Father, for seeking us out and bringing us to You. Selah!

Psalm 66: I Will Declare What He Hath Done for My Soul!

Make a joyful noise unto God, all ye lands: Sing forth the honour of his name: make his praise glorious. Say unto God, How terrible art thou in thy works! through the greatness of thy power shall thine enemies submit themselves unto thee. All the earth shall worship thee, and shall sing unto thee; they shall sing to thy name. Selah. Come and see the works of God: he is terrible in his doing toward the children of men. He turned the sea into dry land: they went through the flood on foot: there did we rejoice in him. He ruleth by his power for ever; his eyes behold the nations: let not the rebellious exalt themselves. Selah. O bless our God, ye people, and make the voice of his praise to be heard: Which holdeth our soul in life, and suffereth not our feet to be moved. For thou, O God, hast proved us: thou hast tried us, as silver is tried. Thou broughtest us into the net; thou laidst affliction upon our loins. Thou hast caused men to ride over our heads; we went through fire and through water: but thou broughtest us out into a wealthy place. I will go into thy house with burnt offerings: I will pay thee my vows, Which my lips have uttered, and my mouth hath spoken, when I was in trouble. I will offer unto thee burnt sacrifices of fatlings, with the incense of rams; I will offer bullocks with goats. Selah. Come and hear, all ye that fear God, and I will declare what he hath done for my soul. I cried unto him with my mouth, and he was extolled with my tongue. If I regard iniquity in my heart, the Lord will not hear me: But verily God hath heard me; he hath attended to the voice of my prayer. Blessed be God, which hath not turned away

> my prayer, nor his mercy from me.

The Lord is the giver of all good things and is so powerful that even His enemies submit to His will. The enemy does not want his slaves to know this because it gives us confidence.

Being a child of God means being on the winning side of every war in our physical battles, but more importantly, in our spiritual battles as well. As we deepen our faith, we begin to see the promises of the Lord fulfilled within our lives. He protects us. He guides us. He sets a table for us before our enemies, and we witness their losses. He is our refuge.

God is always victorious in His battles, and as His children, we get to participate in His victories. These victories bring with them the confidence to know that we will overcome difficult periods and the perseverance to stay faithful in good times and bad, and ultimately, they feed our trust in God. All these things serve to deepen our faith.

At the end of the day, this is what God is asking us all to do: trust in Him.

Stay confident, dear children of God. Fear not; you are held in the refuge of the Lord. You can trust in Him. Honor, praise, and glory to God. Amen.

Psalm 67: O Let the Nations Be Glad and Sing for Joy

> God be merciful unto us, and bless us; and cause his face to shine upon us; Selah. That thy way may be known upon earth, thy saving health among all nations. Let the people praise thee, O God; let all the people praise thee. O let the nations be glad and sing for joy: for thou shalt judge the people righteously, and govern the nations upon earth. Selah. Let the people praise thee, O God; let all the people praise thee. Then shall the earth yield her increase; and God, even our own God, shall bless us. God shall bless us; and all the ends of the earth shall fear him.

When we praise God and are glad and sing for joy, we raise ourselves and our communities toward God. When God sees our praises, it brings His mercy and blessings down upon us. Psalm 67 illustrates the cycle of blessing that is available to every person and, ultimately, to every nation on Earth.

Verse 4, "O let the nations be glad and sing for joy: for thou shalt judge the people righteously, and govern the nations upon earth. Selah."

Two things are happening in this psalm. Firstly, David is praying for his people and asking God to have mercy on them so that others can see that God has blessed them by shining His light upon them. This will cause all people to see that God has shown mercy and is a righteous judge. This will then, secondly, cause all people to reverentially fear the Lord, and they will then begin to sing praises to the Almighty God.

Verse 6, "Then shall the earth yield her increase; and God, even our own God, shall bless us."

This is how the world changes for the better. We first start with ourselves by increasing our faith through glorifying God in our lives. This will then bring down His mercy and blessings upon us. Others will see how God has judged us as righteous and blessed us, and they will begin to praise Him as well. Soon, whole communities will be praising God and being blessed, which will then spread reverential fear of the Lord farther throughout the land. Ultimately, nations will be filled with the mercy and blessings of God, which will lead to other nations praising the Lord. As the number of people, communities, and nations who glorify God increases, the blessings increase until, finally, the whole earth is praising God and being blessed.

Verse 7, "God shall bless us; and all the ends of the earth shall fear him."

Ultimately, this is the vision that God has for us all. What a wonderful world this would be! If we could get the earth to worship and praise God, we could become a world of increase and blessings. Our Father just wants what is best for us, and that always starts and ends with praising and glorifying His loving kindness and mercy. Psalm 67 is a road map to the earth as God desires it to be, and it starts with individuals like us. Thank You, O Lord!

Our faith and praise bring increase and blessings to the earth, one person at a time.

Psalm 68: The Earth Shook, the Heavens Also Dropped at the Presence of God

Let God arise, let his enemies be scattered: let them also that hate him flee before him. As smoke is driven away, so drive them away: as wax melteth before the fire, so let the wicked perish at the presence of God. But let the righteous be glad; let them rejoice before God: yea, let them exceedingly rejoice. Sing unto God, sing praises to his name: extol him that rideth upon the heavens by his name JAH, and rejoice before him. A father of the fatherless, and a judge of the widows, is God in his holy habitation. God setteth the solitary in families: he bringeth out those which are bound with chains: but the rebellious dwell in a dry land. O God, when thou wentest forth before thy people, when thou didst march through the wilderness; Selah: The earth shook, the heavens also dropped at the presence of God: even Sinai itself was moved at the presence of God, the God of Israel. Thou, O God, didst send a plentiful rain, whereby thou didst confirm thine inheritance, when it was weary. Thy congregation hath dwelt therein: thou, O God, hast prepared of thy goodness for the poor. The Lord gave the word: great was the company of those that published it. Kings of armies did flee apace: and she that tarried at home divided the spoil. Though ye have lien among the pots, yet shall ye be as the wings of a dove covered with silver, and her feathers with yellow gold. When the Almighty scattered kings in it, it was white as snow in Salmon. The hill of God is as the hill of Bashan; an high hill as the hill of Bashan. Why leap ye, ye high hills?

this is the hill which God desireth to dwell in; yea, the LORD will dwell in it for ever. The chariots of God are twenty thousand, even thousands of angels: the Lord is among them, as in Sinai, in the holy place. Thou hast ascended on high, thou hast led captivity captive: thou hast received gifts for men; yea, for the rebellious also, that the LORD God might dwell among them. Blessed be the Lord, who daily loadeth us with benefits, even the God of our salvation. Selah. He that is our God is the God of salvation; and unto GOD the Lord belong the issues from death. But God shall wound the head of his enemies, and the hairy scalp of such an one as goeth on still in his trespasses. The Lord said, I will bring again from Bashan, I will bring my people again from the depths of the sea: That thy foot may be dipped in the blood of thine enemies, and the tongue of thy dogs in the same. They have seen thy goings, O God; even the goings of my God, my King, in the sanctuary. The singers went before, the players on instruments followed after; among them were the damsels playing with timbrels. Bless ye God in the congregations, even the Lord, from the fountain of Israel. There is little Benjamin with their ruler, the princes of Judah and their council, the princes of Zebulun, and the princes of Naphtali. Thy God hath commanded thy strength: strengthen, O God, that which thou hast wrought for us. Because of thy temple at Jerusalem shall kings bring presents unto thee. Rebuke the company of spearmen, the multitude of the bulls, with the calves of the people, till every one submit himself with pieces of silver: scatter thou the people that delight in war. Princes shall come out of Egypt; Ethiopia shall soon stretch out her hands unto God. Sing unto God, ye kingdoms of the earth; O sing praises unto the Lord; Selah: To him that rideth upon the heavens of heavens, which were of old; lo, he doth send out his voice, and that a mighty voice. Ascribe ye strength unto God: his excellency is over Israel, and his strength is in the clouds. O God, thou art terrible out of thy holy places: the God of Israel is he that giveth strength and power unto his people. Blessed be God.

Psalm 68 seems to be presenting more details about the time when all nations will praise the Lord in the holy temple and the rebellious will be scattered and flee from our terrible God.

Verse 8, "The earth shook, the heavens also dropped at the presence of God: even Sinai itself was moved at the presence of God, the God of Israel."

Let us take a closer look at what is being described in this psalm.

When God comes to judge the nations:

The righteous will:

1. Be glad.
2. Be exceedingly rejoiceful.
3. Sing praises unto the name of God.
4. Enthusiastically praise Him by His name, JAH (which many believe is a different way of saying the name Yahweh).

The enemies of God will:

1. Be scattered.
2. Flee before God.
3. Be driven away like wax melts in a fire.
4. Perish.

God has proven His power and judgment, and even nature shakes in His presence. He is the just judge.

When He judges the earth, He will:

1. Wound the head of His enemy and those who continue to violate His law.
2. Kill so many of His enemies that the righteous will

       tread through blood on the streets, and dogs will drink the blood.
3. Cause princes to come out of Egypt.
4. Cause Ethiopia to stretch her hands toward Him.
5. Speak in a mighty voice.
6. Rule over Israel through His excellent strength.

Verse 35, "O God, thou art terrible out of thy holy places: the God of Israel is he that giveth strength and power unto his people. Blessed be God." Selah!

It seems that when God comes down, we will know because the signs will be clear. The righteous will rejoice, and the wicked will flee and perish. There will be no confusion for those who can see.

Thank You, Almighty and powerful God of Israel and our God. Amen.

Psalm 69: O God, in the Multitude of Thy Mercy, Hear Me

Save me, O God; for the waters are come in unto my soul. I sink in deep mire, where there is no standing: I am come into deep waters, where the floods overflow me. I am weary of my crying: my throat is dried: mine eyes fail while I wait for my God. They that hate me without a cause are more than the hairs of mine head: they that would destroy me, being mine enemies wrongfully, are mighty: then I restored that which I took not away. O God, thou knowest my foolishness; and my sins are not hid from thee. Let not them that wait on thee, O Lord GOD of hosts, be ashamed for my sake: let not those that seek thee be confounded for my sake, O God of Israel. Because for thy sake I have borne reproach; shame hath covered my face. I am become a stranger unto my brethren, and an alien unto my mother's children. For the zeal of thine house hath eaten me up; and the reproaches of them that reproached thee are fallen upon me. When I wept, and chastened my soul with fasting, that was to my reproach. I made sackcloth also my garment; and I became a proverb to them. They that sit in the gate speak against me; and I was the song of the drunkards. But as for me, my prayer is unto thee, O LORD, in an acceptable time: O God, in the multitude of thy mercy hear me, in the truth of thy salvation. Deliver me out of the mire, and let me not sink: let me be delivered from them that hate me, and out of the deep waters. Let not the waterflood overflow me, neither let the deep swallow me up, and let not the pit shut her mouth upon me. Hear me, O LORD; for thy lovingkindness is good: turn unto me according to the multitude of thy tender mercies. And hide not thy face from thy servant; for I am in trouble: hear me speedily. Draw nigh unto my soul, and redeem it: deliver me because of mine enemies. Thou hast known my reproach, and my shame, and my dishonour: mine adversaries are all before thee. Reproach hath broken my heart; and I am full of heaviness: and I looked for some to take pity, but there was none; and for comforters, but I found none. They gave me also gall for my meat; and in my thirst they gave me vinegar to drink. Let their table become a snare before them: and that which should have been for their welfare, let it become a trap. Let their eyes be darkened, that they see not; and make their loins continually to shake. Pour out thine indignation upon them, and let thy wrathful anger take hold of them. Let their habitation be desolate; and let none dwell in their tents. For they persecute him whom thou hast smitten; and they talk to the grief of those whom thou hast wounded. Add iniquity unto their iniquity: and let them not come into thy righteousness. Let them be blotted out of the book of the living, and not be written with the righteous. But I am poor and sorrowful: let thy salvation, O God, set me up on high. I will praise the name of God with a song, and will magnify him with thanksgiving. This also shall please the LORD better than an ox or bullock that hath horns and hoofs. The humble shall see this, and be glad: and your heart shall live that seek God. For the LORD heareth the poor, and despiseth not his prisoners. Let the heaven and earth praise him, the seas, and every thing that moveth therein. For God will save Zion, and will build the cities of Judah: that they may dwell there, and have it in possession. The seed also of his servants shall inherit it: and they that love his name shall dwell therein.

In so many ways, not only is David one of the founding fathers of Israel, and he was her king in his day, but he seems to be used as a platform that often represents the humanity of the Son of God, Jesus Christ, throughout the Psalms.

In Psalm 69, we can imagine hearing the most intimate and human thoughts of Jesus.

Verse 16, "Hear me, O LORD; for thy lovingkindness is good: turn unto me according to the multitude of thy tender mercies."

Being part flesh is limiting. It means that everything that is thought gets filtered through the brain, which is of the flesh. Anyone who has ever thought knows that the brain is filled with distractions and is centered on the self. So it was with the Son of God. Though He knew what His godly nature was sent to do and the power that He possessed, His thoughts were still being filtered through the fleshly brain. Therefore, it is not impossible to imagine that even Jesus had similar thoughts to what any man would have had.

For example, in verses 17 and 18, it is not difficult to imagine the human Jesus pleading with His Father to save Him as He begins to become aware of all the powerful people who have become His enemies and wish harm upon Him. "And hide not thy face from thy servant; for I am in trouble: hear me speedily. Draw nigh unto my soul, and redeem it: deliver me because of mine enemies," He might have said.

The reality of Jesus Christ was, however, that He did not ever need saving nor redemption, for He had come to save and redeem. But David's words often seem to communicate the hidden thoughts of Jesus, the man, while He was walking the earth and even until His death. Consider verse 21, which seems to foreshadow what happens to Christ while He hangs dying on the cross, "They gave me also gall for my meat; and in my thirst they gave me vinegar to drink."

Now, compare to the book of Matthew (chapter 27, verses 34–35), who was one of the apostles of Christ, "They gave him [Jesus] vinegar to drink mingled with gall: and when he had tasted thereof, he would not drink. And they crucified him."

Study: Who Was David?

So, who was David that God should, at times, use him as an archetype of the Christ to come? Was he a prophet, or did God use David as one who would prepare the world for His coming Son, the Messiah? Let us examine some basic historical and biblical facts of this man, David.

David, Historically

1. David was the second king of Jerusalem, whose reign was later looked back on as a golden era. (The first king was Saul, who would become David's chief enemy.)
2. The date of David's enthronement is approximately 1000 BC.
3. He is known both as a great fighter and a source of poems and songs, some of which are collected in the book of Psalms.
4. He went on to establish an empire by becoming the ruler of many small kingdoms bordering Israel, including Edom, Moab, and Ammon.
5. His empire stretched from Egypt in the south to Lebanon in the north and from the Mediterranean Sea in the west to the desert in the east.
6. He controlled the crossroads of the great empires of the ancient Near East.

David, Biblically

1. Second Samuel 7.
    a. The Lord asks David to build Him a temple:
        i. Verse 4–5, "And it came to pass that night, that the word of the LORD came unto Nathan, saying, Go and tell my servant David, Thus saith the LORD, Shalt thou build me an house for me to dwell in?"

- a. The Lord makes David a king over His people:
    - i. Verse 8–9, "Now therefore so shalt thou say unto my servant David, Thus saith the LORD of hosts, I took thee from the sheepcote, from following the sheep, to be ruler over my people, over Israel: And I was with thee whithersoever thou wentest, and have cut off all thine enemies out of thy sight, and have made thee a great name, like unto the name of the great men that are in the earth."
2. Isaiah 9.
    - a. The prophet Isaiah prophesied that a son will be born:
        - i. Verse 6, "For unto us a child is born, unto us a son is given: and the government shall be upon his shoulder: and his name shall be called Wonderful, Counseller, The mighty God, The everlasting Father, The Prince of Peace."
    - a. And that the throne of David will have no end:
        - i. Verse 7, "Of the increase of his government and peace there shall be no end, upon the throne of David, and upon his kingdom, to order it, and to establish it with judgment and with justice from henceforth even for ever. The zeal of the LORD of hosts will perform this."
3. Acts 13.
    - a. God proclaims that David will fulfill all His will:
        - i. Verse 22, "And when he had removed him, he raised up unto them David to be their king; to whom also he gave testimony, and said, I have found David the son of Jesse, a man after mine own heart, which shall fulfill all my will."
    - a. Out of David's seed, the Messiah will be born:
        - i. Verse 23, "Of this man's seed hath God according to his promise raised unto Israel a Saviour, Jesus."

So, we can see that David does indeed play a very important part in fulfilling the will of God and it is even proclaimed by the Everlasting Father that David is a man after His own heart. By now, we are aware that God is always searching the hearts of men. So, He would know the depths of David's heart. Knowing this, it makes sense that David would be used, in his day, to speak on matters close to God and to have an intimate understanding of His heart, which would also include the heart of His Son, Jesus, who is God incarnate. We could say that very often, the heart of a man manifests in his thoughts, words, and actions, which David seemed to be able to translate into the Psalms.

In Psalm 69, it is hard not to see the suffering of our Savior, Jesus Christ, but also the infinite compassion and mercy in His character. In this way, to read the Psalms is to gain access to the very mind of God and His Son, Jesus.

May we strive to be more like our Lord and creator in our own daily lives.

Psalm 70: O God, Thou Art My Help and My Deliverer

Make haste, O God, to deliver me; make haste to help me, O LORD. Let them be ashamed and confounded that seek after my soul: let them be turned backward, and put to confusion, that desire my hurt. Let them be turned back for a reward of their shame that say, Aha, aha. Let all those that seek thee rejoice and be glad in thee: and let such as love thy salvation say continually, Let God be magnified. But I am poor and needy: make haste unto me, O God: thou art my help and my deliverer; O LORD, make no tarrying.

Psalm 70 is simply a reminder and prayer about the difference in how God deals with the arrogant and manipulative who seek to hurt others versus how He deals with the poor and needy who seek the salvation of God. The first will be put to shame and confusion, and the second will rejoice and be glad. It's as simple as that.

Examination of Conscience

It is always good to take account of where we are on our path at any moment, not to judge ourselves harshly, but to see where we need improvement. Here are a few questions to get you started.

Things I do that intentionally hurt others:

_____

_____

Things I do that unintentionally hurt others:

_____

_____

Ways I am arrogant/selfish:

_____

_____

Ways I am manipulative:

_____

_____

Ways I am humble:

_____

_____

Ways I need God:

_____

_____

How I seek God:

_____

_____

How I give glory to God:

_____

_____

The more we prioritize God in our lives, the more we magnify His significance in our everyday lives. At this moment, where is a relationship with God prioritized in your life (be honest)?

_____

_____

_____

What other priorities compete with God in your life right now?

_____

_____

_____

_____

_____

Dear Lord, help us to always magnify Your presence in our lives, for You are our help, our deliverer, and our salvation. Amen.

Psalm 71: Cast Me Not Off in the Time of Old Age

In thee, O LORD, do I put my trust: let me never be put to confusion. Deliver me in thy righteousness, and cause me to escape: incline thine ear unto me, and save me. Be thou my strong habitation, whereunto I may continually resort: thou hast given commandment to save me; for thou art my rock and my fortress. Deliver me, O my God, out of the hand of the wicked, out of the hand of the unrighteous and cruel man. For thou art my hope, O Lord GOD: thou art my trust from my youth. By thee have I been holden up from the womb: thou art he that took me out of my mother's bowels: my praise shall be continually of thee. I am as a wonder unto many; but thou art my strong refuge. Let my mouth be filled with thy praise and with thy honour all the day. Cast me not off in the time of old age; forsake me not when my strength faileth. For mine enemies speak against me; and they that lay wait for my soul take counsel together, Saying, God hath forsaken him: persecute and take him; for there is none to deliver him. O God, be not far from me: O my God, make haste for my help. Let them be confounded and consumed that are adversaries to my soul; let them be covered with reproach and dishonour that seek my hurt. But I will hope continually, and will yet praise thee more and more. My mouth shall shew forth thy righteousness and thy salvation all the day; for I know not the numbers thereof. I will go in the strength of the Lord GOD: I will make mention of thy righteousness, even of thine only. O God, thou hast taught me from my youth: and hitherto have I declared thy wondrous works. Now also when I am old and grayheaded, O God, forsake me not; until I have shewed thy strength unto this generation, and thy power to every one that is to come. Thy righteousness also, O God, is very high, who hast done great things: O God, who is like unto thee! Thou, which hast shewed me great and sore troubles, shalt quicken me again, and shalt bring me up again from the depths of the earth. Thou shalt increase my greatness, and comfort me on every side. I will also praise thee with the psaltery, even thy truth, O my God: unto thee will I sing with the harp, O thou Holy One of Israel. My lips shall greatly rejoice when I sing unto thee; and my soul, which thou hast redeemed. My tongue also shall talk of thy righteousness all the day long: for they are confounded, for they are brought unto shame, that seek my hurt.

One of the most vulnerable communities in any society is the elderly. These are the people who were active during their younger years, but who now are frailer and may not give the appearance of contributing within society. Often, the elderly can feel like a burden and cast off by the general population. Even David, the mighty king of Jerusalem and the chosen people of God, was feeling vulnerable as he grew older in years. In Psalm 71, David asks God not to forsake him in his old age when his strength has failed him.

David pleads with God to remember how he spoke of the glory of God since his youth and was always a faithful servant.

Verse 5, "For thou art my hope, O Lord GOD: thou art my trust from my youth."

And now he asks God to protect him from those who wish harm toward him and to "be not far from me: O my God, make haste for my help" (verse 12).

David recognizes that even when he is older and frail, he can still be influential within society by continuing to recognize that God is great among the current generations of people.

Verse 18, "Now also when I am old and grayheaded, O God, forsake me not; until I have shewed thy strength unto this generation, and thy power to every one that is to come."

Psalm 71 is about the wisdom and influence of the old and wise among the people. It is a reminder that those who have long lived within the refuge of God can give testimony, by their lives, of the greatness of God.

When we are young, we learn through doing, and we hope that by being a good person, we will be pleasing to God and we will be good citizens. In our naïveté, we imagine that being good people will make us immune from harm and that our days will be spent reaping rewards and happiness.

As we mature and continue to live, however, we regularly run into difficult situations and people who wish to harm us. It can be disillusioning. Often, when the sheen of youth leads into the struggles of life, and we are confronted with hardship, we find ourselves questioning the goodness of God. It is at this time many of us find ourselves using our will to separate from God. It is very common for even the most devout to feel periods of desolation and separation from God during difficult times.

The message of Psalm 71 is one of hope. When we look to our elders who are still praising God, we can become curious and begin to examine their lives as a witness to the greatness of God. By the time someone has reached a good, old age, they have experienced many hardships because life will never be without struggles, but we can also see how God has helped them overcome their hardships and their times of need. The elderly who continue to live within the refuge of God become steady beacons of hope that God exists, that He is loving and kind, and that He protects and redeems His children. These are lives that have been lived and are records of the ways of God.

No matter where you are right now on your journey, whether you have lived a long life or if you are just starting, how you live becomes your story to the world. It can be a story of redemption or one of despair. It is never too late to revise which narrative you are creating. If you continue to lean into the ways of God, your life will become a beacon of hope for the people who come after you, and you, too, can show the glory of God within the fullness of your life!

Verse 23, "My lips shall greatly rejoice when I sing unto thee; and my soul, which thou hast redeemed."

Glory, praise, and honor to You, O Lord!

O Lord, let Your goodness and compassion over my life become a beacon of Your strength to the generations when I am old and frail. Let me always sing of Your goodness!

Psalm 72: Blessed Be the Lord God, the God of Israel, Who Only Doeth Wondrous Things

Give the king thy judgments, O God, and thy righteousness unto the king's son. He shall judge thy people with righteousness, and thy poor with judgment. The mountains shall bring peace to the people, and the little hills, by righteousness. He shall judge the poor of the people, he shall save the children of the needy, and shall break in pieces the oppressor. They shall fear thee as long as the sun and moon endure, throughout all generations. He shall come down like rain upon the mown grass: as showers that water the earth. In his days shall the righteous flourish; and abundance of peace so long as the moon endureth. He shall have dominion also from sea to sea, and from the river unto the ends of the earth. They that dwell in the wilderness shall bow before him; and his enemies shall lick the dust. The kings of Tarshish and of the isles shall bring presents: the kings of Sheba and Seba shall offer gifts. Yea, all kings shall fall down before him: all nations shall serve him. For he shall deliver the needy when he crieth; the poor also, and him that hath no helper. He shall spare the poor and needy, and shall save the souls of the needy. He shall redeem their soul from deceit and violence: and precious shall their blood be in his sight. And he shall live, and to him shall be given of the gold of Sheba: prayer also shall be made for him continually; and daily shall he be praised. There shall be an handful of corn in the earth upon the top of the mountains; the fruit thereof shall shake like Lebanon: and they of the city shall flourish like grass of the earth. His name shall endure for ever: his name shall be continued as long as the sun: and men shall be blessed in him: all nations shall call him blessed. Blessed be the LORD God, the God of Israel, who only doeth wondrous things. And blessed be his glorious name for ever: and let the whole earth be filled with his glory; Amen, and Amen. The prayers of David the son of Jesse are ended.

Psalm 72 is a prayer to the glory of God, who made David a king over the people of Israel. David asks that the Lord judge his own life and give to him the righteousness of God.

Verse 1, "Give the king thy judgments, O God, and thy righteousness unto the king's son."

David recognizes that God is great and should be glorified for His wondrous works.

Psalm 72 gives an account of the greatness of God.

God will:

1. Judge the people with righteousness.
2. Judge the poor with judgment.
3. Save the children of the needy.
4. Break in pieces the oppressor.

And when He comes down:

1. The righteous shall flourish.
2. There will be an abundance of peace.
3. He shall have dominion from the sea.
4. He shall have dominion from the river to the ends of the earth.
5. Those who live in the wilderness shall bow before Him.
6. His enemies shall be like the dust.
7. Kings will bring Him gifts.
8. Kings shall bow before Him.
9. All nations shall serve Him.

He will judge, redeem, and deliver:

1. The needy when they cry.
2. The poor and those who have no helper.
3. He will spare the needy and poor and save their souls.
4. He will redeem the souls of the poor and needy from deceit and violence.
5. Their blood shall be precious in His sight.

Then, God will be:

1. Praised daily.
2. Prayed to continually.
3. His name shall endure forever.
4. His name shall be continued as long as the sun.
5. He will cause men to be blessed in Him.
6. He will be called blessed by all nations.

In the end, David gives a wonderful account of the glory of heaven from the time of judgment until the saints praise Him continually. There is also more than a hint about how God recreates that glory when "He shall come down like rain upon the mown grass: as showers that water the earth" (verse 6). Not only is David prophesying the day of judgment on the last day, but a case could be made that David is professing how God works every time He comes down in Spirit to make for us, His children, heaven on Earth.

It is suggested that we read this psalm three times and consider each interpretation:

1. Our day of judgment after we have passed from physical life on Earth.
2. The day of judgment on the last day when Christ comes down from heaven.
3. Every time the Lord has shown mercy and has dwelt among us in our own lives and in the life of our nations.

Praise, glory, and honor, O Lord! Your wondrous deeds fill our hearts with joy! Amen.

Psalm 73: So Foolish Was I...: I Was as a Beast before Thee

Truly God is good to Israel, even to such as are of a clean heart. But as for me, my feet were almost gone; my steps had well nigh slipped. For I was envious at the foolish, when I saw the prosperity of the wicked. For there are no bands in their death: but their strength is firm. They are not in trouble as other men; neither are they plagued like other men. Therefore pride compasseth them about as a chain; violence covereth them as a garment. Their eyes stand out with fatness: they have more than heart could wish. They are corrupt, and speak wickedly concerning oppression: they speak loftily. They set their mouth against the heavens, and their tongue walketh through the earth. Therefore his people return hither: and waters of a full cup are wrung out to them. And they say, How doth God know? and is there knowledge in the most High? Behold, these are the ungodly, who prosper in the world; they increase in riches. Verily I have cleansed my heart in vain, and washed my hands in innocency. For all the day long have I been plagued, and chastened every morning. If I say, I will speak thus; behold, I should offend against the generation of thy children. When I thought to know this, it was too painful for me; Until I went into the sanctuary of God; then understood I their end. Surely thou didst set them in slippery places: thou castedst them down into destruction. How are they brought into desolation, as in a moment! they are utterly consumed with terrors. As a dream when one awaketh; so, O Lord, when thou awakest, thou shalt despise their image. Thus my heart was grieved, and I was pricked in my reins. So foolish was I, and ignorant: I was as a beast before thee. Nevertheless I am continually with thee: thou hast holden me by my right hand. Thou shalt guide me with thy counsel, and afterward receive me to glory. Whom have I in heaven but thee? and there is none upon earth that I desire beside thee. My flesh and my heart faileth: but God is the strength of my heart, and my portion for ever. For, lo, they that are far from thee shall perish: thou hast destroyed all them that go a whoring from thee. But it is good for me to draw near to God: I have put my trust in the Lord GOD, that I may declare all thy works.

Asaph, appointed by King David to serve as a worship leader in the tabernacle choir, is the author of this psalm, and he is confessing about a time when he slipped back on the path. It was at a time when he found himself envious of the riches of the wicked because it seemed that the wicked had strength and they were not plagued like the more righteous.

Verses 5–6, "They are not in trouble as other men; neither are they plagued like other men. Therefore pride compasseth them about as a chain; violence covereth them as a garment."

These people are arrogant, corrupt, and violent. They speak against the things of God, are oppressive with their words, and imagine themselves to be above those unlike them. And yet, Asaph found himself feeling envy toward those who are "the ungodly, who prosper in the world [and] increase in riches" (verse 12). He imagined that they had boundaries against hardship despite the violence and their wickedness.

Yet, when he began to move himself toward the refuge of His Father in heaven, he started to cleanse himself of this delusionary thinking.

Verse 17, "Until I went into the sanctuary of God; then understood I their end."

Verse 19, "How are they brought into desolation, as in a moment!

they are utterly consumed with terrors."

Once away from those who prosper through ungodly and wicked behavior, Asaph was better able to view them not with envy but with clarity and objectivity. And he saw how the wicked are always cast down into destruction. And thus began the cycle of Asaph's redemption and renewal in the Lord.

Study: The Biblical Cycle of Redemption and Renewal

Throughout the Bible, we are confronted with stories of people who have fallen away from the righteous path of God and what happens to them. There seems to be an ever-present pattern to these stories that many times end in the person, the community of people, or the nation returning to God and once again entering His path of salvation and reward. Sometimes, the people do not return, and every single time that happens, it leads to their destruction.

One of the core events that demonstrate this cycle is the story of Moses and how God brought the people of Israel out of bondage from the Egyptians through him. God saw that His people were oppressed and in hardship through their enslavement at the hands of the Pharaohs, so he sent Moses to free them in His name. Several miracles were performed, including the parting of the Red Sea, before the Israelites were completely free.

However, not long after their captivity from the Egyptians was over, they complained to God and began worshiping false idols and doing other activities that were firmly of the world and not at all on God's path. So, He chastised them by forcing them to be lost in the wilderness for forty years before He brought them into the promised land. During the chastisement, many of His people repented and came back to the ways of God. In the end, the Israelites were brought into their home, and once again, they began to prosper and praise Him for His mercy and greatness.

This cycle continues even to this day and in our own lives when we find ourselves slipping and once again becoming part of the world's system. Perhaps we find ourselves getting caught up in making money and begin to imagine that being dishonest with our source of income is "just business." Or we find ourselves seeking happiness in consumerism and purchasing products and goods over the happiness that comes with God. Maybe we have an addiction that we fall back into and start a new cycle of drug, alcohol, or sexual abuse that eventually leads to petty criminal activities or even worse. Or maybe, just like Asaph, we look out to the world and feel bitterness and envy for the rich and famous because we are struggling in our own lives. Whatever the cause, living in the world's system and relying on it instead of God is slipping off God's path and is where the cycle always begins. Using Psalm 73 as a guide, we can see clearly how Asaph navigated the biblical cycle of redemption and renewal:

1. Living in the world's system.
   a. Putting the ways of the world before God's ways or thinking they are more important.
   b. In Asaph's case, envying the wicked for seemingly not having hardship.
2. Choosing to live outside the ways of the world.
   a. Recognizing that we have slipped back or need help, despising what we have become, and wishing to correct it.
   b. Verse 20, "As a dream when one awaketh; so, O Lord, when thou awakest, thou shalt despise their image."
3. Chastening/suffering/purification of spirit.
   a. Suffering with guilt (or worse) the consequences of our worldly and immoral behavior, like going to jail or losing a spouse/friend or feeling self-loathing for our bad behavior and for offending God.
   b. Verse 14, "For all the day long have I been plagued, and chastened every morning."

4. Revelation of how foolish one has been.
   a. Understanding the full extent of what living in worldly ways means for your life, your soul, and your relationships—especially with God.
   b. Verse 22, "So foolish was I, and ignorant: I was as a beast before thee."
5. Turning toward God's ways and trusting in and praising Him.
   a. Deciding to get on God's path and to walk in His ways through trust in Him.
   b. This eventually leads to feeling joy, which leads to praising His merciful, kind, and loving ways and all His magnificent creations.
   c. Verse 28, "But it is good for me to draw near to God: I have put my trust in the Lord GOD, that I may declare all thy works."

Which part are you currently going through in your cycle of redemption and renewal? Are you putting the ways of the world before the ways of God? Are you beginning to see the consequences of your foolish behavior? Or are you, once again, experiencing the joy that comes from trusting God on the good path?

Wherever you find yourself right now, persevere in the process, even when all seems lost. In the end, when the tides have turned back in your favor, you will find joy and peace of mind.

Keep going!

Psalm 74: O God, How Long Shall the Adversary Reproach?

O God, why hast thou cast us off for ever? why doth thine anger smoke against the sheep of thy pasture? Remember thy congregation, which thou hast purchased of old; the rod of thine inheritance, which thou hast redeemed; this mount Zion, wherein thou hast dwelt. Lift up thy feet unto the perpetual desolations; even all that the enemy hath done wickedly in the sanctuary. Thine enemies roar in the midst of thy congregations; they set up their ensigns for signs. A man was famous according as he had lifted up axes upon the thick trees. But now they break down the carved work thereof at once with axes and hammers. They have cast fire into thy sanctuary, they have defiled by casting down the dwelling place of thy name to the ground. They said in their hearts, Let us destroy them together: they have burned up all the synagogues of God in the land. We see not our signs: there is no more any prophet: neither is there among us any that knoweth how long. O God, how long shall the adversary reproach? shall the enemy blaspheme thy name for ever? Why withdrawest thou thy hand, even thy right hand? pluck it out of thy bosom. For God is my King of old, working salvation in the midst of the earth. Thou didst divide the sea by thy strength: thou brakest the heads of the dragons in the waters. Thou brakest the heads of leviathan in pieces, and gavest him to be meat to the people inhabiting the wilderness. Thou didst cleave the fountain and the flood: thou driedst up mighty rivers. The day is thine, the night also is thine: thou hast prepared the light and the sun. Thou hast set all the borders of the earth: thou hast made summer and winter. Remember this, that the enemy hath reproached, O LORD, and that the foolish people have blasphemed thy name. O deliver not the soul of thy turtledove unto the multitude of the wicked: forget not the congregation of thy poor for ever. Have respect unto the covenant: for the dark places of the earth are full of the habitations of cruelty. O let not the oppressed return ashamed: let the poor and needy praise thy name. Arise, O God, plead thine own cause: remember how the foolish man reproacheth thee daily. Forget not the voice of thine enemies: the tumult of those that rise up against thee increaseth continually.

Psalm 74 talks about the enemy of God and how he has infiltrated all aspects of life in the nation. This psalm pleads to God to have mercy on His children, for they are poor and needy amid the destruction at the hands of the adversary. In other words, Psalm 74 speaks directly about Satan and his ways. Now would be an excellent time to have a closer look at what this means.

Study: The Adversary

In the Scriptures, God names people and creatures for what they are. For example, God changed Abram's name to Abraham because it means "father of multitudes." Elijah is a name that means "Yahweh is my God." David, who is the author of many of these Psalms, means "beloved." Later in Scripture, we read that the angels told Mary to name her son Jesus (or Yeshua), which means "Savior" or "God is salvation." We even see Jesus being referred to as *Immanuel*, which can be translated to mean "God with us." So, it is a common practice for God to name the main characters in His plan with names that mean specific things that apply to their purpose.

Satan is one such character, and he is referred to variously in the Bible as the accuser, an enemy, an opponent, the devil, the serpent, and a dragon, whose sole focus is to deceive, divide, and destroy

God's people and defeat the purpose of God. In fact, the name Satan itself is translated from Hebrew to mean "adversary."

According to the Merriam-Webster dictionary, the word *adversary* means one that contends with, opposes, or resists: an enemy or opponent.

So straight out, without any interpretation at all, we can see that Satan is the opponent of God and is a being that God and His children will have to contend with, resist, and oppose. In other words, Satan is the enemy of God and the godly.

Let's look at what Psalm 74 reveals about the nature of Satan and his minions and what they are doing during the time this psalm was written thousands of years ago.

1. Satan goes into the place where God's children go to worship, and he performs wicked deeds.
2. Satan and his minions disrupt where the godly congregate with their roars and voices.
3. The minions set up their evil battle flags amid the signs where the godly congregate.
4. Where once craftsmen carved works out of trees and found fame, the ungodly followers of Satan use axes and hammers to destroy those works.
5. They have burnt the places where the godly go to worship their holy Father.
6. They destroy the dwelling places of God and cast them to the ground.
7. The minions work together to come up with ways to destroy the holy places where God dwells.
8. Every one of the synagogues of God has been burnt up throughout the land.
9. The foolish enemies of God curse Him and call Him insulting and disrespectful names.

How God has dealt with the adversary in the past:

1. He divided the sea by His strength.

2. He bashed the dragons in the waters.
3. He cut the heads of the leviathan into pieces.
4. He gave the meat of leviathan's heads to the people inhabiting the wilderness to eat.

In other words, God destroyed the enemy and used the meat of His enemy to bless His people living in the wilderness with food, thus humiliating His adversary down to its very body.

In summary:

The dark places of the earth are full of the habitations of cruelty, but God remembers how the foolish reproaches (blames, discredits, or disgraces) Him daily. He does not forget the voice of His enemies and the chaos of those that rise against Him continually. This much, however, is guaranteed: like in the past, God will always (every single time) defeat Satan and his minions. It's something that we, who are the children of God, should find solace in knowing. Thank You, O Lord, for always being victorious in every battle You enter! Amen.

Notes:

_____
_____
_____
_____
_____
_____
_____
_____
_____

Psalm 75: Unto Thee, O God, Do We Give Thanks

> Unto thee, O God, do we give thanks, unto thee do we give thanks: for that thy name is near thy wondrous works declare. When I shall receive the congregation I will judge uprightly. The earth and all the inhabitants thereof are dissolved: I bear up the pillars of it. Selah. I said unto the fools, Deal not foolishly: and to the wicked, Lift not up the horn: Lift not up your horn on high: speak not with a stiff neck. For promotion cometh neither from the east, nor from the west, nor from the south. But God is the judge: he putteth down one, and setteth up another. For in the hand of the LORD there is a cup, and the wine is red; it is full of mixture; and he poureth out of the same: but the dregs thereof, all the wicked of the earth shall wring them out, and drink them. But I will declare for ever; I will sing praises to the God of Jacob. All the horns of the wicked also will I cut off; but the horns of the righteous shall be exalted.

The author of Psalm 75 appears to be advising those whom he calls foolish. If we were to give a common definition for who a "fool" or "foolish person" is, we would probably say it is a silly person who does silly things. In fact, there is an English proverb that says, "A fool and his money are soon parted." In other words, a fool is not someone who we would consider a person who is generally wise and whose life reflects wise decisions.

But what is foolish in the eyes of God?

Proverbs 1:7, "The fear of the LORD is the beginning of knowledge: but fools despise wisdom and instruction."

Psalm 14:1, "The fool hath said in his heart, There is no God. They are corrupt, they have done abominable works, there is none that doeth good."

A fool in context to God is someone who may have access to knowing about God and His ways but who is still determined to believe and act like God does not exist. This is the person to whom Psalm 75 is addressing.

The people who believe in God sing praises to Him and give thanks for His wondrous deeds. But the foolish act as if being an unbeliever is a victory and "lift up their horn" to proclaim their foolishness. Psalm 75 advises that acting foolish like that will affect how God judges them. Not only will these fools not get the fresh wine of God's goodness, but they will also be given the dregs, or sediment, which is left over at the bottom of the barrel. The bitterness of wine that is left behind.

In the end, God will judge us, and as verse 10 reminds us, "All the horns of the wicked also will [He] cut off; but the horns of the righteous shall be exalted." When all is said and done, those who praise God will be raised up, but those who profess that God does not exist will be cut off. Pretty straightforward.

Praise and glory to Thee, my Lord and master. I love You with all my heart. May Your will be done in my heart today and always. Amen.

Psalm 76: When God Arose to Judgment, to Save All the Meek of the Earth

In Judah is God known: his name is great in Israel. In Salem also is his tabernacle, and his dwelling place in Zion. There brake he the arrows of the bow, the shield, and the sword, and the battle. Selah. Thou art more glorious and excellent than the mountains of prey. The stouthearted are spoiled, they have slept their sleep: and none of the men of might have found their hands. At thy rebuke, O God of Jacob, both the chariot and horse are cast into a dead sleep. Thou, even thou, art to be feared: and who may stand in thy sight when once thou art angry? Thou didst cause judgment to be heard from heaven; the earth feared, and was still, When God arose to judgment, to save all the meek of the earth. Selah. Surely the wrath of man shall praise thee: the remainder of wrath shalt thou restrain. Vow, and pay unto the LORD your God: let all that be round about him bring presents unto him that ought to be feared. He shall cut off the spirit of princes: he is terrible to the kings of the earth.

Psalm 76 speaks about the judgment and the wrath of the Lord. The Father will cut down those who imagine themselves to have power, for "He is terrible to the kings of the earth," but He will save the meek on the day of judgment. Everyone will know that the Lord has cast His judgment, and His name will be feared and praised as a result. The earth itself will be silent on the day the Lord makes His presence known to all the earth.

Verse 8, "Thou didst cause judgment to be heard from heaven; the earth feared, and was still."

For those who have meekly given their trust to the Lord and walked in His way, they will feel joy. But those who have cut themselves off will feel the Lord's wrath. However, even when the Lord gives judgment, He will be merciful and hold back the worst.

Verse 10, "Surely the wrath of man shall praise thee: the remainder of wrath shalt thou restrain."

He is a kind and merciful Father, even unto the day of His judgment.

The beginning of this psalm reminds us about the Lord's affiliations on Earth.

Verses 1–2, "In Judah is God known: his name is great in Israel. In Salem also is his tabernacle, and his dwelling place in Zion."

These verses give us an idea of those areas central to the Lord and act as a reminder that it is in these "places" that His name is known and is thought to be great; His tabernacle (or temple) resides, and this is where He dwells. Judah, Israel, Salem, and Zion are referenced throughout the Bible and, in many ways, are interchangeable as places that are synonymous with God's kingdom. Now would be an excellent time to look at the place God dwells, which is Zion, to gain a greater understanding of the kingdom of God.

Study: Zion

Zion is a complex subject to contemplate and study. What is Zion? It's been a question that is often asked. Perhaps now would be a good time to examine "Zion" and some of the ways it is used within the biblical context.

"The LORD loveth the gates of Zion more than all the dwellings of Jacob" (Psalm 87:2).

Zion can refer to several places and may be used interchangeably with:

1. The hill where the most ancient areas of Jerusalem stood.

      a. The mountain of the Lord.
      b. Rock of Israel.
      c. Holy mountain.
2. The city of Jerusalem itself.
      a. Also known as the city of David.
      b. Second Chronicles 5:2: "Then Solomon assembled the elders of Israel, and all the heads of the tribes, the chief of the fathers of the children of Israel, unto Jerusalem, to bring up the ark of the covenant of the LORD out of the city of David, which is Zion."
3. The dwelling place of God.
      a. Psalm 9:11, "Sing praises to the LORD, which dwelleth in Zion: declare among the people his doings."
      b. The kingdom of God.
4. The place where a deliverer will come out of:
      a. Romans 11:26, "And so all Israel shall be saved: as it is written, There shall come out of Sion the Deliverer, and shall turn away ungodliness from Jacob."
5. Questions:
      a. Is Zion a state of being?
      b. Is Zion heaven?
      c. Is heaven on Earth the Zion of this world?

Interesting to research: Will the new Jerusalem, which will be brought down from the heavens on the last day, be the final Zion for all ages?

> And I saw a new heaven and a new earth: for the first heaven and the first earth were passed away; and there was no more sea. And I John saw the holy city, new Jerusalem, coming down from God out of heaven, prepared as a bride adorned for her husband. And I heard a great voice out of heaven saying, Behold, the tabernacle of God is with men, and he will dwell with them, and they shall be his people, and God himself shall be with them, and be their God.
>
>   Revelation 21:1–3

Question: Could Zion be wherever God dwells among His people/children?

Notes:

Psalm 77: In the Day of My Trouble I Sought the Lord

I cried unto God with my voice, even unto God with my voice; and he gave ear unto me. In the day of my trouble I sought the Lord: my sore ran in the night, and ceased not: my soul refused to be comforted. I remembered God, and was troubled: I complained, and my spirit was overwhelmed. Selah. Thou holdest mine eyes waking: I am so troubled that I cannot speak. I have considered the days of old, the years of ancient times. I call to remembrance my song in the night: I commune with mine own heart: and my spirit made diligent search. Will the Lord cast off for ever? and will he be favourable no more? Is his mercy clean gone for ever? doth his promise fail for evermore? Hath God forgotten to be gracious? hath he in anger shut up his tender mercies? Selah. And I said, This is my infirmity: but I will remember the years of the right hand of the most High. I will remember the works of the LORD: surely I will remember thy wonders of old. I will meditate also of all thy work, and talk of thy doings. Thy way, O God, is in the sanctuary: who is so great a God as our God? Thou art the God that doest wonders: thou hast declared thy strength among the people. Thou hast with thine arm redeemed thy people, the sons of Jacob and Joseph. Selah. The waters saw thee, O God, the waters saw thee; they were afraid: the depths also were troubled. The clouds poured out water: the skies sent out a sound: thine arrows also went abroad. The voice of thy thunder was in the heaven: the lightnings lightened the world: the earth trembled and shook. Thy way is in the sea, and thy path in the great waters, and thy footsteps are not known. Thou leddest thy people like a flock by the hand of Moses and Aaron.

There will be times in life when we will be so troubled by situations that are playing out, or we will be processing the depths of our interior trauma that we cannot even form the words to explain how we feel. During these times, we may only be able to cry out, "Help me!" as we sit in our despair, hoping for answers or moments of relief. During these times, it might even feel like our God is not answering us. It might even feel like He has pulled Himself away from us. And this hurts because we are saying, "Lord, I need You," and we do not feel His comfort.

This is the feeling of Psalm 77. The author of this psalm describes the type of despair that is so potent that it causes us to even refuse to be comforted, which adds to the feeling of being alone and isolated.

Verses 2–4, "In the day of my trouble I sought the Lord: my sore ran in the night, and ceased not: my soul refused to be comforted. I remembered God, and was troubled: I complained, and my spirit was overwhelmed. Selah. Thou holdest mine eyes waking: I am so troubled that I cannot speak."

In his desolation, he wonders if God has forgotten him or has taken His grace and mercy from him.

Verse 7, "Will the Lord cast off for ever? and will he be favourable no more?"

What is being described here is a vicious cycle of despair coupled with the fear that one has been abandoned by God, which then sends us into an even deeper despair. Life is like this at times, and we can find ourselves fanning the fires of our misery with all kinds of thoughts, true or not.

In the end, Psalm 77 shows us how to slow down the cycle of despair and how to turn it around so that we, once again, find ourselves in the sanctuary of God's lovingkindness.

Let's take a look at how this psalm unfolds to teach us how to get back to a better frame of mind:

1. I will remember the works of the Lord: surely I will remember thy wonders of old.
2. I will meditate also on all thy work and talk of thy doings:
   a. "Who is so great a god as our God?"
3. Thou art the God that doest wonders.
4. Thou hast declared thy strength among the people.
5. Thou hast with thine arm redeemed thy people.
6. Thou leddest thy people like a flock by the hand of Moses and Aaron.

The author is remembering that God works wonders and has redeemed His chosen people in the past. He then remembers how God led the people out of Egypt and slavery. In other words, we can think back on those times that God has helped us in the past or, if you are a new believer, you can recall how God led you to Him in your own time of trouble. We can also read about the many times God has helped His people through their troubles. God never changes. He has and will always help His people find a way out of trouble.

Psalm 46:1, "God is our refuge and strength, a very present help in trouble."

It is not so much that God has abandoned us in our time of trouble but that we may be refusing to lean into His presence.

By meditating on how He has helped us or others in the past and with the knowledge that He has promised to help us in our day of trouble, we can begin to turn our despair into hope. Hope for a future time when our troubled season will be over. And then we can turn to praise as we review how God helped us through and was with us the entire time. This is His promise.

Worksheet: Help in Our Time of Trouble

Recall a time or two when God helped you or others, even when it may have seemed like He was not present.

_____

_____

_____

_____

_____

_____

_____

_____

_____

_____

_____

_____

You can count on God. He never promises anything that He does not intend to carry out.

Psalm 78: That They Might Set Their Hope in God, and Not Forget the Works of God

Give ear, O my people, to my law: incline your ears to the words of my mouth. I will open my mouth in a parable: I will utter dark sayings of old: Which we have heard and known, and our fathers have told us. We will not hide them from their children, shewing to the generation to come the praises of the LORD, and his strength, and his wonderful works that he hath done. For he established a testimony in Jacob, and appointed a law in Israel, which he commanded our fathers, that they should make them known to their children: That the generation to come might know them, even the children which should be born; who should arise and declare them to their children: That they might set their hope in God, and not forget the works of God, but keep his commandments: And might not be as their fathers, a stubborn and rebellious generation; a generation that set not their heart aright, and whose spirit was not stedfast with God. The children of Ephraim, being armed, and carrying bows, turned back in the day of battle. They kept not the covenant of God, and refused to walk in his law; And forgat his works, and his wonders that he had shewed them. Marvellous things did he in the sight of their fathers, in the land of Egypt, in the field of Zoan. He divided the sea, and caused them to pass through; and he made the waters to stand as an heap. In the daytime also he led them with a cloud, and all the night with a light of fire. He clave the rocks in the wilderness, and gave them drink as out of the great depths. He brought streams also out of the rock, and caused waters to run down like rivers. And they sinned yet more against him by provoking the most High in the wilderness. And they tempted God in their heart by asking meat for their lust. Yea, they spake against God; they said, Can God furnish a table in the wilderness? Behold, he smote the rock, that the waters gushed out, and the streams overflowed; can he give bread also? can he provide flesh for his people? Therefore the LORD heard this, and was wroth: so a fire was kindled against Jacob, and anger also came up against Israel; Because they believed not in God, and trusted not in his salvation: Though he had commanded the clouds from above, and opened the doors of heaven, And had rained down manna upon them to eat, and had given them of the corn of heaven. Man did eat angels' food: he sent them meat to the full. He caused an east wind to blow in the heaven: and by his power he brought in the south wind. He rained flesh also upon them as dust, and feathered fowls like as the sand of the sea: And he let it fall in the midst of their camp, round about their habitations. So they did eat, and were well filled: for he gave them their own desire; They were not estranged from their lust. But while their meat was yet in their mouths, The wrath of God came upon them, and slew the fattest of them, and smote down the chosen men of Israel. For all this they sinned still, and believed not for his wondrous works. Therefore their days did he consume in vanity, and their years in trouble. When he slew them, then they sought him: and they returned and inquired early after God. And they remembered that God was their rock, and the high God their redeemer. Nevertheless they did flatter him with their mouth, and they lied unto him with their tongues. For their heart was not right with him, neither were they stedfast in his covenant. But he, being full of compassion, forgave their iniquity, and destroyed them not: yea, many a time turned he his anger away, and did not stir up all his wrath. For he remembered that they were but flesh; a wind that passeth away, and cometh not again. How oft did they provoke him in the wilderness, and grieve him in the desert! Yea, they turned back and tempted God, and limited the Holy One of Israel. They remembered not his hand, nor the day when he delivered them from the enemy. How he had wrought his signs in Egypt, and his wonders in the field of Zoan: And had turned their rivers into blood; and their floods, that they could not drink. He sent divers sorts of flies among them, which devoured them; and frogs, which destroyed them. He gave also their increase unto the caterpiller, and their labour unto the locust. He destroyed their vines with hail, and their sycomore trees with frost. He gave up their cattle also to the hail, and their flocks to hot thunderbolts. He cast upon them the fierceness of his anger, wrath, and indignation, and trouble, by sending evil angels among them. He made a way to his anger; he spared not their soul from death, but gave their life over to the pestilence; And smote all the firstborn in Egypt; the chief of their strength in the tabernacles of Ham: But made his own people to go forth like sheep, and guided them in the wilderness like a flock. And he led them on safely, so that they feared not: but the sea overwhelmed their enemies. And he brought them to the border of his sanctuary, even to this mountain, which his right hand had purchased. He cast out the heathen also before them, and divided them an inheritance by line, and made the tribes of Israel to dwell in their tents. Yet they tempted and provoked the most high God, and kept not his testimonies: But turned back, and dealt unfaithfully like their fathers: they were turned aside like a deceitful bow. For they provoked him to anger with their high places, and moved him to jealousy with their graven images. When God heard this, he was wroth, and greatly abhorred Israel: So that he forsook the tabernacle of Shiloh, the tent which he placed among men; And delivered his strength into captivity, and his glory into the enemy's hand. He gave his people over also unto the sword; and was wroth with his inheritance. The fire consumed their young men; and their maidens were not given to marriage. Their priests fell by the sword; and their widows made no lamentation. Then the Lord awaked as one out of sleep, and like a mighty man that shouteth by reason of wine. And he smote his enemies in the hinder parts: he put them to a perpetual reproach. Moreover he refused the tabernacle of Joseph, and chose not the tribe of Ephraim: But chose the tribe of Judah, the mount Zion which he loved. And he built his sanctuary like high palaces, like the earth which he hath established for ever. He chose David also his servant, and took him from the sheepfolds: From following the ewes great with young he brought him to feed Jacob his people, and Israel his inheritance. So he fed them according to the integrity of his heart; and guided them by the skilfulness of his hands.

Psalm 78 is an account of the people of Israel and how God has dealt with them from an early age until the time of David. It is one of the longer psalms, but it comes across as a narration of an elder to the upcoming generations.

Verses 6–8,

That the generation to come might know them, even the children which should be born; who should arise and declare them to their children: That they might set their hope in God, and not forget the works of God, but keep his commandments: And might not be as their fathers, a stubborn and rebellious generation; a generation that set not their heart aright, and whose spirit was not steadfast with God.

It is suggested that one mindfully reads this psalm because, in many ways, it sums up the history of God and His chosen people from the time of Jacob and the beginning of the twelve tribes of Israel through to Moses and the Exodus and onto the beginning of the Davidian age. All of this is fascinating. The real story, however, is how God responds to His people even amid some serious rebellion on their part.

Verses 10–11, "They kept not the covenant of God, and refused to walk in his law; And forgat his works, and his wonders that he had shewed them."

If you recall, in Psalm 73, we discussed the biblical cycle of renewal and redemption that is evidenced throughout the Old and New Testaments. Basically, this is about how (a) the people rebel and do not follow God's ways, which leads to (b) facing the consequences of their actions, which then leads to (c) a contrite heart for offending God, which then becomes (d) an understanding of the mercy and grace of God which ultimately leads to(e) praising and thanking God for His goodness and just ways.

Psalm 78 further exemplifies how this works by using the people of Israel as our real-life guides. In the end, the overarching theme of Psalm 78 is that God is patient, kind, merciful, and a just guide until the people cross a line of iniquity and wicked behavior. The wrath of God is then used to punish the ones who continue to offend God despite His lovingkindness. In the end, after God's punishment had spanned a few generations, Psalm 78:70–72 proclaims that God,

> Chose David also his servant, and took him from the sheepfolds: From following the ewes great with young he brought him to feed Jacob his people, and Israel his inheritance. So he fed them according to the integrity of his heart; and guided them by the skilfulness of his hands.

In other words, David was chosen by God to be king and to use his skillfulness to help restore the inheritance of God's covenant with His people and to lead the people back onto God's righteous path by falling back on the integrity of David's heart (which, as you recall, is after God's own heart). The reward to the people of Israel after a period of punishment for iniquitous behavior was to be given another chance with King David and to once again gain favor and reward in the sight of God.

The Lord is so very kind and merciful. Praise and glory to His name! Amen.

Notes:

_____

_____

_____

_____

_____

_____

_____

_____

_____

Psalm 79: O Remember Not against Us Former Iniquities

O God, the heathen are come into thine inheritance; thy holy temple have they defiled; they have laid Jerusalem on heaps. The dead bodies of thy servants have they given to be meat unto the fowls of the heaven, the flesh of thy saints unto the beasts of the earth. Their blood have they shed like water round about Jerusalem; and there was none to bury them. We are become a reproach to our neighbours, a scorn and derision to them that are round about us. How long, LORD? wilt thou be angry for ever? shall thy jealousy burn like fire? Pour out thy wrath upon the heathen that have not known thee, and upon the kingdoms that have not called upon thy name. For they have devoured Jacob, and laid waste his dwelling place. O remember not against us former iniquities: let thy tender mercies speedily prevent us: for we are brought very low. Help us, O God of our salvation, for the glory of thy name: and deliver us, and purge away our sins, for thy name's sake. Wherefore should the heathen say, Where is their God? let him be known among the heathen in our sight by the revenging of the blood of thy servants which is shed. Let the sighing of the prisoner come before thee; according to the greatness of thy power preserve thou those that are appointed to die; And render unto our neighbours sevenfold into their bosom their reproach, wherewith they have reproached thee, O Lord. So we thy people and sheep of thy pasture will give thee thanks for ever: we will shew forth thy praise to all generations.

Have you ever pleaded with God for a wicked person or a group of ungodly people to be given punishment for the disasters they produce through their lives and the chaos that seems to follow them? They are liars, they steal, and they intentionally hurt people, but nothing ever seems to happen to them. They go about life wreaking havoc, and you don't see any evidence that God is punishing them. On the other hand, you try to live a good life. You are honest, you do a good day's work, and you make the effort to love and support people. Perhaps you praise God and have fellowship with Him when you can, and yet, your prayers asking God to stop this perceived enemy of yours from ruining your and other people's lives appear to go unanswered. This is what is happening in Psalm 79.

The author is listing all the terrible deeds that the heathens are doing to his nation and his people. They have defiled the holy temple in Jerusalem. They slaughter the servants of God and leave their flesh to be eaten by beasts and fowl. They harass and scold their saintly neighbors with criticism and contempt for their beliefs. And, yet...and *yet*...still God does nothing to stop this.

It is at times like these that a follower of God can begin to feel like God is using the ungodly to punish them. And like the author of Psalm 79, we too, can begin to examine where we have gone astray in our own lives. Perhaps we worship our idols above God, like money, social media, or vanity. We are and have been sinners, we know, so we plead with God, "How long, LORD? wilt thou be angry for ever? shall thy jealousy burn like fire?" (verse 5).

You see, we want God to stop punishing us for our sins and instead look to the others whose sins are far greater than ours. They are the ones who need punishment, not us. Can God not see how truly bad these neighbors are? Because of this, we cry out, "Pour out thy wrath upon the heathen that have not known thee, and upon the kingdoms that have not called upon thy name" (verse 6).

Take them down! Pour out all Your wrath and leave them devastated, we pray. On the other hand:

Verses 8–9,

> O remember not against us former iniquities: let thy tender mercies speedily prevent us: for we are brought very low. Help us, O God of our salvation, for the glory of thy name: and deliver us, and purge away our sins, for thy name's sake.

In essence, these verses are asking God to forget our past sins and use His mercy to help lift us and rid us of our sins. And then, while You are forgetting our sins, why don't You pour Your wrath down on our enemies, not once but sevenfold?

Verse 12, "And render unto our neighbors sevenfold into their bosom their reproach, wherewith they have reproached thee, O Lord."

If you do this, "So we thy people and sheep of thy pasture will give thee thanks for ever: we will shew forth thy praise to all generations" (verse 13).

None of this is to say that those who pursue ungodly lives and who seek to ruin others' lives and properties are not worthy of the wrath of God. They may be, and we can be sure God will have the last say in the matter. To be sure, the author of this psalm has been brought low by all that is happening around him, and it has been going on for an extended period. He is pleading with God for relief. Yet, one cannot help but notice a double standard and perhaps a certain pride of the author, who seems to be justifying and rationalizing his sins and the sins of his people and focusing all his attention on the dastardly deeds of his neighbors.

Later, when Christ comes, He tells us that we should pray for our enemies and forgive them—turn the other cheek, so to speak. Could this be a reference to Psalm 79, when in the book of Matthew, Jesus is asked about this idea of forgiving our neighbors? Matthew 18:21–22,

> Then came Peter to him, and said, Lord, how oft shall my brother sin against me, and I forgive him? till seven

times? Jesus saith unto him, I say not unto thee, Until seven times: but, Until seventy times seven.

In Psalm 79, the author asks God to punish his neighbor seven times what he gave. Centuries later, Jesus answered this question. "Forgive seventy times seven" that which has been sinned against us.

You know what? That is what God will do: He will forgive us our sins. Shouldn't we at least try to do that in our own lives? Forgive those who have hurt us? It is hard, but it will be so worth it. To forgive is a blessing sent by God because it gives our hearts peace.

The only thing our vengeance toward another person does is to take away the love we have in our hearts for them.

Psalm 80: Turn Us Again, O Lord God of Hosts, Cause Thy Face to Shine; and We Shall Be Saved

Give ear, O Shepherd of Israel, thou that leadest Joseph like a flock; thou that dwellest between the cherubims, shine forth. Before Ephraim and Benjamin and Manasseh stir up thy strength, and come and save us. Turn us again, O God, and cause thy face to shine; and we shall be saved. O LORD God of hosts, how long wilt thou be angry against the prayer of thy people? Thou feedest them with the bread of tears; and givest them tears to drink in great measure. Thou makest us a strife unto our neighbours: and our enemies laugh among themselves. Turn us again, O God of hosts, and cause thy face to shine; and we shall be saved. Thou hast brought a vine out of Egypt: thou hast cast out the heathen, and planted it. Thou preparedst room before it, and didst cause it to take deep root, and it filled the land. The hills were covered with the shadow of it, and the boughs thereof were like the goodly cedars. She sent out her boughs unto the sea, and her branches unto the river. Why hast thou then broken down her hedges, so that all they which pass by the way do pluck her? The boar out of the wood doth waste it, and the wild beast of the field doth devour it. Return, we beseech thee, O God of hosts: look down from heaven, and behold, and visit this vine; And the vineyard which thy right hand hath planted, and the branch that thou madest strong for thyself. It is burned with fire, it is cut down: they perish at the rebuke of thy countenance. Let thy hand be upon the man of thy right hand, upon the son of man whom thou madest strong for thyself. So will not we go back from thee: quicken us, and we will call upon thy name. Turn us again, O LORD God of hosts, cause thy face to shine; and we shall be saved.

Psalm 80 is a good example of the prayers of someone who is exhibiting a contrite heart. In this psalm, the author is trying to understand the relationship he and his people have with God. At that moment, he sees that his people are filled with sadness and, perhaps, remorse. He asks, "O LORD God of hosts, how long wilt thou be angry against the prayer of thy people?" (verse 4).

This is followed by the remembrance of the time when the Lord brought the people out of captivity and set them on a hill where God Himself planted them like a vine that grew throughout the region. In other words, God saved them and gave them a new home, and it prospered.

The Lord nurtured the vine He planted in righteousness, but soon, it began to foster strange and unexalted fruit, much to His dismay. Where before God took His people to a promised land, and the heathens were pushed back, "Thou hast brought a vine out of Egypt: thou hast cast out the heathen, and planted it" (verse 8).

It appears that centuries later, the heathens are now invading the land and appropriating the people of God, "Why hast thou then broken down her hedges, so that all they which pass by the way do pluck her?" (verse 12).

In other words, the fortified boundary that God originally put between His people and the heathens has since broken down, and many of His people have been taken out of their righteous lives and have adopted the ways of the ungodly.

It's an age-old story about the nature of man. Even with the most holy and anointed starts to the life of a person, an enterprise, or a nation, we continue to backslide into the ways of the world time and again. God makes us in his image and likeness, and we turn ourselves into devils and weeds. This is the way of being human.

On the other hand, this psalm is one of hope. Even when we turn away from the Lord, we can always come to our senses and ask to be given another chance. Even when we burn down our house, we can ask God to build it up again.

Verses 18–19, "So will not we go back from thee: quicken us, and we will call upon thy name. Turn us again, O LORD God of hosts, cause thy face to shine; and we shall be saved."

It is never too late. No matter where you've been, what you have done, or who you have hurt, it is never too late to come to God with a contrite, remorseful heart and ask that God help you start again. That, too, is in the nature of people. We can always turn around.

Thank You, Lord, for Your great mercy and compassion in the face of our rejection and offenses.

God understands our human nature and is always willing to help us turn our lives around.

Psalm 81: Oh That My People Had Hearkened unto Me

Sing aloud unto God our strength: make a joyful noise unto the God of Jacob. Take a psalm, and bring hither the timbrel, the pleasant harp with the psaltery. Blow up the trumpet in the new moon, in the time appointed, on our solemn feast day. For this was a statute for Israel, and a law of the God of Jacob. This he ordained in Joseph for a testimony, when he went out through the land of Egypt: where I heard a language that I understood not. I removed his shoulder from the burden: his hands were delivered from the pots. Thou calledst in trouble, and I delivered thee; I answered thee in the secret place of thunder: I proved thee at the waters of Meribah. Selah. Hear, O my people, and I will testify unto thee: O Israel, if thou wilt hearken unto me; There shall no strange god be in thee; neither shalt thou worship any strange god. I am the LORD thy God, which brought thee out of the land of Egypt: open thy mouth wide, and I will fill it. But my people would not hearken to my voice; and Israel would none of me. So I gave them up unto their own hearts' lust: and they walked in their own counsels. Oh that my people had hearkened unto me, and Israel had walked in my ways! I should soon have subdued their enemies, and turned my hand against their adversaries. The haters of the LORD should have submitted themselves unto him: but their time should have endured for ever. He should have fed them also with the finest of the wheat: and with honey out of the rock should I have satisfied thee.

Psalm 81 seems to be God's discussion of the prayer of a contrite heart in Psalm 80. Let us examine what God has to say about this:

1. Thou calledst in trouble, and I delivered thee.
2. I answered thee in the secret place of thunder.
3. I proved thee at the waters of Meribah.

When His people were in trouble, God delivered them. Not only that, but He came to the people and answered them and proved Himself. So now, the Lord has a few things to say, "Hear, O my people, and I will testify unto thee: O Israel, if thou wilt hearken unto me" (verse 8).

1. There shall no strange god be in thee.
    a. Do not invite another spirit but God to live within your spirit.
2. Neither shalt thou worship any strange god.
    a. Do not praise and worship any god but the creator Himself.
3. Open thy mouth wide, and I will fill it.
    a. Speak only the words that God places within us.
    b. Do not speak about things that are not aligned with the words of the one true God.

The Father is pointing out those things that He commanded His people to specifically follow. Let's look at the book of Exodus, chapter 20, verses 2–6, to further clarify what God is speaking about in Psalm 81:

"I am the Lord thy God, which have brought thee out of the land of Egypt, out of the house of bondage" (Exodus 20:2).

1. "Thou shalt have no other gods before me" (verse 3).
2. "Thou shalt not make unto thee any graven image, or any likeness of any thing that is in heaven above, or that is in the earth beneath, or that is in the water under the earth" (verse 4).
3. "Thou shalt not bow down thyself to them, nor serve them" (verse 5).
4. "For I the Lord thy God am a jealous God, visiting the iniquity of the fathers upon the children unto the third

and fourth generation of them that hate me; And shewing mercy unto thousands of them that love me, and keep my commandments" (verses 5–6).

God is saying, "Look, I did these things for you and only asked that you follow these commands." Back to Psalm 81:

1. Verse 11, "But my people would not hearken to my voice; and Israel would none of me."
2. Verse 12, "So I gave them up unto their own hearts' lust: and they walked in their own counsels."

In other words, God presented Himself to His people and asked that they follow Him. When they used their free will for vain lusts, He withdrew His blessings and protections in acquiescence. Our Lord is a humble and meek creator. He will not normally intercede in the lives of people who have cast Him off and do not walk in His good ways. The result is He withdraws from their lives, which in the end leads to disorder, chaos, and destruction 100 percent of the time.

The sad part is that if His people had followed His commands, "He should have fed them also with the finest of the wheat: and with honey out of the rock should I have satisfied thee" (verse 16). All the good things were available to them and would have been given freely

Contemplation: What Do I Put above God in My Own Life?

I don't know about you, but this makes me want to contemplate my own life and examine those areas where I might be putting other things above God. What idols might I be worshipping over the Father that has been so good to me? Perhaps God is offering me all the good things in life, but my idolatry is keeping the fullness of God at bay.

Use these lines to write notes as you contemplate:

_____
_____
_____
_____
_____
_____
_____

Dear Lord, help me identify those areas in my life that have become idols that I have put over worshiping and praising You. Help me to overcome anything that is causing You to withdraw Your good counsel from my life, even if just a little. I ask that You draw closer and give me the strength to always put You first in everything.

Lord, let me never be separated from You.

Psalm 82: He Judgeth among the Gods

God standeth in the congregation of the mighty; he judgeth among the gods. How long will ye judge unjustly, and accept the persons of the wicked? Selah. Defend the poor and fatherless: do justice to the afflicted and needy. Deliver the poor and needy: rid them out of the hand of the wicked. They know not, neither will they understand; they walk on in darkness: all the foundations of the earth are out of course. I have said, Ye are gods; and all of you are children of the most High. But ye shall die like men, and fall like one of the princes. Arise, O God, judge the earth: for thou shalt inherit all nations.

The author of Psalm 82, Asaph, is observing that the children of God have become wicked. Indeed, even the foundation of the earth has fallen off the course that God intended. This psalm is asking for God to judge among the people and to show mercy toward the poor and needy amongst them. For the people of his nation are walking in darkness and have become gods among themselves. They are causing pain and suffering to the poor with their own hands. Asaph recognizes how far the children of God have fallen and issues this stern warning, "I have said, Ye are gods; and all of you are children of the most High. But ye shall die like men, and fall like one of the princes" (verses 6–7).

In other words, though you have access to the power of God as one of His children and are, therefore, like God unto yourself, you can still be judged harshly by God and cast down like any common prince of man. Psalm 82 speaks of the vanity and corrupted power of people, even among those who call themselves children of God.

O Lord, keep us humble in our inheritance as one of Your children. May we never get so vain that we think of ourselves as gods in our own right and cast You aside in our arrogance.

Help us to stay on Your path. Thank You, Lord.

Psalm 83: Hold Not Thy Peace, and Be Not Still, O God

Keep not thou silence, O God: hold not thy peace, and be not still, O God. For, lo, thine enemies make a tumult: and they that hate thee have lifted up the head. They have taken crafty counsel against thy people, and consulted against thy hidden ones. They have said, Come, and let us cut them off from being a nation; that the name of Israel may be no more in remembrance. For they have consulted together with one consent: they are confederate against thee: The tabernacles of Edom, and the Ishmaelites; of Moab, and the Hagarenes; Gebal, and Ammon, and Amalek; the Philistines with the inhabitants of Tyre; Assur also is joined with them: they have holpen the children of Lot. Selah. Do unto them as unto the Midianites; as to Sisera, as to Jabin, at the brook of Kison: Which perished at Endor: they became as dung for the earth. Make their nobles like Oreb, and like Zeeb: yea, all their princes as Zebah, and as Zalmunna: Who said, Let us take to ourselves the houses of God in possession. O my God, make them like a wheel; as the stubble before the wind. As the fire burneth a wood, and as the flame setteth the mountains on fire; So persecute them with thy tempest, and make them afraid with thy storm. Fill their faces with shame; that they may seek thy name, O LORD. Let them be confounded and troubled for ever; yea, let them be put to shame, and perish: That men may know that thou, whose name alone is JEHOVAH, art the most high over all the earth.

In Psalm 83, Asaph asks God to take vengeance on the enemies of God. When this psalm was written, it appears that those who opposed God had taken possession of the holy land and had conspired to make sure the name of Israel was forgotten in history. He then goes on to list a line of different nations in verses 6–11,

> Edom, and the Ishmaelites; of Moab, and the Hagarenes; Gebal, and Ammon, and Amalek; the Philistines with the inhabitants of Tyre; Assur also is joined with them: they have holpen the children of Lot. Selah. Do unto them as unto the Midianites; as to Sisera, as to Jabin, at the brook of Kison: Which perished at Endor: they became as dung for the earth. Make their nobles like Oreb, and like Zeeb: yea, all their princes as Zebah, and as Zalmunna.

Let's examine some of these nations from other parts of the Bible to get an idea of what is being discussed here:

1. Numbers 31:7, "And they warned against the Midianites, as the LORD commanded Moses; and they slew all the males."
2. Judges 7:22, "And the three hundred blew the trumpets, and the LORD set every man's sword against his fellow, even throughout all the host: and the host fled Bethshittah in Zererath, and to the border of the Abelmeholah, unto Tabbath."
3. Judges 4:15, "And the LORD discomfited Sisera, and all his chariots, and all his host, with the edge of the sword before Barak; so that Sisera lighted down off his chariot, and fled away of his feet."
4. Judges 4:24, "And the hand of the children of Israel prospered, and prevailed against Jabin the king of Canaan, until they had destroyed Jabien king of Canaan."
5. Judges 5:21, "The river of Kishon swept them away, that ancient river, the river Kishon. O my soul, thou hast trodden down strength."

We can see that Psalm 83 leans back into the history of Israel to remind God how He has judged the enemies of His people in the past. In many ways, Asaph is asking God to slay the current enemies of Israel in much the same manner. Psalm 83 is an appeal to God to present His wrath in the current day, "That men may know that thou, whose name alone is JEHOVAH, art the most high over all the earth" (verse 18). Asaph knows that God's righteous anger and justice always prevail.

At the same time, this psalm is a lesson in patience. We are to ask God for help and then wait on Him. Over and over, we are reminded that God's will is always victorious. He will always win every battle in which He engages. In many ways, this is a mercy from God. In His lovingkindness, He has engaged the enemies of His people throughout history and has won every battle so that those who believe in Him might see His powerful ways.

Israel still stands, yet none of the nations who have come against him are widely remembered even in our current times. The Lord takes the devices of the enemy and turns them around to use against them. Wait on the Lord, and He will win your battle as well.

"Do not be afraid," says the Lord. "The battle is not yours but Mine."

Psalm 84: For the Lord God Is a Sun and Shield!

How amiable are thy tabernacles, O LORD of hosts! My soul longeth, yea, even fainteth for the courts of the LORD: my heart and my flesh crieth out for the living God. Yea, the sparrow hath found an house, and the swallow a nest for herself, where she may lay her young, even thine altars, O LORD of hosts, my King, and my God. Blessed are they that dwell in thy house: they will be still praising thee. Selah. Blessed is the man whose strength is in thee; in whose heart are the ways of them. Who passing through the valley of Baca make it a well; the rain also filleth the pools. They go from strength to strength, every one of them in Zion appeareth before God. O LORD God of hosts, hear my prayer: give ear, O God of Jacob. Selah. Behold, O God our shield, and look upon the face of thine anointed. For a day in thy courts is better than a thousand. I had rather be a doorkeeper in the house of my God, than to dwell in the tents of wickedness. For the LORD God is a sun and shield: the LORD will give grace and glory: no good thing will he withhold from them that walk uprightly. O LORD of hosts, blessed is the man that trusteth in thee.

Psalm 84 recognizes that the Lord is our sun and our shield. And like so many things in the Bible, which is the living Word of God, there are many ways that this can be perceived.

Let's take a moment to look at the different ways that the Lord truly is our sun and our shield.

Study: Ways That Our God Is the Sun and the Shield

The Sun:

1. He is the source of light on Earth.
   a. He created the sun and continues to be the source of its light.
   b. He is the sun, for He is all things.
2. He is the source of all life on Earth.
   a. Without the sun, nothing would grow.
3. He sheds light in darkness.
   a. He exposes the light of truth in the darkness of deception.
4. John 8:12, "Then spake Jesus again unto them, saying, I am the light of the world: he that followeth me shall not walk in darkness, but shall have the light of life."

The Shield:

1. He is our protection against those who wage war against us.
   a. His presence acts as a barrier against physical and spiritual battles.
2. He shelters us while we go through the storms in life.
   a. He protects us against the full force of our troubles.
3. He is a refuge away from the corruption of the ways of the world.
   a. He acts as a place where we are set aside and protected from being corrupted by the ways of the world.
4. "Thou hast also given me the shield of thy salvation" (2 Samuel 22:36).
   a. All of the Lord's protection is available to us when we are under His salvation.

In the second half of Psalm 84, verse 11, we are promised that not only is He our sun and our shield, but "the Lord will give grace and glory: no good thing will he withhold from them that walk uprightly."

Read that again: no good thing will be withheld from them who walk uprightly. Isn't that amazing? The creator of *all* things and the most powerful force in the universe will *not* withhold any good thing from those who walk the good path with Him. In the end, it all comes down to this, "O LORD of hosts, blessed is the man that trusteth in thee" (verse 12).

Trust in the Lord, and not only will He be our light and protect us, but we will also be blessed, and no good thing will be withheld from us. We just need to trust in Him and His promises. Search your heart right now and examine the state of trust you have in the Lord. Try to work on those areas that stop you from fully trusting in Him. It will be so worth it to place all your trust in Him. His promises are great, and His words are pure.

On a scale of 1 to 10, where is my trust in the Lord at this moment? _____

Thank You, Lord, my Savior, my comforter, my redeemer, my friend, and my King. I love You with all my heart. Help me to trust You more as we walk together. Amen.

Notes:

_____

_____

_____

_____

_____

_____

_____

Psalm 85: Turn Us, O God of Our Salvation

LORD, thou hast been favourable unto thy land: thou hast brought back the captivity of Jacob. Thou hast forgiven the iniquity of thy people, thou hast covered all their sin. Selah. Thou hast taken away all thy wrath: thou hast turned thyself from the fierceness of thine anger. Turn us, O God of our salvation, and cause thine anger toward us to cease. Wilt thou be angry with us for ever? wilt thou draw out thine anger to all generations? Wilt thou not revive us again: that thy people may rejoice in thee? Shew us thy mercy, O LORD, and grant us thy salvation. I will hear what God the LORD will speak: for he will speak peace unto his people, and to his saints: but let them not turn again to folly. Surely his salvation is nigh them that fear him; that glory may dwell in our land. Mercy and truth are met together; righteousness and peace have kissed each other. Truth shall spring out of the earth; and righteousness shall look down from heaven. Yea, the LORD shall give that which is good; and our land shall yield her increase. Righteousness shall go before him; and shall set us in the way of his steps.

The author of Psalm 85 is asking the Lord to turn His children away from their folly and back to the righteousness of His ways. The people of David's time are being compared to Jacob, the son of Isaac and Rebekah, and the grandson of Abraham, with whom God made His covenant. For a time, Jacob was positioned as a cunning and deceitful person who stole the birthright of his twin brother, Esau. In other words, Jacob was a liar and a thief.

Verse 1, "LORD, thou hast been favourable unto thy land: thou hast brought back the captivity of Jacob."

Psalm 85 recognizes that the people of Israel have turned again toward this type of iniquity, which held Jacob captive in his own time. In this sense, we can see that to be held captive means to be held bound by sin in the same sense that evil binds the soul to a life of iniquity.

However, eventually, Jacob was able to turn around, and as a reward, God gave Jacob the great honor of changing his name to Israel and giving him the twelve sons who went on to become the originators of the twelve tribes of Israel.

Psalm 85 asks God to turn His people once again, "Wilt thou not revive us again: that thy people may rejoice in thee?" (verse 6).

This is a psalm that reminds us that the Lord can turn around even the vilest of sinners and put them on a praiseworthy path of reward that glorifies God. We are never too far gone to be turned back to God. Psalm 85 recognizes this and appeals to the mercy of God for help and assistance.

Verses 12–13, "Yea, the LORD shall give that which is good; and our land shall yield her increase. Righteousness shall go before him; and shall set us in the way of his steps."

Thank You, Lord! For You are slow to anger. You are compassionate and merciful with Your beloved children. You will hear us when we pray for help in the day of our captivity, and You will set us back onto the path of Your ways.

Praise and glory are Yours, O Lord!

Psalm 86: For Thou Art Great, and Doest Wondrous Things: Thou Art God Alone

Bow down thine ear, O LORD, hear me: for I am poor and needy. Preserve my soul; for I am holy: O thou my God, save thy servant that trusteth in thee. Be merciful unto me, O Lord: for I cry unto thee daily. Rejoice the soul of thy servant: for unto thee, O Lord, do I lift up my soul. For thou, Lord, art good, and ready to forgive; and plenteous in mercy unto all them that call upon thee. Give ear, O LORD, unto my prayer; and attend to the voice of my supplications. In the day of my trouble I will call upon thee: for thou wilt answer me. Among the gods there is none like unto thee, O Lord; neither are there any works like unto thy works. All nations whom thou hast made shall come and worship before thee, O Lord; and shall glorify thy name. For thou art great, and doest wondrous things: thou art God alone. Teach me thy way, O LORD; I will walk in thy truth: unite my heart to fear thy name. I will praise thee, O Lord my God, with all my heart: and I will glorify thy name for evermore. For great is thy mercy toward me: and thou hast delivered my soul from the lowest hell. O God, the proud are risen against me, and the assemblies of violent men have sought after my soul; and have not set thee before them. But thou, O Lord, art a God full of compassion, and gracious, longsuffering, and plenteous in mercy and truth. O turn unto me, and have mercy upon me; give thy strength unto thy servant, and save the son of thine handmaid. Shew me a token for good; that they which hate me may see it, and be ashamed: because thou, LORD, hast holpen me, and comforted me.

In Psalm 86, David proclaims that the Lord our God is the one and only true God. The gods of the heathen are not like God because not only are they false and unproven gods, but they do not do the types of wondrous works that the God of Israel regularly performs. And because of this, David will "praise thee, O Lord my God, with all my heart: and I will glorify thy name for evermore" (verse 12).

This psalm lists the many ways God has proved Himself to be great and above all other gods, according to David.

Study: How God Has Proven Himself to Be Great?

1. He is righteous.
2. He is ready to forgive.
3. He shows an abundance of mercy to all of them who call upon Him.
4. He will answer His children who call upon Him when they are in trouble.
5. He delivers our souls from the lowest pit of hell.
6. He is full of compassion.
7. He is tenderhearted.
8. He is long-suffering and slow to anger.
9. He is full of mercy.
10. He is full of truth.

Worksheet: How Has God Shown His Greatness in Your Life?

Please take a moment to contemplate and write down how God has shown and proven His greatness to you personally in your own life. Use the list above as a reference.

Thou art great, O Lord!

Psalm 87: The Lord Loveth the Gates of Zion

His foundation is in the holy mountains. The LORD loveth the gates of Zion more than all the dwellings of Jacob. Glorious things are spoken of thee, O city of God. Selah. I will make mention of Rahab and Babylon to them that know me: behold Philistia, and Tyre, with Ethiopia; this man was born there. And of Zion it shall be said, This and that man was born in her: and the highest himself shall establish her. The LORD shall count, when he writeth up the people, that this man was born there. Selah. As well the singers as the players on instruments shall be there: all my springs are in thee.

Psalm 87 speaks about the love our creator has for Zion and directs our attention to Rahab and Babylon as proof of God's love for the "city of God," which is another phrase to illustrate Zion.

As an example of what God contends with on behalf of Zion, let's briefly study the reference to Rahab.

Study: Rahab

1. A poetic reference to Egypt.
   a. Babylon is also very often a spiritual reference to Egypt within the context of the Bible.
2. Used as another poetic reference to indicate pride or arrogance.
3. A mystical sea monster as an emblematic or poetic name for Egypt and the sea.
   a. In medieval Jewish folklore, Rahab is a mythical sea monster, a dragon of the waters, the demonic angel of the sea.

4. Rahab represents the primordial abyss, the water dragon of darkness, comparable to Leviathan and Tiamat.
   a. Rahab later became a particular demon, an inhabitant of the sea, especially associated with the Red Sea.
5. Isaiah 51:9, "Awake, awake, put on strength, O arm of the Lord; awake, as in the ancient days, in the generations of old. Art thou not it that hath cut Rahab, and wounded the dragon?"

So, we can see that Rahab is referenced as a symbol of the spirit of those places that are at odds and, indeed, at war with God and His chosen people. Not only has God conquered this spirit over the generations, but He has made the holy mountain of Zion the place where He laid His foundation.

Verse 2, "The LORD loveth the gates of Zion more than all the dwellings of Jacob."

We can imagine that the gates of Zion are the entrance to the dwelling place of Zion where the mighty general, the Lord of hosts, has conquered and continues to conquer the enemies of His kingdom. The same kingdom that the children of God belong to, take refuge in, and sing songs of praise and glory about.

Thank You, Lord, for continuing to use Your goodness and power to protect Your holy kingdom from the dragons that besiege the gates where Your children stand protected.

Notes:

_____

_____

_____

_____

_____

_____

Psalm 88: For My Soul Is Full of Troubles; My Life Draweth Nigh unto the Grave

O LORD God of my salvation, I have cried day and night before thee: Let my prayer come before thee: incline thine ear unto my cry; For my soul is full of troubles: and my life draweth nigh unto the grave. I am counted with them that go down into the pit: I am as a man that hath no strength: Free among the dead, like the slain that lie in the grave, whom thou rememberest no more: and they are cut off from thy hand. Thou hast laid me in the lowest pit, in darkness, in the deeps. Thy wrath lieth hard upon me, and thou hast afflicted me with all thy waves. Selah. Thou hast put away mine acquaintance far from me; thou hast made me an abomination unto them: I am shut up, and I cannot come forth. Mine eye mourneth by reason of affliction: LORD, I have called daily upon thee, I have stretched out my hands unto thee. Wilt thou shew wonders to the dead? shall the dead arise and praise thee? Selah. Shall thy lovingkindness be declared in the grave? or thy faithfulness in destruction? Shall thy wonders be known in the dark? and thy righteousness in the land of forgetfulness? But unto thee have I cried, O LORD; and in the morning shall my prayer prevent thee. LORD, why castest thou off my soul? why hidest thou thy face from me? I am afflicted and ready to die from my youth up: while I suffer thy terrors I am distracted. Thy fierce wrath goeth over me; thy terrors have cut me off. They came round about me daily like water; they compassed me about together. Lover and friend hast thou put far from me, and mine acquaintance into darkness.

During His lamentations in the garden, did the Father allow Jesus to experience feeling cut off from Him so that Jesus Himself experienced that feeling in the flesh? Psalm 88 could point to this very thing as one interpretation.

When we read this psalm and contemplate how much Jesus suffered in thoughts and prayers in the garden, is it so hard to imagine Him expressing the thoughts that David expresses in Psalm 88? Those same thoughts that so many of us feel from time to time in life during particularly trying times.

Verse 14–16,

> LORD, why castest thou off my soul? why hidest thou thy face from me? I am afflicted and ready to die from my youth up: while I suffer thy terrors I am distracted. Thy fierce wrath goeth over me; thy terrors have cut me off.

That feeling that the Father has abandoned us in our time of need. These are the times that try a person's soul and bring their faith to the surface to examine. Did Jesus Himself cry out in His darkest time?

Verse 18, "Lover and friend hast thou put far from me, and mine acquaintance into darkness."

We may never know, but it is not hard to imagine that even the Son of God wondered where His Father was during His most difficult troubles.

However, it is during these particularly hard times that when we say, "Yes, I will trust in You and Your mercy and compassion," that we find ourselves gain in faith. God has promised us that He is our strength and virtue. Though we may feel that He has abandoned us, He is always beside us, even in our darkest times. Like us, Jesus knew that His Father was His refuge, and a simple turn of thought back to faith will help anyone make it through any experience. The

Father will always bring us back to peace within our souls.

Thank You, Lord, for Your great goodness. You are our refuge. We love You. Amen.

He restores our souls every time. Trust the Lord and stay in faith.

Psalm 89: The Covenant between God and His People

I will sing of the mercies of the LORD for ever: with my mouth will I make known thy faithfulness to all generations. For I have said, Mercy shall be built up for ever: thy faithfulness shalt thou establish in the very heavens. I have made a covenant with my chosen, I have sworn unto David my servant, Thy seed will I establish for ever, and build up thy throne to all generations. Selah. And the heavens shall praise thy wonders, O LORD: thy faithfulness also in the congregation of the saints. For who in the heaven can be compared unto the LORD? who among the sons of the mighty can be likened unto the LORD? God is greatly to be feared in the assembly of the saints, and to be had in reverence of all them that are about him. O LORD God of hosts, who is a strong LORD like unto thee? or to thy faithfulness round about thee? Thou rulest the raging of the sea: when the waves thereof arise, thou stillest them. Thou hast broken Rahab in pieces, as one that is slain; thou hast scattered thine enemies with thy strong arm. The heavens are thine, the earth also is thine: as for the world and the fulness thereof, thou hast founded them. The north and the south thou hast created them: Tabor and Hermon shall rejoice in thy name. Thou hast a mighty arm: strong is thy hand, and high is thy right hand. Justice and judgment are the habitation of thy throne: mercy and truth shall go before thy face. Blessed is the people that know the joyful sound: they shall walk, O LORD, in the light of thy countenance. In thy name shall they rejoice all the day: and in thy righteousness shall they be exalted. For thou art the glory of their strength: and in thy favour

our horn shall be exalted. For the LORD is our defence; and the Holy One of Israel is our king. Then thou spakest in vision to thy holy one, and saidst, I have laid help upon one that is mighty; I have exalted one chosen out of the people. I have found David my servant; with my holy oil have I anointed him: With whom my hand shall be established: mine arm also shall strengthen him. The enemy shall not exact upon him; nor the son of wickedness afflict him. And I will beat down his foes before his face, and plague them that hate him. But my faithfulness and my mercy shall be with him: and in my name shall his horn be exalted. I will set his hand also in the sea, and his right hand in the rivers. He shall cry unto me, Thou art my father, my God, and the rock of my salvation. Also I will make him my firstborn, higher than the kings of the earth. My mercy will I keep for him for evermore, and my covenant shall stand fast with him. His seed also will I make to endure for ever, and his throne as the days of heaven. If his children forsake my law, and walk not in my judgments; If they break my statutes, and keep not my commandments; Then will I visit their transgression with the rod, and their iniquity with stripes. Nevertheless my lovingkindness will I not utterly take from him, nor suffer my faithfulness to fail. My covenant will I not break, nor alter the thing that is gone out of my lips. Once have I sworn by my holiness that I will not lie unto David. His seed shall endure for ever, and his throne as the sun before me. It shall be established for ever as the moon, and as a faithful witness in heaven. Selah. But thou hast cast off and abhorred, thou hast been wroth with thine anointed. Thou hast made void the covenant of thy servant: thou hast profaned his crown by casting it to the ground. Thou hast broken down all his hedges; thou hast brought his strong holds to ruin. All that pass by the way spoil him: he is a reproach to his neighbours. Thou hast set up the right hand of his adversaries; thou hast made all his enemies to rejoice. Thou hast also turned the edge of his sword, and hast not made him to stand in the battle. Thou hast made his glory to cease, and cast his throne down to the ground. The days of his youth hast thou shortened: thou hast covered him with shame. Selah. How long, LORD? wilt thou hide thyself for ever? shall thy wrath burn like fire? Remember how short my time is: wherefore hast thou made all men in vain? What man is he that liveth, and shall not see death? shall he deliver his soul from the hand of the grave? Selah. Lord, where are thy former lovingkindnesses, which thou swarest unto David in thy truth? Remember, Lord, the reproach of thy servants; how I do bear in my bosom the reproach of all the mighty people; Wherewith thine enemies have reproached, O LORD; wherewith they have reproached the footsteps of thine anointed. Blessed be the LORD for evermore. Amen, and Amen.

Psalm 89 examines the covenant that God made with His chosen people through David.

Verses 3–4, "I have made a covenant with my chosen, I have sworn onto David my servant, Thy seed will I establish for ever, and build up thy throne to all generations. Selah."

Verses 20, 22, "I have found David my servant; with holy oil have I anointed him: …The enemy shall not exact upon him; nor the son of wickedness afflict him."

God offers to David:

1. His mercy forever.
2. His covenant shall stand fast.
3. David's seed will endure forever.
4. And his throne will last as the days of heaven.

However,

1. If his children forsake God's law and walk not in His judgment.
2. If they break His statutes and keep not His commandments.

Then, God will:

1. Visit their transgression with the rod.
2. And their iniquity with stripes.

Nevertheless,

1. His loving kindness He will not utterly take away.
2. He will not suffer His faithfulness to fail.

When God made the covenant with His people, that was it. He will not break nor alter the words that have gone out of His lips. He has sworn in His holiness unto David that He will not lie (nor can He because He is truth). When we speak truth, we speak God. It's as simple as that.

Verse 34, "My covenant will I not break, nor alter the thing that is gone out of my lips."

So, according to the Word of God, David's seed shall endure forever, and David will have a throne as the sun before us. God's words are "true," "binding," and "everlasting." If God has spoken, it is as if eternity has opened to hold His words.

Consideration: The Bible as an Epic Story of Adventure

One level of the Bible is the triune God as a magnificent adventure author. The planet that the Bible portrays plays out like an epic, wonderful, exciting, highest imagination of plays. There are wars and dragons, angels and demons, falls and miraculous resurrections. Jesus and His Father's imagination knows no bounds. Pity the people who see only with blinders on their eyes. They miss the wondrous adventure called *life*.

God is the Word. Jesus is the Word incarnate. Holy Spirit is the Word's author set on fire in each of our hearts.

Notes:

Psalm 90: Thou Turnest Man Destruction and Sayest, Return Ye Children of Men

Lord, thou hast been our dwelling place in all generations. Before the mountains were brought forth, or ever thou hadst formed the earth and the world, even from everlasting to everlasting, thou art God. Thou turnest man to destruction; and sayest, Return, ye children of men. For a thousand years in thy sight are but as yesterday when it is past, and as a watch in the night. Thou carriest them away as with a flood; they are as a sleep: in the morning they are like grass which groweth up. In the morning it flourisheth, and groweth up; in the evening it is cut down, and withereth. For we are consumed by thine anger, and by thy wrath are we troubled. Thou hast set our iniquities before thee, our secret sins in the light of thy countenance. For all our days are passed away in thy wrath: we spend our years as a tale that is told. The days of our years are threescore years and ten; and if by reason of strength they be fourscore years, yet is their strength labour and sorrow; for it is soon cut off, and we fly away. Who knoweth the power of thine anger? even according to thy fear, so is thy wrath. So teach us to number our days, that we may apply our hearts unto wisdom. Return, O LORD, how long? and let it repent thee concerning thy servants. O satisfy us early with thy mercy; that we may rejoice and be glad all our days. Make us glad according to the days wherein thou hast afflicted us, and the years wherein we have seen evil. Let thy work appear unto thy servants, and thy glory unto their children. And let the beauty of the

LORD our God be upon us: and establish thou the work of our hands upon us; yea, the work of our hands establish thou it.

The Lord is compassionate and merciful. Even after our destruction in the flood, our Lord had mercy and brought us back from the brink of utter destruction. Time for God is but an illusion. A thousand years are but a moment. After the flood, man once again sprung up like the blades of grass. Psalm 90 seems to bring up the judgment of God on His people, and even after destruction, the Lord showed patience, compassion, and mercy. We can imagine the final judgment being the same way.

The people who were destroyed in the flood were beyond redemption and thus cut off from the love of God. However, the children of God were spared, and God Himself brought them back into life. Soon, they prospered like the blades of grass, though they came to the precipice of destruction. God showed mercy on man and allowed us once again to dwell in His presence.

Verse 17, "And let the beauty of the LORD our God be upon us: and establish thou the work of our hands upon us; yea, the work of our hands establish thou it."

Here are a few Bible verses in addition to Psalm 90 to lean back on when your life is nearing devastation, and you need to remember that God's got this. You can make it through the storm!

1. Deuteronomy 33:27 (emphasis added by the author), "*The eternal God is thy refuge*, and underneath are the everlasting arms: and he shall thrust out the enemy from before thee; and shall say, Destroy them."
2. Ezekiel 11:16 (emphasis added by the author), "Therefore say, Thus saith the Lord GOD; Although I have cast them far off among the heathen, and although I have scattered them among the countries, *yet will I be to them as a little sanctuary* in the countries where they shall come."
3. Isaiah 26:12, "LORD, thou wilt ordain peace for us; for

thou also hast wrought all our works in us." The Lord is the author of all things good and bad, *He allows, and He restores.*

The Lord is a refuge. The Lord is a sanctuary. He allows, and He restores. His children can count on Him in times of trouble.

Thank You, Lord. Glory and praise. Thank You, Lord Almighty, for Your everlasting love, mercy, and compassion! You are our refuge. Praise to You! Amen.

Psalm 91: He That Dwelleth in the Secret Place of the Most High Shall Abide under the Shadow of the Almighty

He that dwelleth in the secret place of the most High shall abide under the shadow of the Almighty. I will say of the LORD, He is my refuge and my fortress: my God; in him will I trust. Surely he shall deliver thee from the snare of the fowler, and from the noisome pestilence. He shall cover thee with his feathers, and under his wings shalt thou trust: his truth shall be thy shield and buckler. Thou shalt not be afraid for the terror by night; nor for the arrow that flieth by day; Nor for the pestilence that walketh in darkness; nor for the destruction that wasteth at noonday. A thousand shall fall at thy side, and ten thousand at thy right hand; but it shall not come nigh thee. Only with thine eyes shalt thou behold and see the reward of the wicked. Because thou hast made the LORD, which is my refuge, even the most High, thy habitation; There shall no evil befall thee, neither shall any plague come nigh thy dwelling. For he shall give his angels charge over thee, to keep thee in all thy ways. They shall bear thee up in their hands, lest thou dash thy foot against a stone. Thou shalt tread upon the lion and adder: the young lion and the dragon shalt thou trample under feet. Because he hath set his love upon me, therefore will I deliver him: I will set him on high, because he hath known my name. He shall call upon me, and I will answer him: I will be with him in trouble; I will deliver him, and honour him. With long life will I satisfy him, and shew him my salvation.

This is so important to know, and the core message of Psalm 91, "He that dwelleth in the secret place of the most High shall abide under the shadow of the Almighty. I will say of the Lord, He is my refuge and my fortress: my God; in him will I trust" (verses 1–2).

When we dwell in the secret place of God, which is inside our beings, we then abide under the shadow of the Almighty, and He will protect us. In addition, we shall:

1. Not be afraid of the terror of the night.
2. Not be afraid of the arrow that flies by day.
3. Not be afraid of the pestilence that walketh in darkness.
4. Not be afraid of the destruction that wastes at noonday.

Because,

1. A thousand shall fall at thy side, and ten thousand at thy right hand, but it will not afflict us.
2. Only with our eyes will we behold and see the reward of the wicked.

All this goodness is available to us because we have made the Lord our refuge and habitation. In return, He will give His angels charge over us to keep us in all ways, and no evil shall befall us, nor shall any plague come near our homes. Those who abide in the Lord shall witness the judgment of the wicked and be spared. Thus, the Lord has spoken through David, and His words are binding and permanent and are all *truth*.

Thank You, Lord, for even in our unworthiness, You give us protection and mercy. We love You and will always trust in You. Amen.

Psalm 92: O Lord, How Great Are Thy Works! And Thy Thoughts Are Very Deep

It is a good thing to give thanks unto the LORD, and to sing praises unto thy name, O most High: To shew forth thy lovingkindness in the morning, and thy faithfulness every night, Upon an instrument of ten strings, and upon the psaltery; upon the harp with a solemn sound. For thou, LORD, hast made me glad through thy work: I will triumph in the works of thy hands. O LORD, how great are thy works! and thy thoughts are very deep. A brutish man knoweth not; neither doth a fool understand this. When the wicked spring as the grass, and when all the workers of iniquity do flourish; it is that they shall be destroyed for ever: But thou, LORD, art most high for evermore. For, lo, thine enemies, O LORD, for, lo, thine enemies shall perish; all the workers of iniquity shall be scattered. But my horn shalt thou exalt like the horn of an unicorn: I shall be anointed with fresh oil. Mine eye also shall see my desire on mine enemies, and mine ears shall hear my desire of the wicked that rise up against me. The righteous shall flourish like the palm tree: he shall grow like a cedar in Lebanon. Those that be planted in the house of the LORD shall flourish in the courts of our God. They shall still bring forth fruit in old age; they shall be fat and flourishing; To shew that the LORD is upright: he is my rock, and there is no unrighteousness in him.

Psalm 92 reveals the justice of the Lord. There are two types of people that the Lord will judge. The first kind is the person who cannot or refuses to hear the knowledge of God's ways, which are deep and require reading, contemplation, and prayer to know. Ultimately, these are the people of iniquity who are or become the enemies of God. When they are judged, "For, lo, thine enemies, O Lord, for, lo, thine enemies shall perish; all the workers of iniquity shall be scattered" (verse 9).

The judgment of God will ultimately lead those who are enemies of God to become scattered from each other and to die both a physical and spiritual death.

On the other hand, the ones who abide in the house of the Lord and know and follow His ways and teachings will be judged accordingly as children of God.

Verses 13–14, "Those that be planted in the house of the LORD shall flourish in the courts of our God. They shall still bring forth fruit in old age; they shall be fat and flourishing."

Not only will the court of God's judgment look favorably on them, but He will see that they flourish even unto old age. Their needs in life will be met, and their spirits will increase and prosper.

It is interesting to note that the distinct difference of judgment between those who are ungodly and those who are the children of God is also how God and His people can illustrate the true nature of God.

Verse 15, "To shew that the LORD is upright: he is my rock, and there is no unrighteousness in him."

When we are observant of the ways of the Lord, we will always see that God is a just judge, and there are no gray areas of judgment with Him. We will be judged as either enemies of God and live with those consequences, or we will be judged as children of God and live out those consequences. This is not to instill a spirit of fear in us but to understand the importance of a reverential fear of the Lord in our daily lives.

We are either for God or against Him. It's that simple. Which side are you currently on at the moment?

Psalm 93: The Lord Reigneth

The LORD reigneth, he is clothed with majesty; the LORD is clothed with strength, wherewith he hath girded himself: the world also is stablished, that it cannot be moved. Thy throne is established of old: thou art from everlasting. The floods have lifted up, O LORD, the floods have lifted up their voice; the floods lift up their waves. The LORD on high is mightier than the noise of many waters, yea, than the mighty waves of the sea. Thy testimonies are very sure: holiness becometh thine house, O LORD, for ever.

Psalm 93 reminds us that the Lord is in control of everything because He reigns over everything. There is no mightier power than God, and once He has established something, it will not be moved. Like in the time of Noah, His power both allows and restores. The flood killed most of the things on Earth, yet He allowed for a new beginning for humankind, and our hope was restored.

Contemplation: The Lord Allows and He Restores

People often complain or use as an excuse not to have faith the fact that God has allowed evil into their life, and therefore, God must be feared or, worse, (He) is evil. Or something to that effect. For it is easier to believe that lie than to walk the sometimes painful path that is His way. Although the Lord may allow hardship, He also has the strength and power to restore us as well.

The truth is that this world is a constant barrage of potential suffering and pain. We can imagine each person standing amid a meteor shower that is projecting rocks and stones toward us. This is the spiritual energy of the earth, which is inhabited by evil as well as good. Each stone or rock represents painful situations or, at its worst, targeted evil designed to bring us down.

This is how we walk this plane daily. God told us that He is our fortress; He is our refuge. Trust in Him, and He will give you rest. Those of us who have taken these words to heart still walk within the rock shower, but many times, we are given shields in our walk, or we are given a more gentle path through the many potential pitfalls of life. But even on this path, pain and suffering cannot be avoided. It is in the nature of this world and of our existence.

Pain and suffering are unavoidable. During these trying times, the faithful lean into trusting God, not away from Him, for we know He walks beside us, guiding us if we listen. His guidance helps bring us through the storms of life with more wisdom, patience, humility, clarity, and all the virtues available to us. We learn from our suffering, and we find a way to grow in good countenance. In many ways, the refuge of God is in the spirit as much as in a safe place. However, to be sure, the physical refuge of God is very real.

Although suffering in life is inevitable, bitterness and hatred are only an option and not the only way to move forward through life. When we recognize that the Lord is a just judge, it helps us overcome the uncertainty of hardship and helps us have hope in the middle of the pain.

Thank You, Lord! Even when You allow pain in our lives, You can also restore and heal our souls in the midst of the pain. You are our refuge and our compassionate King! Amen.

Psalm 94: O God, to Whom Vengeance Belongeth, Shew Thyself

O LORD God, to whom vengeance belongeth; O God, to whom vengeance belongeth, shew thyself. Lift up thyself, thou judge of the earth: render a reward to the proud. LORD, how long shall the wicked, how long shall the wicked triumph? How long shall they utter and speak hard things? and all the workers of iniquity boast themselves? They break in pieces thy people, O LORD, and afflict thine heritage. They slay the widow and the stranger, and murder the fatherless. Yet they say, The LORD shall not see, neither shall the God of Jacob regard it. Understand, ye brutish among the people: and ye fools, when will ye be wise? He that planted the ear, shall he not hear? he that formed the eye, shall he not see? He that chastiseth the heathen, shall not he correct? he that teacheth man knowledge, shall not he know? The LORD knoweth the thoughts of man, that they are vanity. Blessed is the man whom thou chastenest, O LORD, and teachest him out of thy law; That thou mayest give him rest from the days of adversity, until the pit be digged for the wicked. For the LORD will not cast off his people, neither will he forsake his inheritance. But judgment shall return unto righteousness: and all the upright in heart shall follow it. Who will rise up for me against the evildoers? or who will stand up for me against the workers of iniquity? Unless the LORD had been my help, my soul had almost dwelt in silence. When I said, My foot slippeth; thy mercy, O LORD, held me up. In the multitude of my thoughts within me thy comforts delight my soul. Shall the throne of iniquity have fellowship with thee, which frameth mischief by a law? They gather themselves together against the soul of the righteous, and condemn the innocent blood. But the LORD is my defence; and my God is the rock of my refuge. And he shall bring upon them their own iniquity, and shall cut them off in their own wickedness; yea, the LORD our God shall cut them off.

Psalm 94, once again, looks at how the Lord judges amongst the people. It's interesting to note that the author of this psalm is aware of four things:

1. God created our sight and has access to what we see.
2. God created our ears and has access to what we hear.
3. God knows our thoughts.
4. Vengeance is God's to give, not ours.

In as much as He can do these things, He can chastise us in ways that will be helpful to our spiritual growth. Unfortunately, not all people follow the ways that God teaches, nor do they consider His wisdom when making decisions, and this, we are told, is foolish.

Psalm 94:8 asks, "Understand, ye brutish among the people: and ye fools, when will ye be wise?"

At the end of the day, Psalm 94 reminds us again that the Lord will defend the righteous, and He will cut off the wicked. And this is the judgment of the Lord in one simple thought. Be defended by God or be cast off into darkness. The choice is all ours to make.

Thank You, Lord, for all Your wisdom and knowledge and for taking this humble, broken servant as an unworthy student. Praise be forever. Amen.

Psalm 95: For the Lord Is a Great God, and a King above All

> O come, let us sing unto the LORD: let us make a joyful noise to the rock of our salvation. Let us come before his presence with thanksgiving, and make a joyful noise unto him with psalms. For the LORD is a great God, and a great King above all gods. In his hand are the deep places of the earth: the strength of the hills is his also. The sea is his, and he made it: and his hands formed the dry land. O come, let us worship and bow down: let us kneel before the LORD our maker. For he is our God; and we are the people of his pasture, and the sheep of his hand. To day if ye will hear his voice, Harden not your heart, as in the provocation, and as in the day of temptation in the wilderness: When your fathers tempted me, proved me, and saw my work. Forty years long was I grieved with this generation, and said, It is a people that do err in their heart, and they have not known my ways: Unto whom I sware in my wrath that they should not enter into my rest.

Psalm 95 starts with a list of some of the great and praiseworthy things about God.

1. He is the rock of our salvation.
2. He is a great God.
3. He is the King above all other gods.
4. He made all the places on the earth high and low.
5. He owns all the places on the earth, the sea, and dry land.
6. He is our God, and we are His sheep.

It is good to acknowledge all these things and to give praise to God for His glory and wondrous deeds. However, as this psalm points out, if we harden our hearts to the glory of God and His miraculous ways, we will not be brought into His place of rest, which is both here on Earth and in heaven. Hear His voice, and all good things will be yours.

Verses 7–8, "For he is our God; and we are the people of his pasture, and the sheep of his hand. To day if ye will hear his voice, Harden not your heart."

Do not harden your heart to the voice of the Lord, but listen and allow His words to restore your peace.

Thank You, Lord. I ask that You continue to allow me to hear Your voice and that You soften my heart to Your ways now and into the future. Praise and glory and honor to You, Lord.

Psalm 96: O Sing unto the Lord a New Song: Sing unto the Lord

> O sing unto the LORD a new song: sing unto the LORD, all the earth. Sing unto the LORD, bless his name; shew forth his salvation from day to day. Declare his glory among the heathen, his wonders among all people. For the LORD is great, and greatly to be praised: he is to be feared above all gods. For all the gods of the nations are idols: but the LORD made the heavens. Honour and majesty are before him: strength and beauty are in his sanctuary. Give unto the LORD, O ye kindreds of the people, give unto the LORD glory and strength. Give unto the LORD the glory due unto his name: bring an offering, and come into his courts. O worship the LORD in the beauty of holiness: fear before him, all the earth. Say among the heathen that the LORD reigneth: the world also shall be established that it shall not be moved: he shall judge the people righteously. Let the heavens rejoice, and let the earth be glad; let the sea roar, and the fulness thereof. Let the field be joyful, and all that is therein: then shall all the trees of the wood rejoice Before the LORD: for he cometh, for he cometh to judge the earth: he shall judge the world with righteousness, and the people with his truth.

Many times throughout the Bible, we are instructed to "sing a new song." Psalm 96 asks all the earth to "sing unto the Lord a new song" and to "declare his glory among the heathen, his wonders among all people." But what exactly does it mean to sing a new song? Let's briefly examine this concept to gain a greater understanding of what is being presented.

Study: Sing a New Song

One way to begin a discussion on any topic is to look at the language and examine what exactly is being presented. So, let us start with defining each word of this phrase as is found in the dictionary as well as a brief biblical history of the word.

1. *Sing* (verb) definition: to utter words in succession with musical modulations of the words.
   a. The first time we see the word "sing" in the Bible is in the Old Testament. Exodus 15:1, "Then sang Moses and the children of Israel this song unto the LORD, and spake, saying, I will sing unto the LORD, for he hath triumphed gloriously: the horse and his rider hath he thrown into the sea."
   b. This was clearly an act of praise to God for saving and freeing His people from the bondage of slavery to the Egyptians.
   c. Because of this, we can infer that, in at least one biblical sense, to sing is to use musical modulation with words to praise and thank the Lord.
2. *New* (adjective). There are quite a few definitions for the word "new:"
   - Having recently come into existence: recent, modern.
   - Having been seen, used, or known for a short time: novel, unfamiliar.
   - Being other than the former or old. (A new car.)
   - Having been in a relationship or condition but a short time. (A new mother.)
   - Beginning as the resumption or repetition of a previous act or thing. (A new day.)
   - Made or become fresh. (Woke a new person.)
   - Different from one of the same categories that have existed previously. (A new religion.)
   - Of dissimilar origin and usually of superior quality. (A new strain of hybrid corn.)

    b.   One of the most famous uses of the word "new" is in the New Testament, when Paul claims the following in 2 Corinthians 5:17, "Therefore if any man be in Christ, he is a new creature: old things are passed away; behold, all things are become new."
3. *Song* (noun): a short poem or other set of words set to music or meant to be sung.
　　a.　Song differs from "sing" in as much as "song" is the substance of words and melody, and "sing" is the action of using the words and melodies to produce musical modulations. In short, "song" is a thing, and "sing" is an action. A song can exist without the action of someone singing it.
　　b.　We have already discussed that Exodus initiates the terms "sing" and "song." Biblically, these terms are used in conjunction with expressions to and about God. Generally, this involves thanks and praise.
　　c.　In Deuteronomy 31:19–22, we are presented with Moses issuing this ordinance to the people of Israel, "Now therefore write ye this song for you, and teach it the children of Israel: put it in their mouths, that this song may be a witness for me against the children of Israel. For when I shall have brought them into the land which I sware unto their fathers, that floweth with milk and honey; and they shall have eaten and filled themselves, and waxen fat; then will they turn unto other gods, and serve them, and provoke me, and break my covenant. And it shall come to pass, when many evils and troubles are befallen them, that this song shall testify against them as a witness; for it shall not be forgotten out of the mouths of their seed: for I know their imagination which they go about, even now, before I have brought them into the land which I sware. Moses therefore wrote this song the same day, and taught it the children of Israel."

      d. Read that again. At the time that these words were uttered by Moses, this was the new song that was created after the song of praise that was mentioned in Exodus.

      e. If we examine what is being written, we see that Moses is expressing a prophetic vision for the people of Israel:
- The people will be brought into the land of milk and honey, and eventually, once they are satiated and comfortable, they will begin to turn to other gods, breaking the covenant with God, and then the God of Israel will separate Himself from His people leaving them to the evils and troubles of living off His path.
- In the end, the new song of Moses will follow the people of Israel as a witness for all generations. (Spoiler alert: including our current generations.)

      f. Using the definitions of "new" above, we can conclude that this song was not only new in the sense that it had recently come into existence, but it was also a prophetic song that is a different kind of song than the former kind of song which was one of thanks and praise.

4. In conclusion, there are many ways that a song can become "new," and it is good to contemplate ways a song in the Bible can be seen as or created as a "new" song.

    a. Is the song merely just a different song or is it meant to be a fresh take on an old song?

    b. Like the song in Deuteronomy, is this song a tale of prophecy or history, or is it a continuation of the type of song in Exodus, one of thanks and praise?

    c. When we are asked to "sing a new song" unto God, are we being asked to sing a song that expresses a type of relationship or condition to God that has recently changed or deepened?

In what way is God asking you to sing to Him a new song in your own life right now? Note it here:

_____

_____

_____

_____

_____

_____

_____

There are so many ways we can sing and interpret songs written to God.

Psalm 97: The Lord Reigneth

The LORD reigneth; let the earth rejoice; let the multitude of isles be glad thereof. Clouds and darkness are round about him: righteousness and judgment are the habitation of his throne. A fire goeth before him, and burneth up his enemies round about. His lightnings enlightened the world: the earth saw, and trembled. The hills melted like wax at the presence of the LORD, at the presence of the Lord of the whole earth. The heavens declare his righteousness, and all the people see his glory. Confounded be all they that serve graven images, that boast themselves of idols: worship him, all ye gods. Zion heard, and was glad; and the daughters of Judah rejoiced because of thy judgments, O LORD. For thou, LORD, art high above all the earth: thou art exalted far above all gods. Ye that love the LORD, hate evil: he preserveth the souls of his saints; he delivereth them out of the hand of the wicked. Light is sown for the righteous, and gladness for the upright in heart. Rejoice in the LORD, ye righteous; and give thanks at the remembrance of his holiness.

Psalm 97 is a glorious psalm of the ultimate triumph of good over evil when the Lord will show Himself. These things will happen when God comes to Earth:

1. The multitudes will be glad.
2. Clouds and darkness shall surround Him.
3. The spirit of righteousness and judgment will be shown to inhabit His throne.
4. Fire will go before Him and burn up His enemies.
    a. God and the wicked cannot coexist in the same space.
    b. Fire purifies His path.
    c. Fire destroys His enemies.

5. Lightning will enlighten the world.
6. The earth will tremble.
7. The hills will melt like wax in the presence of the Lord.
8. The heavens will declare His righteousness.
9. All the people will see His glory.

For those who serve false idols:

1. They will be made angry.
2. They will see that God is above all the gods they serve, including themselves.
3. They won't understand what is happening.

For *all* that know and love the Lord and hate evil:

1. God will preserve the souls of His saints.
2. He will deliver them out of the hand of the wicked.
3. Light will be sown for the righteous.
4. Gladness will be for the upright in heart.
5. The Lord will ask the righteous to rejoice and give thanks in the remembrance of His holiness.

It looks like, although the power of God is mighty and will strike fear in the hearts of all people, it will soon become apparent that the Lord has come to preserve and reward His righteous children. To those who oppose Him, He will make it very clear that He is the Lord above all things and that their idols are worthless. This will be nothing less than a full presentation of how the Lord has triumphed over evil and its minions and the raising up of all His children who followed Him and remembered His holiness.

Be not afraid, for the Lord will be there for all who love Him. Fear not even in the last days! Thank You, my glorious friend and Lord. You are the most holy in all creation! Amen.

Psalm 98: The Lord Hath Made Known His Salvation

O sing unto the LORD a new song; for he hath done marvellous things: his right hand, and his holy arm, hath gotten him the victory. The LORD hath made known his salvation: his righteousness hath he openly shewed in the sight of the heathen. He hath remembered his mercy and his truth toward the house of Israel: all the ends of the earth have seen the salvation of our God. Make a joyful noise unto the LORD, all the earth: make a loud noise, and rejoice, and sing praise. Sing unto the LORD with the harp; with the harp, and the voice of a psalm. With trumpets and sound of cornet make a joyful noise before the LORD, the King. Let the sea roar, and the fulness thereof; the world, and they that dwell therein. Let the floods clap their hands: let the hills be joyful together Before the LORD; for he cometh to judge the earth: with righteousness shall he judge the world, and the people with equity.

Psalm 98 presents an amazing look into the day that the Lord made His salvation known in front of those who worship idols and other gods, which is what a "heathen" generally means in the context of the Bible.

Verse 2, "The LORD hath made known his salvation: his righteousness hath he openly shewed in the sight of the heathen."

In continuation of Psalm 97, we see more evidence of what comes about during the judgment of God whenever He descends onto Earth victoriously. But first, let's examine the first verse, which explains a little more about how the victory was won, "O sing unto the LORD a new song; for he hath done marvellous things: his right hand, and his holy arm, hath gotten him the victory."

The Lord is entirely responsible for the victory for it was His right hand and His holy arm that got Him the victory. And it was His victory—not the people's, not the king's, not the human army's victory. It was entirely God's victory.

The way God won the victory was the way He seems to win all battles:

1. Marvelous things.
   a. Supernatural effort.
2. His right hand.
   a. Psalm 118:16, "The right hand of the LORD is exalted: the right hand of the LORD doeth valiantly."
   b. In general, the right hand of God is a metaphor for the all-encompassing strength and salvation of the Lord.
   c. We also learn later that His Son, the Messiah, sits at His right hand for eternity, so it is good to consider this aspect as well.
3. His holy arm.
   a. In general, His holy arm refers to the Lord working through His children on Earth.
   b. It is sometimes necessary for the Lord to utilize the physical presence of His people to carry out and be present during aspects of the victory.
   c. Here, we learn that when people are used as His instruments, they become His holy arm extended to the battlefield as He Himself manages the victory.

As we have been discussing in the past few psalms, once again, we are asked to sing a new song unto the Lord because He has gotten the victory. If we are to interpret which type of "new song" we are to sing, perhaps we should consider the circumstances of the victory.

On one level, in verse 3, we see that the Lord "hath remembered his mercy and his truth toward the house of Israel." So, perhaps the new song is born out of a battle between Israel and its enemies? A new song about a new victory of God over the enemies of Israel.

However, when we continue this same verse (verse 3), we see that "all the ends of the earth have seen the salvation of our God." In true biblical fashion, we begin to see the multidimensional aspect of the Word of God. Yes, the term "salvation" can simply mean that God showed His mercy and saved Israel from harm in battle, but generally, when we are discussing "salvation" from a biblical standpoint, it is interpreted to mean the salvation or deliverance of one from their sinful behavior.

In this sense, it would not be a stretch to interpret the new song as a continuation of the old song that started in the desert with Moses. God showed His loving mercy toward the people of Israel and His salvation from their destruction, even amid their own sinful and idolatrous behavior. In this psalm, God continues to prove His promise that He will not allow the total annihilation of His people. Once again, He has shown mercy and saved His children from the full consequence of their poor behavior, and the people sing a new song of thanks and praise for once again sparing them full punishment.

This brings us to yet another level of interpretation, which we begin to see in the final verse of Psalm 98, "Before the LORD; for he cometh to judge the earth: with righteousness shall he judge the world, and the people with equity."

This points to the prophecy of a time when the Lord comes down to judge the earth as is revealed throughout the Old and New Testament, but especially in the New Testament book of Revelations. We have already taken notice that the victory of God has been procured not only by His holy arm but also by His right hand. This can be interpreted to also represent His Son, Jesus Christ, who rose from the dead after crucifixion and ascended into heaven to be seated at the right hand of His Father.

From a Christian perspective, the final victory of good over evil, which began on the cross, will take place at a time when the Son of God will come down to Earth on a cloud to judge all of mankind. In this interpretation, the new song to sing is born out of something the world has never seen before and will be the best version of all things that have come before.

No matter how we look at this psalm, one thing is clear: the song the children of God has and will sing is "a joyful noise unto the LORD," and the song was and will be a "loud noise [of] rejoice … praise" (verse 4).

Thank You, our eternal Father of love, mercy, and good judgment.

Our thanks and praise are always on our lips, for You have given us victory over our own lives and also eternal victory over evil.

Psalm 99: Let Them Praise Thy Great and Terrible Name; for It Is Holy

The LORD reigneth; let the people tremble: he sitteth between the cherubims; let the earth be moved. The LORD is great in Zion; and he is high above all the people. Let them praise thy great and terrible name; for it is holy. The king's strength also loveth judgment; thou dost establish equity, thou executest judgment and righteousness in Jacob. Exalt ye the LORD our God, and worship at his footstool; for he is holy. Moses and Aaron among his priests, and Samuel among them that call upon his name; they called upon the LORD, and he answered them. He spake unto them in the cloudy pillar: they kept his testimonies, and the ordinance that he gave them. Thou answeredst them, O LORD our God: thou wast a God that forgavest them, though thou tookest vengeance of their inventions. Exalt the LORD our God, and worship at his holy hill; for the LORD our God is holy.

Study: Holiness

The concept of holiness is one we all think we understand but which few of us can really define. So, let's take a brief look at what it means to be "holy."

Divinity:

In general, people tend to view the term "holy" in terms of being, as the Webster Dictionary defines it, "exalted or worthy of complete devotion as one perfect in goodness and righteousness." In other words, if one is holy, then one is focused on emulating the divinity and true nature of God, the most holy.

Psalm 99 expresses praise and thanks to God for holiness. In this case, the author of the psalm recognizes that the name of God itself is holy.

Verse 3, "Let them praise thy great and terrible name; for it is holy."

In other words, saying the very name of God is to speak holiness, and by speaking holiness, we are brought closer to the divinity of God.

Purity:

Another way to look at holiness is to see it in terms of purity versus impurity. In a spiritual sense, to be pure in holiness is to be clean and untainted by the stain of sin. And to become clean, one must be cleansed. This can be equally true from an evil standpoint. If we have been cleansed of all connection to anything holy, it is possible for us then to be pure evil.

But most of us are somewhere in the middle between pure holiness and pure evilness. We find ourselves impure in holiness in a biblical sense and are stained by mixing in the dirt and filth of sinful behaviors. Some of us are deep into the ways of the world and filled with the filthy stench of sin. However, when we step out of the "world" and take on our rightful inheritance as children of God, we start to clean up. First Corinthians 6:19–20 gives us a very good accounting of this,

> What? know ye not that your body is the temple of the Holy Ghost which is in you, which ye have of God, and ye are not your own? For ye are bought with a price: therefore glorify God in your body, and in your spirit, which are God's.

In this sense, it is never too late for the impure—which is every one of us because only God is pure holiness—to begin the process of cleaning up our sinful behaviors. The truth is that our bodies are the temples of the Holy Spirit, and by striving to keep them cleansed of sin and maintain an environment that is pleasing to the Holy Spirit, it pleases our heavenly Father. So, in this way, when we begin to cleanse our lives of chronic sin and seek to create a pure temple worthy of the Holy Spirit dwelling within, we are working on making ourselves more holy.

Set Apart:

A third way of holiness refers to a state of being set apart from defilement. Through research, we become aware that the Hebrew word translated to be "holy" comes from a term that actually means "to separate." Thus, what is holy is separated from common use or held sacred, especially by virtue of it being clean and pure. That which is holy is set apart from the more mundane and common.

In fact, this concept of being separated is a core concept in the New Testament. Jesus Himself spoke the following,

> But I have a baptism to be baptized with; and how am I straitened till it be accomplished! Suppose ye that I am come to give peace on earth? I tell you, Nay; but rather division: For from henceforth there shall be five in one house divided, three against two, and two against three. The father shall be divided against the son, and the son against the father; the mother against the daughter, and the daughter against the mother; the mother in law against her daughter in law, and the daughter in law against her mother in law.
>
> Luke 12:50–53

Jesus came to Earth to divide the pure from the impure. The holy from the unholy. His children from the heathen. He did not come to bring universal peace but to set apart His chosen from the rest of the world. In other words, the point of God coming to Earth through His Son was to make "holy" the faithful believers of God. And why set apart a whole group of people from the rest? To showcase the differences between those with faith and who trust in God and those who don't. Ultimately, this leads us to focus light on those seeking to be holy, which then leads to giving God thanks and praise for His goodness. Without a Holy God, there would be no holiness. God and His name are the source of all holiness.

The world would like us to think that being "holy" is boring and that only people who do not like to have fun set out on the holy path. We are told that holiness is only for the people who think they are better than everyone and are judgmental of those who like to "live life to the fullness" or some such euphemism for engaging in sinful behavior. But the truth is that we were all born to be temples to the Holy Spirit and that by maintaining a life that honors God and His ways, we are living in a way that honors our true nature as a child of God. This is where our true joy comes from—a joy that is everlasting and ever-present.

And what is the first step to holiness?

Trust in the Lord.

He's got your back and will help you along your way. He wants nothing more than to see you at the end of the path as He welcomes you into heaven.

The only thing we must do is to take the first step on the holy path and honor the commitment to keep going.

Psalm 100: It Is He Hath Made Us

Make a joyful noise unto the LORD, all ye lands. Serve the LORD with gladness: come before his presence with singing. Know ye that the LORD he is God: it is he that hath made us, and not we ourselves; we are his people, and the sheep of his pasture. Enter into his gates with thanksgiving, and into his courts with praise: be thankful unto him, and bless his name. For the LORD is good; his mercy is everlasting; and his truth endureth to all generations.

Psalm 100 is a song of praise and a reminder that we are creatures whom God has created. In His mercy and goodness, He made us His people and the sheep of His pastures. This psalm also gives a glimpse into aspects of His pasture.

1. We enter the gates to get to it.
2. And we go into His courts.

Once we are there:

1. We come into His presence with singing.
2. We are in a spirit of thanksgiving and praise.
3. We are to be thankful and bless His name.
4. We will know that He is good and that His mercy will last forever.

Occasionally, a psalm comes along that speaks toward the Lord's heavenly place, and we get a glimpse of what is to come. During our lives, we will have hardships, losses, and sorrow. Sometimes, we will live in the abundance of God's favor, and sometimes, we will feel His desolation. The road can be fraught with temptations and ways to pull us off course. At the same time, while we strive to follow God's ways and live as His child, we will find His mercy and compassion in our darkest hours and our paths will at times be paved with miracles and reward.

Psalm 100 is a reminder that at the end of it all, we will find ourselves entering His gates in a heavenly place where we will be seated in a court as the rightful heirs of the King of all kings. In this place, we will know that our Father is all goodness and mercy, and our songs of thanks, praise, and glory shall ring out throughout the halls of His home—which is now our home as well. Keep going; the end will be so worth it. Continue to "make a joyful noise unto the LORD, all ye lands."

One day, the gates will open, and you, too, will walk into an eternity of joy in the presence of the Lord.

Psalm 101: I Will Behave Myself Wisely in a Perfect Way

> I will sing of mercy and judgment: unto thee, O LORD, will I sing. I will behave myself wisely in a perfect way. O when wilt thou come unto me? I will walk within my house with a perfect heart. I will set no wicked thing before mine eyes: I hate the work of them that turn aside; it shall not cleave to me. A froward heart shall depart from me: I will not know a wicked person. Whoso privily slandereth his neighbour, him will I cut off: him that hath an high look and a proud heart will not I suffer. Mine eyes shall be upon the faithful of the land, that they may dwell with me: he that walketh in a perfect way, he shall serve me. He that worketh deceit shall not dwell within my house: he that telleth lies shall not tarry in my sight. I will early destroy all the wicked of the land; that I may cut off all wicked doers from the city of the LORD.

It is widely believed that perfection cannot be achieved, and simply trusting in God and having faith in His goodness is enough. And while this is true—we cannot be perfect, for we come with a fallen and sinful nature—it is our duty, as children of God, to seek perfection. Psalm 101 is a call to action for all of us and a reminder that we are to be aware of the level of perfection of our hearts.

Verse 2, "I will behave myself wisely in a perfect way. O when wilt thou come unto me? I will walk within my house with a perfect heart."

As one of the ways to "walk with a perfect heart," David proclaims to the Lord all the things that he will and will not do *with* those who have turned aside from God, otherwise known as the ungodly.

He will:

1. Set no wicked thing before his eyes.
   a. No viewing of things that are evil or of an evil nature.
2. Hate the work of them that turn aside and will not cleave to them.
   a. Have no connection with those who have turned away from God.
3. Cause a froward heart to depart from him.
   a. Froward: A person who is contrary and disobedient.
4. Cut off those who slander another.
   a. i.e., gossipers and liars.
5. Not suffer with those who are haughty and proud in heart.

On a more positive note, he will:

1. Cast his eyes upon the faithful of the land so he will dwell with them.
2. Dwell with those who walk in a perfecting way.
   a. In other words, he will dwell with those who are faithful to God's ways.
3. Not dwell with the deceitful so their lies will not land on his ears.
4. Vow to destroy all the wicked of the land.

Psalm 101 is very good advice to follow when choosing who to let go and who to keep in your life, and it is a template on how to stay on the path as we walk in God's ways. The people we walk with can play an important role in our lives and we should use much care and discernment in whom we choose to spend our time with. Anyone who has chosen wrong and has lived through the consequences of that choice can give witness to that!

Worksheet: Examination of Our Relationships

Using this psalm and the lists above, spend a few minutes thinking about your closest relationships. Now, write down some of the characteristics of the people *you* spend your time with. Be honest. Have you chosen well?

_____

_____

_____

_____

_____

_____

_____

Now, consider how you present yourself in relationships. What characteristics do you bring into your closest relationships? Are there areas where you excel? Are there areas where you could use improvement?

_____

_____

_____

_____

_____

_____

_____

Notes:

Psalm 102: Hide Not Thy Face from Me in the Day When I Am in Trouble

Hear my prayer, O LORD, and let my cry come unto thee. Hide not thy face from me in the day when I am in trouble; incline thine ear unto me: in the day when I call answer me speedily. For my days are consumed like smoke, and my bones are burned as an hearth. My heart is smitten, and withered like grass; so that I forget to eat my bread. By reason of the voice of my groaning my bones cleave to my skin. I am like a pelican of the wilderness: I am like an owl of the desert. I watch, and am as a sparrow alone upon the house top. Mine enemies reproach me all the day; and they that are mad against me are sworn against me. For I have eaten ashes like bread, and mingled my drink with weeping, Because of thine indignation and thy wrath: for thou hast lifted me up, and cast me down. My days are like a shadow that declineth; and I am withered like grass. But thou, O LORD, shalt endure for ever; and thy remembrance unto all generations. Thou shalt arise, and have mercy upon Zion: for the time to favour her, yea, the set time, is come. For thy servants take pleasure in her stones, and favour the dust thereof. So the heathen shall fear the name of the LORD, and all the kings of the earth thy glory. When the LORD shall build up Zion, he shall appear in his glory. He will regard the prayer of the destitute, and not despise their prayer. This shall be written for the generation to come: and the people which shall be created shall praise the LORD. For he hath looked down from the height of his sanctuary; from heaven did the LORD behold the earth; To hear the groaning of the prisoner; to loose those that are appointed to death; To

> declare the name of the LORD in Zion, and his praise in Jerusalem; When the people are gathered together, and the kingdoms, to serve the LORD. He weakened my strength in the way; he shortened my days. I said, O my God, take me not away in the midst of my days: thy years are throughout all generations. Of old hast thou laid the foundation of the earth: and the heavens are the work of thy hands. They shall perish, but thou shalt endure: yea, all of them shall wax old like a garment; as a vesture shalt thou change them, and they shall be changed: But thou art the same, and thy years shall have no end. The children of thy servants shall continue, and their seed shall be established before thee.

In Psalm 102, David is lamenting his troubles, and his pain and misery are made worse by his perception that God has abandoned him "because of thine indignation and thy wrath: for thou hast lifted me, and cast me down" (verse 10). In other words, David recognizes that he has sinned against God, and this has angered the Lord, and he is now paying the price.

"Hide not Thy face!" David cries out in his affliction.

When God turns His head away from us, we feel His chastisement with even more force. Even in His perceived turning away, our pain is amplified. Though to His faithful, God has promised to always be with us, even in our affliction, and we must trust that.

It is during these times when we convince ourselves that the Lord, whom we praise and who is all merciful, has abandoned us that we suffer more needlessly than we should. During our day of trouble, we should cultivate the habit of leaning less on our own understanding of the situation and more on our faith and trust in the Lord.

One of the greatest examples of this is Christ's patient wearing of His crown of thorns during His crucifixion. Lord Jesus knew the pain of the thorns was necessary to His suffering to fulfill the total and complete salvation of His children. During His deepest trials, Christ leaned into His Father's plan/will, and with His great suffering came His great redemption of the world.

This is like what penance is for the contrite of heart. Acts of suffering in atonement for the pain of sin bring about our redemption in the sight of the Lord. This is ultimately the way of God's path.

Using Psalm 102 as an example, we can see that the penitential cycle of the children of God who face real or imagined chastisement goes something like this:

1. Our current afflictions will pass.
   a. Our suffering will not last.
2. The Lord will not forsake us.
   a. The Lord is always beside us during our times of need.
3. We will overcome.
   a. We will succeed in moving past our afflictions.
4. The goodness of the Lord endures forever.
   a. We recognize that the Lord is always good.
5. His children will always continue to be.
   a. We shall not perish in the way the ungodly perish, but we will have everlasting life.
6. His children will be established for all generations.
   a. We will continue to live through our future family generations.

Though we are human and have a sinful nature, our Lord is ever compassionate and merciful toward His children. Our suffering is a part of the human experience and when we walk with God, we are aware that we offend the Father through sin, and this creates suffering within. In the end, however, God has promised to walk beside us as we navigate our lives, and ultimately, He will bring us to everlasting life with Him in heaven. He is our guide, and one of the ways we pay Him respect is by recognizing that when we veer off path, we should ask to be forgiven.

That's a small price to pay for the reward of a heavenly life, wouldn't you say?

Thank You, Lord. You are the Most High. You are our compassion. You are our Savior and King. I love You with all my heart. Amen.

Notes:

Psalm 103: The Lord Is Merciful and Gracious, Slow to Anger, and Plenteous in Mercy

Bless the LORD, O my soul: and all that is within me, bless his holy name. Bless the LORD, O my soul, and forget not all his benefits: Who forgiveth all thine iniquities; who healeth all thy diseases; Who redeemeth thy life from destruction; who crowneth thee with lovingkindness and tender mercies; Who satisfieth thy mouth with good things; so that thy youth is renewed like the eagle's. The LORD executeth righteousness and judgment for all that are oppressed. He made known his ways unto Moses, his acts unto the children of Israel. The LORD is merciful and gracious, slow to anger, and plenteous in mercy. He will not always chide: neither will he keep his anger for ever. He hath not dealt with us after our sins; nor rewarded us according to our iniquities. For as the heaven is high above the earth, so great is his mercy toward them that fear him. As far as the east is from the west, so far hath he removed our transgressions from us. Like as a father pitieth his children, so the LORD pitieth them that fear him. For he knoweth our frame; he remembereth that we are dust. As for man, his days are as grass: as a flower of the field, so he flourisheth. For the wind passeth over it, and it is gone; and the place thereof shall know it no more. But the mercy of the LORD is from everlasting to everlasting upon them that fear him, and his righteousness unto children's children; o such as keep his covenant, and to those that remember his commandments to do them. The LORD hath prepared his throne in the heavens; and his kingdom ruleth over all. Bless the LORD, ye his angels, that excel in strength, that do his commandments, hearkening unto the voice of his word. Bless ye the LORD, all ye his hosts; ye ministers of his, that do his pleasure. Bless the LORD, all his works in all places of his dominion: bless the LORD, O my soul

Verse 8, "The LORD is merciful and gracious, slow to anger, and plenteous in mercy."

Why does the Lord care about us so much, even to the point of being exceedingly merciful for our poor and sometimes highly offensive behavior? It's a question worth asking, isn't it?

In the body of Psalm 103, we are given clues as to why the Lord has such an abundance of mercy toward His children. Besides the fact that we are made in the image of God, which is a super powerful thing to contemplate when you get a chance, we are given a glimpse into the mind of God and why His tender mercy and lovingkindness are directed toward us. In true biblical fashion, these notions at first appear to be simple but, ultimately, when broken down, begin to paint a deeper and more complex picture than is first presumed.

But first, let's take a very brief look at what the breadth of the Lord's mercy toward us looks like according to this psalm:

1. He will not rebuke us nor be angry at us forever.
2. He does not give us full punishment for our offenses—even if it seems like He has.
   a. The punishment could have been much worse.
3. The level of His mercy is greater than we can even imagine.
4. In His grace, He removes our transgressions from us.

Study: So, Why Does God Show Mercy toward His Children?

Verse 13 seems to sum it up nicely, "Like as a father pitieth his children, so the LORD pitieth them that fear him."

Yes, you read that correctly. All the mercies the Lord shows His children are because, basically, He feels sorry for us, according to this psalm. The supreme master and creator of all things—who knows everything there is to know and will ever be known—takes pity on us. Think about that for a moment. God knows something we don't know, and this causes Him to pity us.

What could He possibly know? There are clues dotted all over the Bible regarding the way of the world and how hard it is to walk the narrow path of God.

> Enter ye in at the strait gate: for wide is the gate, and broad is the way, that leadeth to destruction, and many there be which go in thereat: Because strait is the gate, and narrow is the way, which leadeth unto life, and few there be that find it.
>
> Matthew 7:13–14

The world we live in is a deluge of potentially sinful enterprises. Every day that we wake up leads us into another day of overwhelming temptations and evil thoughts that we must fight off if we wish to stay on the straight and narrow path. Our bodies ache to partake in our favorite addictions (be it drugs, food, drink, lust, or whatever), even though we know that they are killing us. We wish harm upon others in our thoughts as we drive, work, shop, or wait in line that we wrestle to contain and turn away from. Opportunities to deceive, defraud, steal, betray, or worse toward our friends, family, or strangers compass us daily. There is not a day—dare we say, a moment—in our daily lives that we are not being met with potential offenses against God. Sometimes, we manage to overcome those moments and persevere on the good path, but sometimes, we succumb.

God knows all of this. He has told us that He is with us on the path. Keeping that in mind, the Lord experiences our daily lives with us.

It is hard, very hard, to stay on the path. In His love for us, He pities what we go through, and when we are weak, He shows us mercy. He saw that we fought off the temptation time and again but that we were hit with it at a weak moment, and we succumbed. He saw our remorse and felt our pains of guilt. He helped us turn the page when we read His Word to console us through a sinful moment. The Father knows it all and has compassion for us.

As we gain in holiness ourselves and cultivate a stronger habit of discernment, we begin to see the potential pitfalls of life as they approach us. By using prayer and leaning on God's will, it begins to get easier to avoid offenses and stay on the path. This is one of the gifts of humility. Humility understands that without God and His help and mercy, we would be on the path toward destruction ourselves. It is God Himself who plucked us from that path and joined us on the narrow path that leads to life.

On the other hand, those who are happily on the wide path toward destruction are filled with pride. Not only do they fail to turn from temptation, but they pursue temptation as a way of life. In their pride, they cannot see that they have a heavenly Father who has taken pity on them and who is ready to pluck them from the wide path as well. They are not even humble enough to know they need to be pitied because, as far as they are concerned, the ways of the world are the only ways they see. They are blind to the good path and, as we see all the time throughout the Bible, they will perish in the end.

The good news is that it is never too late to turn away from the world and step onto the good path toward the everlasting banquet of heaven in communion with our Father who loves us. It starts with becoming humble by recognizing that there is a supreme power over your life and trusting in Him enough to begin handing over your will to His will. You will never regret making that choice! Is it easy? No. But unlike the wide path toward destruction, you will feel real joy and find out what true love feels like. The narrow path is not easy, but it is always the path that leads to true fulfillment. It leads to everlasting life with the Holy Trinity.

Thank You, Lord, for understanding the difficulties in this life and taking pity on us as we make our way toward everlasting life with You. Thank You for loving us. Amen.

Psalm 104: O Lord, How Manifold Are Thy Works!*

Bless the LORD, O my soul. O LORD my God, thou art very great; thou art clothed with honour and majesty. Who coverest thyself with light as with a garment: who stretchest out the heavens like a curtain: Who layeth the beams of his chambers in the waters: who maketh the clouds his chariot: who walketh upon the wings of the wind: Who maketh his angels spirits; his ministers a flaming fire: Who laid the foundations of the earth, that it should not be removed for ever. Thou coveredst it with the deep as with a garment: the waters stood above the mountains. At thy rebuke they fled; at the voice of thy thunder they hasted away. They go up by the mountains; they go down by the valleys unto the place which thou hast founded for them. Thou hast set a bound that they may not pass over; that they turn not again to cover the earth. He sendeth the springs into the valleys, which run among the hills. They give drink to every beast of the field: the wild asses quench their thirst. By them shall the fowls of the heaven have their habitation, which sing among the branches. He watereth the hills from his chambers: the earth is satisfied with the fruit of thy works. He causeth the grass to grow for the cattle, and herb for the service of man: that he may bring forth food out of the earth; And wine that maketh glad the heart of man, and oil to make his face to shine, and bread which strengtheneth man's heart. The trees of the LORD are full of sap; the cedars of Lebanon, which he hath planted; Where the birds make their nests: as for the stork, the fir trees are her house. The high hills are a refuge for the wild goats; and the rocks for the conies. He appointed the moon for seasons: the sun knoweth his going down. Thou makest darkness, and it is night: wherein all the beasts of the forest do creep forth. The young lions roar after their prey, and seek their meat from God. The sun ariseth, they gather themselves together, and lay them down in their dens. Man goeth forth unto his work and to his labour until the evening. O LORD, how manifold are thy works! in wisdom hast thou made them all: the earth is full of thy riches. So is this great and wide sea, wherein are things creeping innumerable, both small and great beasts. There go the ships: there is that leviathan, whom thou hast made to play therein. These wait all upon thee; that thou mayest give them their meat in due season. That thou givest them they gather: thou openest thine hand, they are filled with good. Thou hidest thy face, they are troubled: thou takest away their breath, they die, and return to their dust. Thou sendest forth thy spirit, they are created: and thou renewest the face of the earth. The glory of the LORD shall endure for ever: the LORD shall rejoice in his works. He looketh on the earth, and it trembleth: he toucheth the hills, and they smoke. I will sing unto the LORD as long as I live: I will sing praise to my God while I have my being. My meditation of him shall be sweet: I will be glad in the LORD. Let the sinners be consumed out of the earth, and let the wicked be no more. Bless thou the LORD, O my soul. Praise ye the LORD.

Verse 24, "O LORD, how manifold are thy works! in wisdom hast thou made them all: the earth is full of thy riches."

*A key verse in all the Bible.

Psalm 104 paints a glorious picture of the creations of God on Earth. The beginning verses concentrate on the majesty of God:

1. He is clothed with honor and majesty.

2. He is covered with light as His garment.
3. He stretches out over the heavens like a curtain.

In His majesty, the Lord created the foundations of His dwelling on Earth in the water, the clouds, and the wind.

Verse 3, "Who layeth the beams of his chambers in the waters: who maketh the clouds his chariot: who walketh upon the wings of the wind."

In other words, this is how God travels around His creation of Earth. (It is suggested you read that verse again.)

In addition, He has given us the angels, who are spirits who help the Lord minister the flaming fire—which is also the Spirit of God. We can see that the angels are an extension of God who helps minister His will. Psalm 104 lays out how God works within His creation. We get a glimpse into the workings of God's mind, and we can see that it is very ordered. God's ways are always ordered and never chaotic and disordered. Using Psalm 104, let us take a brief look at an example of how the orderliness of God works:

1. God made the mountains.
2. The water flows down the mountains into the valley.
3. On the way down, the water gives refreshment to all His creatures.
4. The water also gives life to the trees and crops.
5. Once in the valley, the beasts drink the water, eat the crops, and thrive.

Now, let's turn our eyes toward verse 14, "He causeth the grass to grow for the cattle, and herb for the service of man: that he may bring forth food out of the earth."

Man is now brought into the picture. Not only has God made the grass to feed the cattle so they may thrive, but He then put the herb within the grass so that man can not only eat the herb but season the meat of the cow. In addition to meat, the creations of God can be used to create other types of food for man.

Verse 15, "And wine that maketh glad the heart of man, and oil to make his face to shine, and bread which strengtheneth man's heart."

The Lord has made provision for all His creatures, but for man, He has made them as a way to co-create with God. As people, we are to find the provisions set out by God and to create new and wonderful things from them. We are to create a new song of God's wonderous manifold of works by using them to enrich our lives. This is the gift our Father has given to those who share in His image: *who would be us*.

On the other hand, the sinners will be consumed by the earth and forgotten. If we cut ourselves off from God and do not follow in His ways, then we will die and be forgotten. Our foundations will be like sand and wash away.

Satan and his minions would like nothing more than to keep you from understanding that humans were created above the beasts and have been given a higher rank than God's other creations. If we are convinced that we have no higher value than any other creation on Earth, then we are playing right into their lies, which leads to depression, low esteem, and other disordered thinking that keeps us trapped in the slavery of his evil ways.

However, the Bible—that is, the Word of God—has something to say about this, and Hebrews chapter 2, verses 6–8, is an excellent, direct message concerning our place within God's creation,

> But one in a certain place testified, saying, What is man, that thou art mindful of him? or the son of man, that thou visitest him? Thou madest him a little lower than the angels; thou crownedst him with glory and honour, and didst set him over the works of thy hands: Thou hast put all things in subjection under his feet. For in that he put all in subjection under him, he left nothing that is not put under him. But now we see not yet all things put under him.

Whereas God gives His creatures their natural or created provision, God gives man, His human sub-angels with free will on Earth, the means to work and create additional provision. The wheat becomes bread through man's sweat. The fish becomes meat. The trees become homes. God expects and has blessed man with the wherewithal to be productive through work. We co-create with our God. In return for this great blessing, we are to sing praises to our Most High creator. Or as verse 33 of this psalm states, "I will sing unto the LORD as long as I live: I will sing praise to my God while I have my being."

By understanding God's blessings, we then understand His great love for us and our knowing that creates gratitude for taking care of us, His children. Thankfulness and praise are the natural reaction to this knowledge. In return, God increases His blessings on us. This is the ever-mounting higher cycle of life with God. He provides; we thank and praise. He provides a higher level of goodness; we praise more, and on it goes.

Thank You for the provisions You have made for every one of Your creations. You are all goodness, O Most High! Amen.

Thank You for Your manifold of wondrous works and for giving us the honor of being good stewards over all Your creations!

Psalm 105: He Is the Lord Our God: His Judgments Are in All the Earth

O give thanks unto the LORD; call upon his name: make known his deeds among the people. Sing unto him, sing psalms unto him: talk ye of all his wondrous works. Glory ye in his holy name: let the heart of them rejoice that seek the LORD. Seek the LORD, and his strength: seek his face evermore. Remember his marvellous works that he hath done; his wonders, and the judgments of his mouth; O ye seed of Abraham his servant, ye children of Jacob his chosen. He is the LORD our God: his judgments are in all the earth. He hath remembered his covenant for ever, the word which he commanded to a thousand generations. Which covenant he made with Abraham, and his oath unto Isaac; And confirmed the same unto Jacob for a law, and to Israel for an everlasting covenant: Saying, Unto thee will I give the land of Canaan, the lot of your inheritance: When they were but a few men in number; yea, very few, and strangers in it. When they went from one nation to another, from one kingdom to another people; He suffered no man to do them wrong: yea, he reproved kings for their sakes; Saying, Touch not mine anointed, and do my prophets no harm. Moreover he called for a famine upon the land: he brake the whole staff of bread. He sent a man before them, even Joseph, who was sold for a servant: Whose feet they hurt with fetters: he was laid in iron: Until the time that his word came: the word of the LORD tried him. The king sent and loosed him; even the ruler of the people, and let him go free. He made him lord of his house, and ruler of all his substance: To bind his princes at his pleasure;

and teach his senators wisdom. Israel also came into Egypt; and Jacob sojourned in the land of Ham. And he increased his people greatly; and made them stronger than their enemies. He turned their heart to hate his people, to deal subtilly with his servants. He sent Moses his servant; and Aaron whom he had chosen. They shewed his signs among them, and wonders in the land of Ham. He sent darkness, and made it dark; and they rebelled not against his word. He turned their waters into blood, and slew their fish. Their land brought forth frogs in abundance, in the chambers of their kings. He spake, and there came divers sorts of flies, and lice in all their coasts. He gave them hail for rain, and flaming fire in their land. He smote their vines also and their fig trees; and brake the trees of their coasts. He spake, and the locusts came, and caterpillers, and that without number, And did eat up all the herbs in their land, and devoured the fruit of their ground. He smote also all the firstborn in their land, the chief of all their strength. He brought them forth also with silver and gold: and there was not one feeble person among their tribes. Egypt was glad when they departed: for the fear of them fell upon them. He spread a cloud for a covering; and fire to give light in the night. The people asked, and he brought quails, and satisfied them with the bread of heaven. He opened the rock, and the waters gushed out; they ran in the dry places like a river. For he remembered his holy promise, and Abraham his servant. And he brought forth his people with joy, and his chosen with gladness: And gave them the lands of the heathen: and they inherited the labour of the people; That they might observe his statutes, and keep his laws. Praise ye the LORD.

Psalm 105 talks about the justice of the Lord and uses the covenant that He made with His chosen people to illustrate how He protects them and serves justice against their enemies, even from the time of Abraham.

Verses 8–10,

> He hath remembered his covenant forever, the word which he commanded to a thousand generations. Which covenant he made with Abraham, and his oath unto Isaac; And confirmed the same unto Jacob for a law, and to Israel for an everlasting covenant.

God does not change. His Word never alters. He will never take His promise away.

What was shall be. Always and forever.

Because God had chosen these people to be His people, and His covenant was everlasting, "He suffered no man to do them wrong: yea, he reproved kings for their sakes; Saying, Touch not mine anointed, and do my prophets no harm" (verses 14–15).

And when man and king inflicted pain on His chosen people, He brought down His sword of justice in the form of punishment. In Psalm 105, we see a list of the punishments of God against the nations who did His people wrong.

1. When Joseph, son of Jacob (aka Israel), was sent into the land and was taken in as a servant, the rulers laid him in iron and hurt his feet with fetters, so God sent a famine into the land.
    a. The famine lasted until the Word of God tried them.
    b. The king understood the power of Joseph's God and freed him.
    c. Joseph then came into power within the nation, had the power to bind princes, and taught wisdom to the senators.
    d. In other words, God's person was allowed into the very halls of power within the nation that enslaved him, and he began changing it from within using God's wisdom, and then the nation, as well as Joseph, flourished.

2. Jacob entered Egypt, which was also known as the land of Ham, and the number of the people of Israel began to increase so much that they became stronger than the enemies of God within the nation.
   a. This caused the people of Egypt to begin hating the children of Israel, and through a subtle campaign, the Egyptians tricked God's people into slavery, where they were then treated very harshly.
   b. After many years, God took pity on His people and sent in Moses, who was taken in as a child and grew up to be like a son to the Pharoah.
      i. Again, God's own person was taken into the very places that had power over the slaves of Israel.
   c. Years later, after Moses fled the Egyptians, by God's command, he brought his older brother, Aaron, back into the house of Pharoah with him, and they asked for God's chosen people to be freed.
   d. When the people were not freed, God gave Moses the power to show the people of Egypt the strong arm of His justice with signs and wonders in the form of plagues.
      i. Each time Pharoah refused to free the chosen people as his slaves, the signs became harsher until the firstborn child of every Egyptian was slain.
      ii. This was the last and most decisive plague against the Egyptians and caused Pharoah to finally submit to the will of God.
   e. The chosen were then freed in a most amazing and wonderous way—God parted the Red Sea—and His chosen people began their journey eventually back to the promised land.

God's justice always sets the record straight and always ends in His will being accomplished in the most perfect manner. And why is this the case? Verses 42–45 of this psalm answer this with the utmost clarity

> For he remembered his holy promise, and Abraham his servant. And he brought forth his people with joy, and his chosen with gladness: And gave them the lands of the heathen: and they inherited the labour of the people; that they might observe his statutes, and keep his laws. Praise ye the LORD.

God made a promise, and He intended to keep it regardless of the circumstances. His will is always done. We must never forget that the Lord is the great arbiter of justice. This is why we should not seek our vengeance and patiently wait on the ways of the Lord. Can anyone deny the perfect justice and punishments of the great plagues of Egypt? No man could have been so thorough. People will fail us, but the Lord will never fail us, for He alone never changes and always keeps His word. This brings us great peace and hope.

Thank You, Lord, for being the only consistent presence that we can rely on in our lives. Praise and glory to You!

Psalm 106: Many Times Did He Deliver Them

Praise ye the LORD. O give thanks unto the LORD; for he is good: for his mercy endureth for ever. Who can utter the mighty acts of the LORD? who can shew forth all his praise? Blessed are they that keep judgment, and he that doeth righteousness at all times. Remember me, O LORD, with the favour that thou bearest unto thy people: O visit me with thy salvation; That I may see the good of thy chosen, that I may rejoice in the gladness of thy nation, that I may glory with thine inheritance. We have sinned with our fathers, we have committed iniquity, we have done wickedly. Our fathers understood not thy wonders in Egypt; they remembered not the multitude of thy mercies; but provoked him at the sea, even at the Red sea. Nevertheless he saved them for his name's sake, that he might make his mighty power to be known. He rebuked the Red sea also, and it was dried up: so he led them through the depths, as through the wilderness. And he saved them from the hand of him that hated them, and redeemed them from the hand of the enemy. And the waters covered their enemies: there was not one of them left. Then believed they his words; they sang his praise. They soon forgat his works; they waited not for his counsel: But lusted exceedingly in the wilderness, and tempted God in the desert. And he gave them their request; but sent leanness into their soul. They envied Moses also in the camp, and Aaron the saint of the LORD. The earth opened and swallowed up Dathan, and covered the company of Abiram. And a fire was kindled in their company; the flame burned up the wicked. They made a calf in Horeb, and worshipped the molten image. Thus they changed their glory into the similitude of an ox that eateth grass. They forgat God their saviour, which had done great things in Egypt; Wondrous works in the land of Ham, and terrible things by the Red sea. Therefore he said that he would destroy them, had not Moses his chosen stood before him in the breach, to turn away his wrath, lest he should destroy them. Yea, they despised the pleasant land, they believed not his word: But murmured in their tents, and hearkened not unto the voice of the LORD. Therefore he lifted up his hand against them, to overthrow them in the wilderness: To overthrow their seed also among the nations, and to scatter them in the lands. They joined themselves also unto Baalpeor, and ate the sacrifices of the dead. Thus they provoked him to anger with their inventions: and the plague brake in upon them. Then stood up Phinehas, and executed judgment: and so the plague was stayed. And that was counted unto him for righteousness unto all generations for evermore. They angered him also at the waters of strife, so that it went ill with Moses for their sakes: Because they provoked his spirit, so that he spake unadvisedly with his lips. They did not destroy the nations, concerning whom the LORD commanded them: But were mingled among the heathen, and learned their works. And they served their idols: which were a snare unto them. Yea, they sacrificed their sons and their daughters unto devils, And shed innocent blood, even the blood of their sons and of their daughters, whom they sacrificed unto the idols of Canaan: and the land was polluted with blood. Thus were they defiled with their own works, and went a whoring with their own inventions. Therefore was the wrath of the LORD kindled against his people, insomuch that he abhorred his own inheritance. And he gave them into the hand of the heathen; and they that hated them ruled over them. Their enemies also oppressed them, and they were brought into subjection under their hand. Many times did he deliver them; but they provoked him with their counsel, and were brought low for their iniquity. Nevertheless he regarded their affliction, when he heard their cry: And he remembered for them his covenant, and repented according to the multitude of his mercies. He made them also to be pitied of all those that carried them captives. Save us, O LORD our God, and gather us from among the heathen, to give thanks unto thy holy name, and to triumph in thy praise. Blessed be the LORD God of Israel from everlasting to everlasting: and let all the people say, Amen. Praise ye the LORD.

In Psalm 105, we talked about how God made a promise to protect His people, and we looked at how the strong arm of justice comes down on those who seek to harm and enslave His chosen people. During that discussion, we talked about how God parted the Red Sea and led His children, *eventually*, to the promised land.

Psalm 106 gives a rundown of the ways God's people sinned against God, even during their salvation from Egypt. These sins were great and horrendous. They are as follows according to this psalm:

1. The chosen fathers did not understand the wonders of Egypt.
2. They forgot all the mercies of God during their flight…but they even had the audacity to provoke God with unfaith at the shore of the Red Sea.
3. Nevertheless, God saved them from their enemies by parting the Red Sea and allowing His people to pass and His enemies to drown. His people praised Him at this sight.
4. But they soon forgot these works and did not seek God's counsel.
5. Instead of praying for God's will, the chosen out of Egypt:
    1. Lusted after each other.
    2. Tempted God with their greed.
    3. They envied Moses and Aaron.

4. They made a calf and worshiped the molten image.
5. They gave praise and glory to the idol, not their God.
6. They completely forgot about what God did in Egypt for them.
7. They joined Baal at the sacrifices of the dead.
8. They angered God at the waters of strife.
9. They sacrificed their sons and daughters unto devils.
10. They killed their children and sacrificed them at the altar and idols of Canaan.
11. They defiled themselves with their works and inventions.

God punished them with plagues and illness, but in the end, He had mercy on His people and saved them from the afflictions time after time. The people repented and once again sang Him praises and gave Him glory, and the Lord never forgot the covenant He made with the people He chose. Thank You, Lord.

It would be nice if we could just point our fingers and condemn the people of long ago who sinned against God even after He saved them from the horrors of slavery in Egypt. After all, it was a long time ago, and people were different then and, dare we say, more barbaric. In this present time, we would never take God for granted and forget the mercy He has shown us in our lives, would we?

Unfortunately, this is not true. Even in our modern times, we frequently fall back into offending God. We aren't very different from those of the past. The good news is that, as long as we live, we can always change our ways and get back into God's grace and mercy. Let's examine how that works:

The Biblical Cycle of God's Mercy, Grace, and Redemption

1. We praise God for showing us His mercy.
2. God graces us with abundance and lovingkindness.
3. We begin to forget God, His mercy, and forgiving nature.
4. Once again, we begin to sin against the Father.
5. God allows us to separate ourselves from Him.
6. We enter desolation and torment in His absence.
7. We ask, pray, and beg God for mercy.
8. God shows us mercy and redeems us.
9. We praise God for showing us His mercy.

And the cycle continues at varying degrees throughout our lives and the lives of our nations.

Let us pray:

Thy will be done in my life today. O Lord, allow me to recognize in my own life where I fall within Your cycle of mercy, grace, and redemption so that I may never sin against You willfully. When I do, bring swift justice and mercy so my sin may be short-lived and my praise and glory of You be my ongoing life. I ask this in the name of Jesus, Your Son and my merciful Savior. Amen.

Notes:

_____

_____

_____

_____

Psalm 107: He Sent His Word, and Healed Them, and Delivered Them from Their Destructions

O give thanks unto the LORD, for he is good: for his mercy endureth for ever. Let the redeemed of the LORD say so, whom he hath redeemed from the hand of the enemy; And gathered them out of the lands, from the east, and from the west, from the north, and from the south. They wandered in the wilderness in a solitary way; they found no city to dwell in. Hungry and thirsty, their soul fainted in them. Then they cried unto the LORD in their trouble, and he delivered them out of their distresses. And he led them forth by the right way, that they might go to a city of habitation. Oh that men would praise the LORD for his goodness, and for his wonderful works to the children of men! For he satisfieth the longing soul, and filleth the hungry soul with goodness. Such as sit in darkness and in the shadow of death, being bound in affliction and iron; Because they rebelled against the words of God, and contemned the counsel of the most High: Therefore he brought down their heart with labour; they fell down, and there was none to help. Then they cried unto the LORD in their trouble, and he saved them out of their distresses. He brought them out of darkness and the shadow of death, and brake their bands in sunder. Oh that men would praise the LORD for his goodness, and for his wonderful works to the children of men! For he hath broken the gates of brass, and cut the bars of iron in sunder. Fools because of their transgression, and because of their iniquities, are afflicted. Their soul abhorreth all manner of meat; and they draw near unto the gates of death. Then they cry unto the LORD in their trouble, and he saveth them out of their distresses. He sent his word, and healed them, and delivered them from their destructions. Oh that men would praise the LORD for his goodness, and for his wonderful works to the children of men! And let them sacrifice the sacrifices of thanksgiving, and declare his works with rejoicing. They that go down to the sea in ships, that do business in great waters; These see the works of the LORD, and his wonders in the deep. For he commandeth, and raiseth the stormy wind, which lifteth up the waves thereof. They mount up to the heaven, they go down again to the depths: their soul is melted because of trouble. They reel to and fro, and stagger like a drunken man, and are at their wits' end. Then they cry unto the LORD in their trouble, and he bringeth them out of their distresses. He maketh the storm a calm, so that the waves thereof are still. Then are they glad because they be quiet; so he bringeth them unto their desired haven. Oh that men would praise the LORD for his goodness, and for his wonderful works to the children of men! Let them exalt him also in the congregation of the people, and praise him in the assembly of the elders. He turneth rivers into a wilderness, and the watersprings into dry ground; A fruitful land into barrenness, for the wickedness of them that dwell therein. He turneth the wilderness into a standing water, and dry ground into watersprings. And there he maketh the hungry to dwell, that they may prepare a city for habitation; And sow the fields, and plant vineyards, which may yield fruits of increase. He blesseth them also, so that they are multiplied greatly; and suffereth not their cattle to decrease. Again, they are minished and brought low through oppression, affliction, and sorrow. He poureth contempt upon princes, and causeth them to wander in the wilderness, where there is no way. Yet setteth he the poor on high from affliction, and maketh him families like a flock. The righteous shall see it, and rejoice: and all iniquity shall stop her mouth. Whoso is wise, and will observe these things, even they shall understand the lovingkindness of the LORD.

Verse 1, "Give thanks unto the LORD, for he is good: for his mercy endureth for ever."

Psalm 107 takes what we learned in Psalm 106 and sets forth example after example of the ways the biblical cycle of God's grace is shown throughout the ages and even today. One of the most mysterious and wonderful parts of reading the Bible is that we find out that God's Word is truly a living phenomenon, and we see that clearly in this psalm.

It would be easy for us to read the words of Psalm 107 and think that what is being discussed are those things that happened in the past. That this psalm is filled with nothing more than dusty, old words about a dusty, old time in history. And boy, oh boy, that is exactly what Satan would love for us to think. "Sure, all this is good and stuff, but that is the past. God doesn't care about you today. You are too far gone. God's not coming to save you now," Satan would tell us. You see, that kind of dialogue in our minds keeps us in his cycle: the cycle of destruction that can eventually lead to complete and utter separation from God and into the pits of hell.

Perhaps now would be a good time to briefly examine the other side of God's grace, which leads to life everlasting: the side that leads to the destruction of the soul and utter separation from God in the eternal fire.

Are you ready?

The Biblical Cycle of Satan's Destruction and Everlasting Death

Let's look and examine the verses of Psalm 107 that seem to present this cycle:

1. Verse 5, "Hungry and thirsty, their soul fainted in them."
2. Verse 10, "Such as sit in darkness and in the shadow of death, being bound in affliction and iron."
3. Verses 26–27, "They go down again to the depths: their soul is melted because of trouble. They reel to and fro, and stagger like a drunken man, and are at their wit's end."
4. Verse 39, "Again, they are minished and brought low through oppression, affliction, and sorrow."

In other words, when we become separated from God through our actions and behaviors, we begin the cycle of destruction in the following ways:

1. We hunger and thirst for the things that cause our souls to grow dim and nearly wither.
    a. We stop looking for God's presence and start to seek the ways of the world.
    b. This causes the spirit of light to grow dim within our souls.
2. We then find ourselves in the spirit of darkness and become bound to our affliction like in an iron vice.
    a. Once the spirit of darkness has overtaken our souls, we find ourselves more and more addicted to the ways of the world.
    b. We then get to a point in our addiction where the pull of our worldly desires is so strong that it feels like we are physically in an iron vice of addiction.
    c. Whereas the mercy of God frees our spirit of affliction, the spirit of darkness strives to keep us bound.
3. We find ourselves in the mental, physical, and spiritual

depths where it feels as if our very soul is melting in the pit of fire.
   a. Like a living hell, our soul feels like it is being tormented by fire.
   b. This causes us to be in a constant state of chaos and overwhelming anxiety.
   c. Whereas God promises refreshment of the soul, the spirit of darkness seeks torment and destruction of the soul.
4. This brings us into an ever-mounting lower cycle of oppression, affliction, and sorrow.
   a. The chaos and anxiety that come with the oppression and binding of addiction begets more chaos and anxiety, which then brings sorrow and more chaos and anxiety in a never-ending cycle downward.
5. Finally, we hit rock bottom and find ourselves in utter hopelessness, which is the true nature of the spirit of destruction: no hope whatsoever.

But then what happens?

Verse 20, "He sent his word, and healed them, and delivered them from their destructions."

In other words, our nature is never irredeemable. Though we may seem separated from the light of God, there is always a flickering spark of the divine within—though sometimes it is very dim. It is only after physical death that all light is extinguished if we have continued to choose the darkness over the light and we then become engulfed in the pitch-black shadow forever. The colors of light no longer reflect.

Whereas heaven is all color and light, hell is shadow and blackness and void, which doesn't seem like a very good place to spend eternity, does it?

In the end, Psalm 107 reads like the story of God's mercy on His people and how the Father sent His Word to save His children.

It's hard not to see that the sacrifice of Jesus Christ on the cross for the salvation of mankind is the ultimate fulfillment of this psalm. In His love for us, the Father sent His Son so that we may have everlasting life and be saved from utter destruction. This is the greatest mercy of God in all of the biblical cycles of God's grace and mercy—past, present, and future.

And those who don't understand shall be brought low with oppression, but "those who see it and are wise shall understand the loving kindness of the Lord" (verse 43) (paraphrased by the author).

Praise and glory to the Lord. Amen.

Psalm 108: Give Us Help from Trouble; for Vain Is the Help of Man

O God, my heart is fixed; I will sing and give praise, even with my glory. Awake, psaltery and harp: I myself will awake early. I will praise thee, O LORD, among the people: and I will sing praises unto thee among the nations. For thy mercy is great above the heavens: and thy truth reacheth unto the clouds. Be thou exalted, O God, above the heavens: and thy glory above all the earth; That thy beloved may be delivered: save with thy right hand, and answer me. God hath spoken in his holiness; I will rejoice, I will divide Shechem, and mete out the valley of Succoth. Gilead is mine; Manasseh is mine; Ephraim also is the strength of mine head; Judah is my lawgiver; Moab is my washpot; over Edom will I cast out my shoe; over Philistia will I triumph. Who will bring me into the strong city? who will lead me into Edom? Wilt not thou, O God, who hast cast us off? and wilt not thou, O God, go forth with our hosts? Give us help from trouble: for vain is the help of man. Through God we shall do valiantly: for he it is that shall tread down our enemies.

God is the great arbiter of justice. It is vainglorious for us to think our judgment is equal to God's. As people with a fallen nature, we judge people and situations through an imperfect, self-centered, and sinful-natured lens.

Psalm 108 is a reminder that there is power in the stillness while we wait for the Lord's justice. When we are still in our actions and instead sing praises to the Lord while we wait, we allow God's holiness to speak into all situations. Out of this holiness comes His divine justice, which is perfect justice.

When we forsake the wisdom of God in any situation and do not remain still through meditation, reading the Bible, and prayer, we put our judgment above God's, and the outcome will be uncertain or, worse, go horribly wrong. For He has told us time and again:

1. Lean not on your own understanding.
2. Vengeance is Mine.

These are not vain words. God's ways are not our ways. Perfection is not always immediately recognized by our human thinking. And this goes for judging the people in our lives who we feel are harming us in some way as well. The only thing our judgment of another person does is to take away the love we have for them in our hearts. When we are still and wait on God's timing, not only can we retain the love of the Lord in our hearts, but in time, we shall see that "through God we shall do valiantly: for he it is that shall tread down our enemies" (verse 13).

We, therefore, need not pass judgment in our hearts on our fellowman no matter how vile and wicked they seem. For the Lord is a just judge, and in time, all men are judged according to their deeds. Our job as children of God is to love one another. And trust in the Lord. Praise and glory to the Father, the Son, and the Holy Ghost.

Worksheet: God's Perfect Justice in My Own Life

Spend a few moments and try to think of a time or two when you waited out a situation instead of acting on it, and the outcome seemed like the perfect solution, perhaps even supernaturally perfect. Perhaps it involved finding the perfect job or meeting someone that exceeded your expectations. Maybe it involved a dispute with a friend, a family member, or a stranger. Whatever the situation, use these lines to make note here:

_____

_____

_____

_____

_____

_____

_____

_____

_____

_____

_____

_____

_____

_____

_____

_____

Thank You for showing us Your mercy as we grow in faith.

Psalm 109: He Shall Be Judged

Hold not thy peace, O God of my praise; For the mouth of the wicked and the mouth of the deceitful are opened against me: they have spoken against me with a lying tongue. They compassed me about also with words of hatred; and fought against me without a cause. For my love they are my adversaries: but I give myself unto prayer. And they have rewarded me evil for good, and hatred for my love. Set thou a wicked man over him: and let Satan stand at his right hand. When he shall be judged, let him be condemned: and let his prayer become sin. Let his days be few; and let another take his office. Let his children be fatherless, and his wife a widow. Let his children be continually vagabonds, and beg: let them seek their bread also out of their desolate places. Let the extortioner catch all that he hath; and let the strangers spoil his labour. Let there be none to extend mercy unto him: neither let there be any to favour his fatherless children. Let his posterity be cut off; and in the generation following let their name be blotted out. Let the iniquity of his fathers be remembered with the LORD; and let not the sin of his mother be blotted out. Let them be before the LORD continually, that he may cut off the memory of them from the earth. Because that he remembered not to shew mercy, but persecuted the poor and needy man, that he might even slay the broken in heart. As he loved cursing, so let it come unto him: as he delighted not in blessing, so let it be far from him. As he clothed himself with cursing like as with his garment, so let it come into his bowels like water, and like oil into his bones. Let it be unto him as the garment which covereth him, and for a girdle wherewith he is girded continually. Let this be the reward of mine adversaries from the LORD, and of them that speak evil against my soul. But do thou for me, O GOD the Lord, for thy name's sake: because thy mercy is good, deliver thou me. For I am poor and needy, and my heart is wounded within me. I am gone like the shadow when it declineth: I am tossed up and down as the locust. My knees are weak through fasting; and my flesh faileth of fatness. I became also a reproach unto them: when they looked upon me they shaked their heads. Help me, O LORD my God: O save me according to thy mercy: That they may know that this is thy hand; that thou, LORD, hast done it. Let them curse, but bless thou: when they arise, let them be ashamed; but let thy servant rejoice. Let mine adversaries be clothed with shame, and let them cover themselves with their own confusion, as with a mantle. I will greatly praise the LORD with my mouth; yea, I will praise him among the multitude. For he shall stand at the right hand of the poor, to save him from those that condemn his soul.

In Psalm 109, David asks the Lord to curse and condemn his enemies.

Verse 17, "As he loved cursing, so let it come unto him: as he delighted not in blessing, so let it be far from him."

For his enemies:

1. The mouth of the wicked and the mouth of the deceitful are opened against him.
2. They compass about him with words of hatred.
3. They fought against him without a cause.
4. They rewarded him with evil when he gave good.
5. They set the wicked over him.
6. They let Satan stand at his right hand.

Because of these offenses against him, David asks the Lord for the following:

1. Let his enemies' days be few.
2. Let someone else take his office.
3. Let his children be fatherless.
4. Let his wife be a widow.
5. Let his children always be vagabonds and beggars.
6. Let the extortioner catch all he has.
7. Let strangers spoil his labor.
8. Let none show him mercy.
9. Let none favor his fatherless children.
10. Let his posterity be cut off and blotted out of history.
11. Let the iniquity of his fathers be remembered by the Lord that He may cut off the memory of them from the earth.

In other words, let the enemies have no favor or memory of them throughout history. Have them erased from history.

David asks that his enemies be rewarded with just reward.

1. Because his enemy showed no mercy, let him be shown no mercy.
2. Because he loved cursing, let him be cursed.
3. Because he delighted not in blessing; let blessings be far from him.
4. Reward his enemies with the same that they gave out.

However, David asks for the Lord's mercy for himself and his people and appeals to the Father's special compassion for the poor, needy, and broken-hearted. David implores the Lord to show him mercy and reward him with blessings.

Verse 27, "That they may know that this is thy hand; that thou, LORD, hast done it."

In return, David will:

1. Greatly praise the Lord with his mouth.
2. Praise him among the multitudes.

For it is recognized that the Lord will "stand at the right hand of the poor, to save him from those who condemn his soul" (verse 31).

This psalm appears to foreshadow how God judges souls on the throne. What we do in life comes back to us at our judgment. If we curse our brothers and sisters, we will then be cursed and perish. If we show mercy and compassion to our brothers and sisters, we will be shown mercy and compassion on our day of judgment.

For what was, is, and ever shall be. God never changes. Here, we see a litany of the behaviors of the enemy, while David represents the poor in spirit and brokenhearted faithful. Psalm 109 shows the judgment and just rewards for both. On which side do you want to stand on your day of judgment? What just rewards are you building in your life?

_____

_____

_____

Thank You, Lord, for giving me a chance to continue to tweak my life in Your direction so I may be judged kindly and find everlasting life with You.

Psalm 110: Sit Thou at My Right Hand

> The LORD said unto my Lord, Sit thou at my right hand, until I make thine enemies thy footstool. The LORD shall send the rod of thy strength out of Zion: rule thou in the midst of thine enemies. Thy people shall be willing in the day of thy power, in the beauties of holiness from the womb of the morning: thou hast the dew of thy youth. The LORD hath sworn, and will not repent, Thou art a priest for ever after the order of Melchizedek. The Lord at thy right hand shall strike through kings in the day of his wrath. He shall judge among the heathen, he shall fill the places with the dead bodies; he shall wound the heads over many countries. He shall drink of the brook in the way: therefore shall he lift up the head.

Psalm 110 reads prophetically and appears to reference the Messiah who had not yet come as of David's reign.

Verse 1, "The LORD said unto my Lord, Sit thou at my right hand, until I make thine enemies thy footstool."

Let us consider this passage in the New Testament that refers to the words in Psalm 110 directly and further establishes this verse as prophetic. The following exchange takes place while Jesus Christ is speaking in the temple among the priests and people,

> And Jesus answered and said, while he taught in the temple, How say the scribes that Christ is the Son of David? For David himself said by the Holy Ghost, The LORD said to my Lord, Sit thou on my right hand, till I make thine enemies thy footstool. David therefore himself calleth him Lord; and whence is he then his son? And the common people heard him gladly.
>
> Mark 12:35–37

In other words, Jesus put to rest the notion that He was merely the Son of David, for even David called Him Lord. "The LORD [God, the Father] said to my Lord [God, the Son], Sit thou at my right hand." Two Lords. Not one Lord and one Son. In this, David recognized that the Messiah would be called a Lord unto himself and not merely a son of man, which Jesus further confirms in Mark was put into David's heart by the Holy Spirit.

Study: The Messiah

As we have discussed throughout these psalms, there are verses dotted about that illuminate certain aspects or speak prophetically about the Messiah, whom the Jewish people were expecting to appear and save them. Because Psalm 110 speaks clearly about this long-awaited Messiah, now would be a good time to take a closer look at who David and the other authors of the Psalms are speaking about and how it was fulfilled in Jesus Christ many years later.

The Messiah:

1. The Lord will send as a rod of strength…
   a. The rod was viewed as a symbol of authority and protection.
   b. The rod can also be used to refer to being used in correction as in a shepherd who uses his rod to keep his sheep in line.
2. …Out of Zion.
   a. This rod of strength shall be sent out of Zion.
   b. Or, more generally, out of the city of David, the Jewish community, and/or out of the heavenly Zion.
3. He will rule His people in the midst of their enemies.
   a. When the Messiah walks the earth, He will be stationed in a place where He has many enemies.
4. He will come from a holy womb.
   a. In Luke 1:41–43 in the New Testament, we see Mary's cousin Elisabeth, then also pregnant with John the Baptist, speak to Mary upon seeing her, "And it came

to pass, that, when Elisabeth heard the salutation of Mary, the babe leaped in her womb; and Elisabeth was filled with the Holy Ghost. And she spake out with a loud voice, and said, Blessed art thou among women, and blessed is the fruit of thy womb. And whence is this to me, that the mother of my Lord should come to me?"
5. He will be a priest in the order of Melchizedek.
    a. Genesis 14:18, "And Melchizedek king of Salem brought forth bread and wine: and he was the priest of the most high God."
    b. New Testament, Mark 14:22–23, "And as they did eat, Jesus took bread, and blessed, and brake it, and gave to them, and said, Take, eat: this is my body. And he took the cup, and when he had given thanks, he gave it to them: and they all drank of it."
6. He will stand next to the right hand of the Lord.
    a. New Testament, Mark 16:19, "So then after the Lord [Christ] had spoken unto them, he was received up into heaven, and sat on the right hand of God."

We are then confronted with the second part of the purpose of the Messiah in this psalm, which many people thought would be accomplished in its entirety when the Messiah finally first walked the earth. Upon further discernment and contemplation, we can see in Psalm 110 that the Messiah has two comings to Earth: one that has been and one to come. The first, which has been illustrated above and ends in Him sitting at the right hand of the Father, and part two, which is further expressed in Psalm 110 and which we will examine below. Some people call this the second coming of the Messiah.

During the second coming of the Messiah on Earth:

1. He will strike through kings in His *day* of wrath.
    a. Literally, one day will come, and the kings of this earth shall be stricken.

b. Ezekiel 7:19, "They shall cast their silver in the streets, and their gold shall be removed: their silver and their gold shall not be able to deliver them in the day of the wrath of the LORD: they shall not satisfy their souls, neither fill their bowels: because it is the stumbling block of their iniquity."
  c. Revelation 6:17, "For the great day of his wrath is come; and who shall be able to stand?"
2. He will judge among the nations.
  a. Isaiah 2:4, "And he shall judge among the nations, and shall rebuke many people: and they shall beat their swords into plowshares, and their spears into pruning-hooks: nation shall not lift up sword against nation, neither shall they learn war any more."
  b. He will come to judge nations and stop wars.
3. He will fill the places with dead bodies.
  a. Amos 8:2–3, "And he said, Amos, what seest thou? And I said, A basket of summer fruit. Then said the LORD unto me, The end is come upon my people of Israel; I will not again pass by them any more. And the songs of the temple shall be howlings in that day, saith the Lord GOD: there shall be many dead bodies in every place; they shall cast them forth with silence."
  b. Revelation 11:8, "And their dead bodies shall lie in the street of the great city, which spiritually is called Sodom and Egypt, where also our Lord *was* crucified."
  c. In other words, the dead bodies pile up after Jesus has been crucified.
4. He will wound the heads over many nations.
  a. The leaders of many nations will be wounded.
  b. We do not know if this will be physical wounding, spiritual wounding, or a combination of both.
5. He will drink of the brook in the way.
  a. There are quite a few times that a brook is mentioned within the Bible, so this sign of the Messiah is more than a bit cryptic, but one cannot help but think of the

living waters, which we discussed earlier in Psalm 63.
  b. Perhaps this prophesy by Zechariah can illuminate the waters that will be taken in drink on the day of the second coming:
      i. Zechariah 14:8, "And it shall be in that day, that living waters shall go out from Jerusalem; half of them toward the former sea, and half of them toward the hinder sea: in summer and in winter shall it be."
6. Therefore, He will lift up the head.
  a. Because He drinks from the brook of the living water, he will, therefore, lift up the head.
      i. One is dependent on the other.
      ii. He drinks, and therefore, the head is lifted up.
  b. Here are a couple of Bible verses that give us more information about what "lifting up the head" may be referring to:
      i. Psalm 24:9 (emphasis added by the author), "*Lift up your heads*, O ye gates; even lift them up, ye everlasting doors; and the King of glory shall come in."
      ii. Luke 21:27–28 (emphasis added by the author), "And then shall they see the Son of man coming in a cloud with power and great glory. And when these things begin to come to pass, then look up, and *lift up your heads*; for your redemption draweth nigh."
      iii. The King of glory shall come in when our redemption draws near.

The promise of a Messiah is woven so intricately within the books of the Bible, and it is good for us to examine and contemplate this concept. Let us pray for discernment as we ponder this psalm and the hope for redemption and everlasting thanks and praise to the King of glory which awaits us in this life and beyond. Thank You, O Most High God and Lord of lords! Amen.

Notes:

Psalm 111: I Will Praise the Lord with My Whole Heart

Praise ye the LORD. I will praise the LORD with my whole heart, in the assembly of the upright, and in the congregation. The works of the LORD are great, sought out of all them that have pleasure therein. His work is honourable and glorious: and his righteousness endureth for ever. He hath made his wonderful works to be remembered: the LORD is gracious and full of compassion. He hath given meat unto them that fear him: he will ever be mindful of his covenant. He hath shewed his people the power of his works, that he may give them the heritage of the heathen. The works of his hands are verity and judgment; all his commandments are sure. They stand fast for ever and ever, and are done in truth and uprightness. He sent redemption unto his people: he hath commanded his covenant for ever: holy and reverend is his name. The fear of the LORD is the beginning of wisdom: a good understanding have all they that do his commandments: his praise endureth for ever.

Psalm 111 gives an accounting of some of the many great and righteous characteristics of the Lord, which we can contemplate to not only help us grow our faith but also when we are giving thanks and praise for His glory. The characteristics of God in Psalm 111 are as follows:

1. His works are great and can be a source of pleasure to those who observe and ponder them.
2. His work is honorable and glorious.
    a. In other words, the work done by the Lord never dishonors Him or His children and is always a source

of glory to Him.
3. His righteousness endures forever.
   a. He will never *not* be righteous.
4. His works were given to us to be a source of wonder and to always be recalled.
5. He is gracious and full of compassion.
   a. Gracious: merciful, kind, forgiving.
   b. Compassion: understanding, tender-hearted, loving.
6. He feeds those who have a reverential fear of Him.
   a. He supplies His children with what they need in body, soul, and mind.
7. He will always be mindful of the covenant He has with His children.
8. He shows His people the power of His works.
9. He takes from the ungodly and gives to His children their inheritance.
10. His works are all truth and justice.
11. His commandments are clear and unshakeable.
12. His commandments last forever and are done in truth and uprightness.
13. He redeems His people.
14. His covenant has been commanded to last forever.
15. Holy and reverent is His name.

In the end, Psalm 111 offers us a summary of one of the most important lessons in all of the Bible, and it is suggested that we contemplate the fullness of verse 10 and apply it to our own walk in faith.

Verse 10, "The fear of the LORD is the beginning of wisdom: a good understanding have all they that do his commandments: his praise endureth for ever."

Worksheet: Psalm 111 and Verse 10

Here are some questions you may use to help with your contemplations of this psalm and, in particular, verse 10:

1. How is a reverential fear of the Lord the beginning of wisdom?

   _____
   _____
   _____
   _____

2. When we follow and do His commandments, what kind of understanding do we gain?

   _____
   _____
   _____
   _____

3. How will knowing what is contained in Psalm 111 cause us to praise Him forever?

   _____
   _____
   _____
   _____

Notes:

_____
_____
_____

Psalm 112: Blessed Is He That Delighteth Greatly in His Commandments

> Praise ye the LORD. Blessed is the man that feareth the LORD, that delighteth greatly in his commandments. His seed shall be mighty upon earth: the generation of the upright shall be blessed. Wealth and riches shall be in his house: and his righteousness endureth for ever. Unto the upright there ariseth light in the darkness: he is gracious, and full of compassion, and righteous. A good man sheweth favour, and lendeth: he will guide his affairs with discretion. Surely he shall not be moved for ever: the righteous shall be in everlasting remembrance. He shall not be afraid of evil tidings: his heart is fixed, trusting in the LORD. His heart is established, he shall not be afraid, until he see his desire upon his enemies. He hath dispersed, he hath given to the poor; his righteousness endureth for ever; his horn shall be exalted with honour. The wicked shall see it, and be grieved; he shall gnash with his teeth, and melt away: the desire of the wicked shall perish.

In Psalm 111, we discussed the goodness of God and how His faithful gain understanding and wisdom in knowing His commandments. In Psalm 112, we go into a little more detail about those who "delighteth greatly in His commandments."

For one thing, those who follow and walk in His commandments are blessed—which is, essentially, a state of being favored by God. Who doesn't want that? Praise ye the Lord.

Some of the other things that manifest in the lives of the blessed people of God, who delighteth in His commandments, as observed in Psalm 112, are:

1. His seed shall be mighty upon the earth.
   a. In fact, the whole generation of those who follow His commands shall be blessed.
2. Wealth and riches shall be in his house.
3. His righteousness shall endure forever.
4. Light will ariseth in the darkness.
5. He will be gracious and full of compassion and righteousness.
6. He shall not be afraid of evil tidings.
7. His horn shall be exalted with honor.

And there are ways we can examine the lives of those who are blessed and see that they are truly upright by their actions. Psalm 112 lists a few of these traits:

1. A good man sheweth favor and lendeth.
2. He guideth his affairs with discretion, "not as fools, but as wise" (Ephesians 5:15).
3. He shall not be moved by the temptations of worldly ways.
4. He hath given to the poor.
5. His righteousness endures forever.
6. His heart is fixed on trusting in the Lord.

On the other hand, *the desire of the wicked* shall perish. Point blank, period.

Verse 10, "The wicked shall see it, and be grieved; he shall gnash with his teeth, and melt away: the desire of the wicked shall perish."

Throughout the Bible, this sentiment is expressed in clear and undeniable terms: the blessed will endure forever, and the wicked will perish.

Which side of that equation do you want to be in your own life and the beyond? Are you for God or against Him?

Psalm 113: He Raiseth up the Poor Out of the Dust

> Praise ye the LORD. Praise, O ye servants of the LORD, praise the name of the LORD. Blessed be the name of the LORD from this time forth and for evermore. From the rising of the sun unto the going down of the same the LORD'S name is to be praised. The LORD is high above all nations, and his glory above the heavens. Who is like unto the LORD our God, who dwelleth on high, Who humbleth himself to behold the things that are in heaven, and in the earth! He raiseth up the poor out of the dust, and lifteth the needy out of the dunghill; That he may set him with princes, even with the princes of his people. He maketh the barren woman to keep house, and to be a joyful mother of children. Praise ye the LORD.

Psalm 113 was, in many ways, summed up many years later in the Gospels, particularly in verses such as Mark 10:31 when Jesus proclaimed, "But many that are first shall be last; and the last first."

This was Jesus presenting clearly that when we are arrogant and think we are above those with less than us, we are putting ourselves in the back of the line—or farther away from God. Our Lord is meek and humble and, as such, feels an affinity to those who share these characteristics. Does this mean that merely having an abundance of riches in this life automatically makes us unworthy of the front of the line? No, it does not. But it is a very human thing to imagine that the amount of "things" we have in this life somehow automatically puts us ahead of those who have less. And although this may be true for this world, in the world that walks with the Lord, none of those matters.

Matthew 19:21, "Jesus said unto him, If thou wilt be perfect, go and sell that thou hast, and give to the poor, and thou shalt have treasure in heaven: and come and follow me."

In other words, following Christ and spending eternity in heaven with the Holy Trinity, are worth more than all the riches that the earth could ever provide.

Jesus was making a point.

Psalm 113 reminds us that when we humble ourselves, we begin to see the truly important things. We see how the Lord works, and this leads us to a better understanding of God's ways and His desire for our lives, for "who is like unto the Lord our God, who dwelleth on high"? (verse 5).

We begin to become more like our heavenly Father when we follow this advice, "Who humbleth himself to behold the things that are in heaven, and in the earth!" (verse 6).

Using God's eyes, we can see the reality of all the things that are in heaven and Earth. It takes a humble heart to see past the riches of the world and view things the way God desires us to see them.

For one, those who are humble see that there are things in heaven and on the earth. It is through humility that one can see past one's ego to recognize that there is a heaven and an earth that are of God.

1. Some of the things that man in humility can see is that God:
   a. Psalm 113:7–8, "He raiseth up the poor out of the dust, and lifteth the needy out of the dunghill; That he may set him with princes, even with the princes of his people."
   b. That they may sit with kings at their table.
2. We see this same sentiment in other parts of the Bible, for instance:
   a. First Samuel 2:8, "He raiseth up the poor out of the

> dust, and lifteth up the beggar from the dunghill, to set them among princes, and to make them inherit the throne of glory: for the pillars of the earth are the LORD'S, and he hath set the world upon them."
> 3. In addition, the Lord also makes barren women to keep house and to be a joyful mother of children.

Nothing is impossible with God. He can and does take the poor and needy from a lowly spot to a great height in front of the world. He can make the barren woman a mother with a home full of children. God is the worker of miracles. It takes a humble heart to recognize that the Lord is above all, and in His righteousness, all the riches of the world will never cause Him to favor one of us over another. Psalm 113 reminds us that our riches will be more of an obstacle if we put them before the Lord and His ways.

A good way to end this discussion is to remember this:

Mark 10:15, "Verily I say unto you, Whosoever shall not receive the kingdom of God as a little child, he shall not enter therein."

In other words, learn to rely on our Father in heaven in the same way that a child relies on their earthly father—at least those good fathers who are responsible for their children. Just trust in Him and put Him above all the rest, and you will see that your walk is in His will, and you, too, will praise His glory because "from the rising of the sun unto the going down of the same the LORD'S name is to be praised" (verse 3). Amen.

Notes:

_____

_____

_____

_____

_____

Psalm 114: Tremble, Thou Earth, at the Presence of the Lord

> When Israel went out of Egypt, the house of Jacob from a people of strange language; Judah was his sanctuary, and Israel his dominion. The sea saw it, and fled: Jordan was driven back. The mountains skipped like rams, and the little hills like lambs. What ailed thee, O thou sea, that thou fleddest? thou Jordan, that thou wast driven back? Ye mountains, that ye skipped like rams; and ye little hills, like lambs? Tremble, thou earth, at the presence of the Lord, at the presence of the God of Jacob; Which turned the rock into a standing water, the flint into a fountain of waters.

Psalm 114 is a psalm about how the Lord showed favor to His people during difficult times. The Lord can move mountains and cause the sea to flee to bring His people to safety and health. Nothing is impossible for the Lord.

Verses 7–8, "Tremble, thou earth, at the presence of the Lord, at the presence of the God of Jacob; Which turned the rock into standing water, the flint into a fountain of water."

Even the earth trembles in the presence of God. This suggests that He is a very present God and can and does dwell among His creations on Earth.

Study: The Lord Dwells among His People

The concept of the Lord dwelling among His creations is explored in many places within the Bible. One of the most famous biblical explorations of God dwelling among His people can be found in the story of the Jewish people's exodus from Egypt. Let's look at some of the highlights:

Exodus:

1. Chapter 6:
    a. Verse 2, "And God spake unto Moses, and said unto him, I am the LORD."
    b. Verses 6–7, "Wherefore say unto the children of Israel, I am the LORD, and I will bring you out from under the burdens of the Egyptians, and I will rid you out of their bondage, and I will redeem you with a stretched out arm, and with great judgments: And I will take you to me for a people, and I will be to you a God: and ye shall know that I am the LORD your God, which bringeth you out from under the burdens of the Egyptians."
2. Chapter 19:
    a. Verse 6, "And ye shall be unto me a kingdom of priests, and an holy nation. These are the words which thou shalt speak unto the children of Israel."
3. Chapter 25:
    a. Verse 8 (emphasis added by the author), "And let them make me a sanctuary; *that I may dwell among them.*"
4. Chapter 29:
    a. Verses 45–46 (emphasis added by the author), "And *I will dwell among the children of Israel*, and will be their God. And they shall know that I am the LORD their God, that brought them forth out of the land of Egypt, *that I may dwell among them*; I am the LORD their God."

The word "dwell" is defined as "to live in or at a specified place." So, here we see the Lord Himself proclaiming that He will dwell (or live) among the people of Israel. God never says anything that does not come to pass, so we can believe that He dwelt within the group of His people, which He freed from Egypt. In other words, He was right there among them.

As people, we tend to see this concept as a metaphor for God being spiritually around the people, as in His Spirit dwelt among the people. Or perhaps it means dwelling mentally in prayer with the people. Or even, in the case of the exodus from Egypt, perhaps we envision God dwelling as a burning bush amongst His people or perhaps in the sanctuary of the ark of the covenant, which had yet to be built when the above words were spoken.

In many ways, each of these concepts is true: He will dwell (or live) among His people. Whichever way we choose to believe how He meant this, we can be sure that God was right there with His people, not in some faraway place, removed from where His people were.

Which is an amazing thing when we consider it.

Interestingly, many years later, the Lord sent His Son to dwell among His people. During the Egyptian exodus, the Lord dwelt among His people in much the same way that Jesus, His Son, dwelt physically and spiritually among His people. What a powerful visual that is when we juxtapose the God of Israel dwelling among His people with the Son of the God of Israel dwelling among His people in very nearly the same place.

I don't know about you, but that blows my mind: the perfect, orderly mind of God presenting His truth in such a strong way. "I will dwell among you."

Furthermore, as the leaders of Israel were instructed to become a nation of priests, so too were the apostles and the followers of Christ asked to go out among the nations and preach. They became the priests of Christ.

It is not hard to consider that in much the same way the people of God were freed from the bonds of Egyptian slavery by the God that dwelt among them, Christ saved the people from the bonds of slavery to sin while He, in turn, dwelt among the people.

Was Egypt a foreshadowing of salvation on the cross? All the same lessons are there. If this piques your interest, and you have the time, you may want to deep dive into the ways the crucifixion of Christ on the cross fulfilled the Jewish exodus from Egypt. If anything, you will gain valuable insight into the history of God dwelling among His people.

Thank You, Lord, for dwelling among nations, societies, and even individual people. You are the Most High, just, and very present Lord: our refuge and our salvation. With love, your humble servant. Amen.

Notes:

Psalm 115: Not unto Us, O Lord, but unto Thy Name Give Glory

Not unto us, O LORD, not unto us, but unto thy name give glory, for thy mercy, and for thy truth's sake. Wherefore should the heathen say, Where is now their God? But our God is in the heavens: he hath done whatsoever he hath pleased. Their idols are silver and gold, the work of men's hands. They have mouths, but they speak not: eyes have they, but they see not: They have ears, but they hear not: noses have they, but they smell not: They have hands, but they handle not: feet have they, but they walk not: neither speak they through their throat. They that make them are like unto them; so is every one that trusteth in them. O Israel, trust thou in the LORD: he is their help and their shield. O house of Aaron, trust in the LORD: he is their help and their shield. Ye that fear the LORD, trust in the LORD: he is their help and their shield. The LORD hath been mindful of us: he will bless us; he will bless the house of Israel; he will bless the house of Aaron. He will bless them that fear the LORD, both small and great. The LORD shall increase you more and more, you and your children. Ye are blessed of the LORD which made heaven and earth. The heaven, even the heavens, are the LORD'S: but the earth hath he given to the children of men. The dead praise not the LORD, neither any that go down into silence. But we will bless the LORD from this time forth and for evermore. Praise the LORD.

Verse 3, "But our God …hath done whatsoever he hath pleased."

Deep in the heart of Psalm 115, is the notion that God is all-powerful and He has the power to do whatever He pleases. The people of strange gods and ideas (aka the heathen) ask, "Where is your God?" And the response is, essentially, everything you see, He hath done because He has the power to do it, and it pleases Him.

When we humble our hearts and understand the great and all-powerful nature of God, we begin to understand exactly what that means. God is all-powerful. In other words, the entirety of all power belongs to God or rather is God. There is nothing that is power that is not of God.

In our vanity, we may believe that we have the power within ourselves and we seek to gain more power through different worldly strategies: riches, fame, military might, etc. Some may even resort to sorcery and witchcraft to bring more power to themselves. These devices for gaining power are a delusion, for any power that man may ever imagine he has achieved is because God has allowed it through our free will, and that power is, ultimately, at the mercy of God. It can be taken away in the twinkling of an eye.

When we begin to realize (or even consider) that human-sourced power is a mere shadow of the real power of God, we begin to understand true nature. When we understand true nature and realize that surrender to the power of God brings us into true power, we begin to become sanctified. Sanctity is the surrender of self-sourced power to the true power of God.

And as with all things of God, this is an inexhaustible exercise. The more we surrender, the more of God's power we possess, and the more sanctified we become. It is another ever-mounting higher cycle that permeates life with the Lord as the center of our lives.

The people who abuse the power that God has allowed to them by trying to achieve selfish and unworthy ends (aka being wicked) find that they begin to lose the real power that is available to them by becoming more and more cut off from God. Their abuse of power leads to less true power, which leads to less connection to God, which then leads to more selfish abuse of power. This is the downward spiral of those who are on the path to destruction.

However, surrendering to the power of God is always available throughout our earthly existence. We can always change to the sanctifying path and begin or continue mounting higher while we walk this earth.

God is hope and all good things. He will never abandon us. However, once we are judged after our death and He sees that we don't belong to Him through our own choices and rejection of Him, He will cut us off forever, and we will perish. It's just the way it works. We had the chance to embrace Him throughout our lives and we never did.

Every soul lost hurts the Lord deeply. Everyone was made in love of God and seeing a soul reject Him is always a great loss for Him. This is why we pray for souls. As children of God, we always seek to help relieve the suffering of our creator, and His greatest suffering comes from losing souls.

Thank You, Lord, for the great love You have for Your children and for being the true power within our lives. We pray that everyone humbles themselves to surrender to Your will. Amen.

Psalm 116: I Was Brought Low, and He Helped Me

I love the LORD, because he hath heard my voice and my supplications. Because he hath inclined his ear unto me, therefore will I call upon him as long as I live. The sorrows of death compassed me, and the pains of hell gat hold upon me: I found trouble and sorrow. Then called I upon the name of the LORD; O LORD, I beseech thee, deliver my soul. Gracious is the LORD, and righteous; yea, our God is merciful. The LORD preserveth the simple: I was brought low, and he helped me. Return unto thy rest, O my soul; for the LORD hath dealt bountifully with thee. For thou hast delivered my soul from death, mine eyes from tears, and my feet from falling. I will walk before the LORD in the land of the living. I believed, therefore have I spoken: I was greatly afflicted: I said in my haste, All men are liars. What shall I render unto the LORD for all his benefits toward me? I will take the cup of salvation, and call upon the name of the LORD. I will pay my vows unto the LORD now in the presence of all his people. Precious in the sight of the LORD is the death of his saints. O LORD, truly I am thy servant; I am thy servant, and the son of thine handmaid: thou hast loosed my bonds. I will offer to thee the sacrifice of thanksgiving, and will call upon the name of the LORD. I will pay my vows unto the LORD now in the presence of all his people, In the courts of the LORD'S house, in the midst of thee, O Jerusalem. Praise ye the LORD.

Psalm 116 reminds us that the poor, needy, and lowly are precious to the Lord because this is when we are most open to being saved. When we find ourselves at a low point and in need of help, as we all will at some point in our lives, and we are physically, mentally, and/or spiritually suffering, and all human avenues have failed us, we will feel like we hit rock bottom. When we feel like we are all alone and there is no one to help us, this is when we are the most open to redemption.

In our pain, we cry out, "God, help me!"

Man has been given free will and it is a very powerful force. When the free will of a man is dominant in his life, he can achieve much in this world through his own devices. God has made man to do much on his own.

However, because we live in a fallen world, the enemy knows how to manipulate and coerce the free will of man. It is precisely this coercion by the enemy that begins to bend a man. The enemy cares not about the free will of man. He hates it because it is a precious gift given to man by the creator. The truth is that the enemy will use all measures necessary to bind up and coerce man into giving up the true power of God and be dominated by the tricks and ways of his dominion.

Very often, this looks like setting aside the power within the honor of right living and, little by little, making selfish and, many times, harmful and/or illegal maneuvers.

Verse 3, "The sorrows of death compassed me, and the pains of hell gat hold upon me: I found trouble and sorrow."

These actions bind us further and further to the enemy and his ways. We can find ourselves in a downward spiral, which the enemy loves because any lost soul pains God.

People are merely fodder for the enemy to inflict pain on God. There is no concern for the pain caused to man. However, it is during the lowest times in man's life when he is the neediest, that he has a chance to set aside his ego and call out to God for help.

This gives God the chance to help His child break the bonds of flesh and be remade into a new being walking the path with God.

Verse 16, "O LORD, truly I am thy servant; I am thy servant, and the son of thine handmaid: thou hast loosed my bonds."

Once a man surrenders himself to God, commits to living a virtuous life, and finds himself becoming sanctified in his new life, it is very difficult to turn back to being bound up again. God Himself has promised to help those who turn away from sin and walk in His path.

Psalm 116 is another reminder of the mercy God has for His people. And it is followed by Psalm 117, which is thanks and praise for the mercy of God.

Will you take the cup of salvation and call upon the name of the Lord in your time of trouble?

Psalm 117: For His Merciful Kindness Is Great toward Us

> O praise the LORD, all ye nations: praise him, all ye people. For his merciful kindness is great toward us: and the truth of the LORD endureth for ever. Praise ye the LORD.

Psalm 117 talks about how our Father is so merciful and filled with lovingkindness that it is right for all the nations of the earth to praise Him. And not only that, but this merciful love of the Most High and His truth will endure forever. It's not as if the Lord gives us mercy one day, and then, the next day, He is depleted of all His mercy. That is more of a human thing—our mercy can last but a day and then we are back cursing our enemies. The Lord is all merciful for all time. He is mercy itself in the same way that He is love or truth itself.

Now would be an excellent time to briefly study the concept of "mercy," for it is a topic that permeates the text of both the Old and New Testaments and is one of those concepts that forms a core value of life with God.

Study: Mercy

The concept of mercy is an ancient one and extends way before the actual word "mercy" began to be used in common language. In fact, we see that the word "mercy" itself was not in common usage until the twelfth century AD and is an evolution of the Latin *"mercedem"* and early French *"merci."* Both words came about long after the original Hebrew texts in which many parts of the ancient Bible were written.

When we start to go way back and look at where the concept of mercy originated, it is a good idea to wrap our heads around the perspective of the original gatekeepers of the biblical stories, especially during their ancient beginning. So we need to imagine how the Old Testament orators were living during the time the very concept of mercy was put into language. And this is where it gets interesting.

Imagine being a part of a group of people who were set aside from the rest of humanity to carry the torch for the one true God. Not only did this God show wondrous signs to His people, but He presented Himself to dwell among them and to forgive and show mercy to His children when they went astray. He sent prophets and great men to speak for Him so that the people were aware of His true existence. And one of the main aspects of God is the persistent "mercy" He shows His people.

According to the Ancient Hebrew Research Center, a group whose mission is to uncover the language, culture, and philosophy of the Bible (primarily in the Old Testament) during its ancient origins, the Hebrew word generally used to convey "mercy" is rooted in the verb sometimes used to convey "to be kind." Mercy is a kindness, so that makes perfect sense. However, when we look even further back than that, we can see that the root of the root of mercy comes from a concrete noun that is generally used for "stork."

It is thought that the stork's neck provides the clue, the AHRC surmised. Storks are a persistent part of nature around the places found in the Bible, so the people would be very familiar with what a stork looks like. It is thought that the way the neck of a stork is curved and causes the head of the stork to bow down, as one does when we are paying respect and showing kindness to another, illustrates our God showing mercy to His people.

In His infinite kindness, the Lord takes pity on us in our times of poor behavior and bows His head in His meek and humble way as He shows us the kindness of mercy rather than the heat of His wrath—which is probably what we very often deserve, let's be honest.

Isn't our Father amazing? The creator of all things has consistently, over the many generations of man, bowed His head and took pity on His children by showing us mercy. Even when we commit the most atrocious and vile of sins, He eventually shows us mercy when we repent and trust in Him. He is that good. And, guess what? That mercy and truth endures forever. He will never, ever change.

Let's give praise to our most kind and merciful Father! Thank You, Lord! Praise and glory to You, O Lord! Amen.

Psalm 118: This Is the Day Which the Lord Hath Made

O give thanks unto the LORD; for he is good: because his mercy endureth for ever. Let Israel now say, that his mercy endureth for ever. Let the house of Aaron now say, that his mercy endureth for ever. Let them now that fear the LORD say, that his mercy endureth for ever. I called upon the LORD in distress: the LORD answered me, and set me in a large place. The LORD is on my side; I will not fear: what can man do unto me? The LORD taketh my part with them that help me: therefore shall I see my desire upon them that hate me. It is better to trust in the LORD than to put confidence in man. It is better to trust in the LORD than to put confidence in princes. All nations compassed me about: but in the name of the LORD will I destroy them. They compassed me about; yea, they compassed me about: but in the name of the LORD I will destroy them. They compassed me about like bees; they are quenched as the fire of thorns: for in the name of the LORD I will destroy them. Thou hast thrust sore at me that I might fall: but the LORD helped me. The LORD is my strength and song, and is become my salvation. The voice of rejoicing and salvation is in the tabernacles of the righteous: the right hand of the LORD doeth valiantly. The right hand of the LORD is exalted: the right hand of the LORD doeth valiantly. I shall not die, but live, and declare the works of the LORD. The LORD hath chastened me sore: but he hath not given me over unto death. Open to me the gates of righteousness: I will go into them, and I will praise the LORD: This gate of the LORD, into which the righteous shall enter. I will praise thee: for thou hast heard me, and art become my salvation. The stone which the builders refused is become the head stone of the corner. This is the LORD'S doing; it is marvellous in our eyes. This is the day which the LORD hath made; we will rejoice and be glad in it. Save now, I beseech thee, O LORD: O LORD, I beseech thee, send now prosperity. Blessed be he that cometh in the name of the LORD: we have blessed you out of the house of the LORD. God is the LORD, which hath shewed us light: bind the sacrifice with cords, even unto the horns of the altar. Thou art my God, and I will praise thee: thou art my God, I will exalt thee. O give thanks unto the LORD; for he is good: for his mercy endureth for ever.

Verse 24, "This is the day which the LORD hath made; we will rejoice and be glad in it."

Surely, this is one of the most famous verses in the Bible. "This is the day which the LORD hath made; we will rejoice and be glad." The all-powerful Lord made this and every day, and that alone is enough to give thanks and praise. In fact, not only is this fact enough to prompt us to give thanks and praise to our wonderful God, but Psalm 118, verse 24, suggests that it is mandatory to thank God for each and every day He makes for us. "We *will* rejoice and be glad" (emphasis added by the author).

If we delve a little further into Psalm 118, we can see that most of the verses refer, again, to the mercy that God showed after a period of trouble.

Verse 5, "I called upon the LORD in distress: the LORD answered me, and set me in a large place."

The Lord answers us by bringing us from a small place of confinement and fear in our day of trouble to a large, expansive place where we feel free and unencumbered by anxiety and the troubles of the day. In response to the mercy God shows us, we are to give thanks.

Verse 29, "O give thanks unto the LORD; for he is good; for his mercy endureth for ever."

While Psalm 118 is about the all-powerful God and His consistent mercy, there is also an undercurrent of what is to come. Like many passages in the Bible, each verse can reference a multitude of scenarios, which is why the Bible itself is a miraculous document. Let's explore one scenario that we can see in Psalm 118.

Study: Jesus as the Mercy of God

What if the "day" the Lord hath made is also a single day in history? What if the day that He made is the day when His Son died on the cross for our salvation? Could Psalm 118 also be referring to that day when we "will rejoice and be glad"?

Let's consider a few verses from Psalm 118 in the context of Jesus Christ:

Verses 21 and 22 seem to reference Jesus, the Son of God:

> b. "I will praise thee: for thou hast heard me, and art become my salvation. The stone which builders refused to become the head stone of the corner."

Is Jesus the rejected who became the headstone of the corner, as is revealed in Psalm 118? Let's take a look at some examples from the New Testament:

1. Matthew 21:42, "Jesus saith unto them, Did ye never read in the scriptures, The stone which the builders rejected, the same is become the head of the corner: this is the Lord's doing, and it is marvellous in our eyes?"
2. Ephesians 2:20, "And are built upon the foundation of the apostles and prophets, Jesus Christ himself being the chief corner stone."

Verses 14–16 of Psalm 118 speak of the right hand of the Lord,

> The LORD is my strength and song, and is become my salvation. The voice of rejoicing and salvation is in the tabernacles of the righteous: the right hand of the LORD doeth valiantly. The right hand of the LORD is exalted: the right hand of the LORD doeth valiantly.

This is speaking of the courage and determination of the right hand of the Lord who doeth valiantly.

Many years later, the apostles of Christ bear witness to seeing Jesus brought up into heaven and sitting at the right hand of God:

1. Consider Mark 16:15, 19, "And he [Jesus] said unto them, Go ye into all the world, and preach the gospel to every creature. ...So then after the Lord had spoken unto them, he was received up into heaven, and sat on the right hand of God."
2. In Luke 20:42, David, an author of many psalms, is referenced to speaking about the right hand of the Lord like this, "And David himself saith in the book of Psalms, The LORD said unto my Lord, Sit thou on my right hand." Two Lords. One on a throne and one sitting on the right hand of the Lord.

It is easy to see by examining Scripture that Jesus is the referenced cornerstone of the church and is its salvation, who sits valiantly at the right hand of God. And because, once again, Psalm 118 references the mercy of God, we can see that Jesus, too, is a manifestation of God's mercy.

Psalm 118:29, "O give thanks unto the LORD; for he is good: for his mercy endureth for ever."

God imagined bringing His mercy into dwell among His people, and that became manifest in Jesus. The salvation by Jesus on the cross is the greatest manifestation of the mercy of God in human history. The mercy of God is not always in the ways that this world imagines. Consider what we learned in Psalm 117 when we examined "mercy" itself. In that, we saw that the early Jewish people looked upon a stork and saw their meek and humble God bowing His head in kindness and forgiveness when His children messed up. Instead of harsh punishment, the Father gave mercy. Now, consider the cross and the moment when Christ died to give us the great mercy of everlasting salvation. When He took His last breath and bowed His head in death.

"It is finished."

The greatest gesture of mercy to the children of God was finished. The Father gave His Son as a sacrifice for the salvation of all. Imagine that kind of love.

Let us all rejoice and be glad for the everlasting mercy of God! Sing Him praise and glory! Amen.

Psalm 119: How to Remain Righteous in an Unrighteous World

Aleph. Blessed are the undefiled in the way, who walk in the law of the LORD. Blessed are they that keep his testimonies, and that seek him with the whole heart. They also do no iniquity: they walk in his ways. Thou hast commanded us to keep thy precepts diligently. O that my ways were directed to keep thy statutes! Then shall I not be ashamed, when I have respect unto all thy commandments. I will praise thee with uprightness of heart, when I shall have learned thy righteous judgments. I will keep thy statutes: O forsake me not utterly.

Beth. Wherewithal shall a young man cleanse his way? by taking heed thereto according to thy word. With my whole heart have I sought thee: O let me not wander from thy commandments. Thy word have I hid in mine heart, that I might not sin against thee. Blessed art thou, O LORD: teach me thy statutes. With my lips have I declared all the judgments of thy mouth. I have rejoiced in the way of thy testimonies, as much as in all riches. I will meditate in thy precepts, and have respect unto thy ways. I will delight myself in thy statutes: I will not forget thy word.

Gimel. Deal bountifully with thy servant, that I may live, and keep thy word. Open thou mine eyes, that I may behold wondrous things out of thy law. I am a stranger in the earth: hide not thy commandments from me. My soul breaketh for the longing that it hath unto thy judgments at all times. Thou hast rebuked the proud that are cursed, which do err from thy commandments. Remove from me reproach and contempt; for I have kept thy testimonies. Princes also did sit and speak against me: but thy servant did meditate in thy statutes. Thy testimonies also are my delight and my counsellers.

Daleth. My soul cleaveth unto the dust: quicken thou me according to thy word. I have declared my ways, and thou heardest me: teach me thy statutes. Make me to understand the way of thy precepts: so shall I talk of thy wondrous works. My soul melteth for heaviness: strengthen thou me according unto thy word. Remove from me the way of lying: and grant me thy law graciously. I have chosen the way of truth: thy judgments have I laid before me. I have stuck unto thy testimonies: O LORD, put me not to shame. I will run the way of thy commandments, when thou shalt enlarge my heart.

He. Teach me, O LORD, the way of thy statutes; and I shall keep it unto the end. Give me understanding, and I shall keep thy law; yea, I shall observe it with my whole heart. Make me to go in the path of thy commandments; for therein do I delight. Incline my heart unto thy testimonies, and not to covetousness. Turn away mine eyes from beholding vanity; and quicken thou me in thy way. Stablish thy word unto thy servant, who is devoted to thy fear. Turn away my reproach which I fear: for thy judgments are good. Behold, I have longed after thy precepts: quicken me in thy righteousness.

Vau. Let thy mercies come also unto me, O LORD, even thy salvation, according to thy word. So shall I have wherewith to answer him that reproacheth me: for I trust in thy word. And take not the word of truth utterly out of my mouth; for I have hoped in thy judgments. So shall I keep thy law continually for ever and ever. And I will walk at liberty: for I seek thy precepts. I will speak of thy testimonies also before kings, and will not be ashamed. And I will delight myself in thy commandments, which I have loved. My hands also will I lift up unto thy commandments, which I have loved; and I will meditate in thy statutes.

Zain. Remember the word unto thy servant, upon which thou hast caused me to hope. This is my comfort in my affliction: for thy word hath quickened me. The proud have had me greatly in derision: yet have I not declined from thy law. I remembered thy judgments of old, O LORD; and have comforted myself. Horror hath taken hold upon me because of the wicked that forsake thy law. Thy statutes have been my songs in the house of my pilgrimage. I have remembered thy name, O LORD, in the night, and have kept thy law. This I had, because I kept thy precepts.

Cheth. Thou art my portion, O LORD: I have said that I would keep thy words. I intreated thy favour with my whole heart: be merciful unto me according to thy word. I thought on my ways, and turned my feet unto thy testimonies. I made haste, and delayed not to keep thy commandments. The bands of the wicked have robbed me: but I have not forgotten thy law. At midnight I will rise to give thanks unto thee because of thy righteous judgments. I am a companion of all them that fear thee, and of them that keep thy precepts. The earth, O LORD, is full of thy mercy: teach me thy statutes.

Teth. Thou hast dealt well with thy servant, O LORD, according unto thy word. Teach me good judgment and knowledge: for I have believed thy commandments. Before I was afflicted I went astray: but now have I kept thy word. Thou art good, and doest good; teach me thy statutes. The proud have forged a lie against me: but I will keep thy precepts with my whole heart. Their heart is as fat as grease; but I delight in thy law. It is good for me that I have been afflicted; that I might learn thy statutes. The law of thy mouth is better unto me than thousands of gold and silver.

Jod. Thy hands have made me and fashioned me: give me understanding, that I may learn thy commandments. They that fear thee will be glad when they see me; because I have hoped in thy word. I know, O LORD, that thy judgments are right, and that thou in faithfulness hast afflicted me. Let, I pray thee, thy merciful kindness be for my comfort, according to thy word unto thy servant. Let thy tender mercies come unto me, that I may live: for thy law is my delight. Let the proud be ashamed; for they dealt perversely with me without a cause: but I will meditate in thy precepts. Let those that fear thee turn unto me, and those that have known thy testimonies. Let my heart be sound in thy statutes; that I be not ashamed.

Caph. My soul fainteth for thy salvation: but I hope in thy word. Mine eyes fail for thy word, saying, When wilt thou comfort me? For I am become like a bottle in the smoke; yet do I not forget thy statutes. How many are the days of thy servant? when wilt thou execute judgment on them that persecutes me? The proud have digged pits for me, which are not after thy law. All thy commandments are faithful: they persecute me wrongfully; help thou me. They had almost consumed me upon earth; but I forsook not thy precepts. Quicken me after thy lovingkindness; so shall I keep the testimony of thy mouth.

Lamed. For ever, O LORD, thy word is settled in heaven. Thy faithfulness is unto all generations: thou hast established the earth, and it abideth. They continue this day according to thine ordinances: for all are thy servants. Unless thy law had been my delights, I should then have perished in mine affliction. I will never forget thy precepts: for with them thou hast quickened me. I am thine, save me: for I have sought thy precepts. The wicked have waited for me to destroy me: but I will consider thy testimonies. I have seen an end of all perfection: but thy commandment is exceeding broad.

Mem. O how love I thy law! it is my meditation all the day. Thou through thy commandments hast made me wiser than mine enemies: for they are ever with me. I have more understanding than all my teachers: for thy testimonies are my meditation. I understand more than the ancients, because I keep thy precepts. I have refrained my feet from every evil way, that I might keep thy word. I have not departed from thy judgments: for thou hast taught me. How sweet are thy words unto my taste! yea, sweeter than honey to my mouth! Through thy precepts I get understanding: therefore I hate every false way.

Nun. Thy word is a lamp unto my feet, and a light unto my path. I have sworn, and I will perform it, that I will keep thy righteous judgments. I am afflicted very much: quicken me, O LORD, according unto thy word. Accept, I beseech thee, the freewill offerings of my mouth, O LORD, and teach me thy judgments. My soul is continually in my hand: yet do I not forget thy law. The wicked have laid a snare for me: yet I erred not from thy precepts. Thy testimonies have I taken as an heritage for ever: for they are the rejoicing of my heart. I have inclined mine heart to perform thy statutes alway, even unto the end.

Samech. I hate vain thoughts: but thy law do I love. Thou art my hiding place and my shield: I hope in thy word. Depart from me, ye evildoers: for I will keep the commandments of my God. Uphold me according unto thy word, that I may live: and let me not be ashamed of my hope. Hold thou me up, and I shall be safe: and I will have respect unto thy statutes continually. Thou hast trodden down all them that err from thy statutes: for their deceit is falsehood. Thou puttest away all the wicked of the earth like dross: therefore I love thy testimonies. My flesh trembleth for fear of thee; and I am afraid of thy judgments.

Ain. I have done judgment and justice: leave me not to mine oppressors. Be surety for thy servant for good: let not the proud oppress me. Mine eyes fail for thy salvation, and for the word of thy righteousness. Deal with thy servant according unto thy mercy, and teach me thy statutes. I am thy servant; give me understanding, that I may know thy testimonies. It is time for thee, LORD, to work: for they have made void thy law. Therefore I love thy commandments above gold; yea, above fine gold. Therefore I esteem all thy precepts concerning all things to be right; and I hate every false way.

Pe. Thy testimonies are wonderful: therefore doth my soul keep them. The entrance of thy words giveth light; it giveth understanding unto the simple. I opened my mouth, and panted: for I longed for thy commandments. Look thou upon me, and be merciful unto me, as thou usest to do unto those that love thy name. Order my steps in thy word: and let not any iniquity have dominion over me. Deliver me from the oppression of man: so will I keep thy precepts. Make thy face to shine upon thy servant; and teach me thy statutes. Rivers of waters run down mine eyes, because they keep not thy law.

Tzaddi. Righteous art thou, O LORD, and upright are thy judgments. Thy testimonies that thou hast commanded are righteous and very faithful. My zeal hath consumed me, because mine enemies have forgotten thy words. Thy word is very pure: therefore thy servant loveth it. I am small and despised: yet do not I forget thy precepts. Thy righteousness is an everlasting righteousness, and thy law is the truth. Trouble and anguish have taken hold on me: yet thy commandments are my delights. The righteousness of thy testimonies is everlasting: give me understanding, and I shall live.

Koph. I cried with my whole heart; hear me, O LORD: I will keep thy statutes. I cried unto thee; save me, and I shall keep thy testimonies. I prevented the dawning of the morning, and cried: I hoped in thy word. Mine eyes prevent the night watches, that I might meditate in thy word. Hear my voice according unto thy lovingkindness: O LORD, quicken me according to thy judgment. They draw nigh that follow after mischief: they are far from thy law. Thou art near, O LORD; and all thy commandments are truth. Concerning thy testimonies, I have known of old that thou hast founded them for ever.

Resh. Consider mine affliction, and deliver me: for I do not forget thy law. Plead my cause, and deliver me: quicken me according to thy word. Salvation is far from the wicked: for they seek not thy statutes. Great are thy tender mercies, O LORD: quicken me according to thy judgments. Many are my persecutors and mine enemies; yet do I not decline from thy testimonies. I beheld the transgressors, and was grieved; because they kept not thy word. Consider how I love thy precepts: quicken me, O LORD, according to thy lovingkindness. Thy word is true from the beginning: and every one of thy righteous judgments endureth for ever.

Schin. Princes have persecuted me without a cause: but my heart standeth in awe of thy word. I rejoice at thy word, as one that findeth great spoil. I hate and abhor lying: but thy law do I love. Seven times a day do I praise thee because of thy righteous judgments. Great peace have they which love thy law: and nothing shall offend them. LORD, I have hoped for thy salvation, and done thy commandments. My soul hath kept thy testimonies; and I love them exceedingly. I have kept thy precepts and thy testimonies: for all my ways are before thee.

Tau. Let my cry come near before thee, O LORD: give me understanding according to thy word. Let my supplication come before thee: deliver me according to thy word. My lips shall utter praise, when thou hast taught me thy statutes. My tongue shall speak of thy word: for all thy commandments are righteousness. Let thine hand help me; for I have chosen thy precepts. I have longed for thy salvation, O LORD; and thy law is my delight. Let my soul live, and it shall praise thee; and let thy judgments help me. I have gone astray like a lost sheep; seek thy servant; for I do not forget thy commandments.

A sampling of verses from Psalm 119,

1. Verse 1, "Blessed are the undefiled in the way, who walk in the law of the LORD."
2. Verse 9, "Wherewithal shall a young man cleanse his way? by taking heed thereto according to thy word."
3. Verse 35, "Make me to go in the path of thy commandments; for therein do I delight."
4. Verse 48, "My hands also will I lift up unto thy commandments, which I have loved; and I will meditate in thy statutes."
5. Verse 112, "I have inclined mine heart to perform thy statutes alway, even unto the end."
6. Verse 127, "Therefore I love thy commandments above gold; yea, above fine gold."
7. Verse 128, "Therefore I esteem all thy precepts concerning all things to be right; and I hate every false way."
8. Verse 140, "Thy word is very pure: therefore thy servant loveth it."
9. Verse 158, "I beheld the transgressors, and was grieved; because they kept not thy word."

10. Verse 165, "Great peace have they which love thy law: and nothing shall offend them."

Psalm 119 is a culmination of much of the wisdom and knowledge that is offered in the Psalms and how individual personalities process their understanding within their writings. It is like a montage of righteous believers delivering their testimonies on what they need and how they pursue living under the commandments of the Lord. These testimonies include living among the wicked and how to turn away from them, prayers for understanding the Lord's ways, requesting merciful judgment for turning away from their transgressions, and offering praise for kind judgment. In the end, the summary appears to be:

Follow and love the right ways of the Lord above any reward this world can offer unto the end, and you will find great peace while you live here, and the Lord will protect you from all offenses against you.

Let's consider the precepts of Psalm 119 for a more thorough look at what is being discussed in the psalm and how we can practice this in our own lives to strengthen our faith as we walk with God.

Verse 4, "Thou hast commanded us to keep thy precepts diligently."

Highlights: The Precepts Contained in Psalm 119

(Precept: a general rule designed to regulate behavior.)

1. Be not the proud, for they are cursed and do err from the commandments.
2. Do not engage in contempt and reproach; do not judge others harshly and do not harshly communicate with them.
3. Do not gossip and speak against anyone.
4. Do not lie or have lying ways.
5. Choose the way of truth.
6. Choose the way of understanding.
7. Choose the path of thy commandments.

8. Do not incline your heart to covetousness or envy.
9. Turn away from the vanity of self.
10. Choose the path of a servant.
11. Meditate on the laws of God.
12. Speak up on the laws in front of even the kings.
13. Persevere in the way of His commandments even when the proud shows derision.
14. The horrors of wicked men who forsake the law should not drive you off the pilgrimage of the law.
15. Do not delay in keeping the commandments.
16. Even when the wicked attack and steal from you, keep the commandments.
17. It is good for me that I have been afflicted that I might learn Thy statutes.
18. The law is better than all the riches of the earth.
19. Hope in the Word of the Lord.
20. Remember that the proud have dug pits for those to get us off the commands; do not fall for it; persevere in the law.
21. Love thy law and meditate on it all day.
22. Refrain from every evil way to keep His Word.
23. The judgment of the Lord teaches us.
24. Through the precepts, we get understanding.
25. Hate every false way.
26. Incline thy heart to perform thy statutes always—even unto the end.
27. Depart from evil-doers.
28. Esteem all thy precepts concerning all things to be right and hate every false way.

Special Contemplation: Consummate Pleasure

We need to learn to be happy in those simple moments that represent a life lived in heaven. We need to see all moments as simple. This is the way of the saint.

Thank You for teaching us Your favorable ways, dear Father. Amen.

Psalm 120: I Am for Peace: But When I Speak, They Are for War

> In my distress I cried unto the LORD, and he heard me. Deliver my soul, O LORD, from lying lips, and from a deceitful tongue. What shall be given unto thee? or what shall be done unto thee, thou false tongue? Sharp arrows of the mighty, with coals of juniper. Woe is me, that I sojourn in Mesech, that I dwell in the tents of Kedar! My soul hath long dwelt with him that hateth peace. I am for peace: but when I speak, they are for war.

A modern look at Psalm 120 is to imagine living in a place and being surrounded by the deceitful tongue of propaganda.

Verse 2, "Deliver my soul, O LORD, from lying lips, and from a deceitful tongue."

Verse 7, "I am for peace: but when I speak, they are for war."

Every day, we hear the lying lips of the propagandist speak words that cause the people around us to become agitated and angry. Like the ancient people of Mesech and Kedar, theirs is a cry for war.

But we are people of peace. The thought of war distresses us. So, we find ourselves crying out to the Lord in prayer, "Help save my soul from those who hate peace!"

This psalm reminds us that as people of faith who walk with the Lord, we are going to find ourselves living among those who speak to the exact opposite worldview that we may have. They are for war, using any means necessary, including deceit, to move the people in their direction. But we continue to speak peace.

It can be very frustrating and play heavy on our souls to live among those who hate peace. But we must continue to pray to our Father; He will hear us.

Hear our prayers for peace, Abba, Father.

Psalm 121: The Lord Is Thy Keeper ...He Shall Preserve Thy Soul

> I will lift up mine eyes unto the hills, from whence cometh my help. My help cometh from the LORD, which made heaven and earth. He will not suffer thy foot to be moved: he that keepeth thee will not slumber. Behold, he that keepeth Israel shall neither slumber nor sleep. The LORD is thy keeper: the LORD is thy shade upon thy right hand. The sun shall not smite thee by day, nor the moon by night. The LORD shall preserve thee from all evil: he shall preserve thy soul. The LORD shall preserve thy going out and thy coming in from this time forth, and even for evermore.

Psalm 121 reminds us that our Father is always near us to keep us safe. He shades us from the sun during the day and the moon at night. Day and night, He preserves us from evil. He does not sleep but is always our keeper. In fact, "The Lord shall preserve thy going out and thy coming in from this time forth, and even for evermore" (verse 8).

The Lord will always preserve us or maintain us in our current state or form (and, in this case, that means as a child of God) forever. That is some promise. Let's consider some other Bible verses that present a clear picture of what it means to be preserved by the Lord:

1. Isaiah 25:4, "For thou hast been a strength to the poor, a strength to the needy in his distress, a refuge from the storm, a shadow from the heart, when the blast of the terrible ones is as a storm against the wall."
2. Psalm 16:8, "I have set the LORD always before me; because he is at my right hand, I shall not be moved."

3. Psalm 109:31, "For he shall stand at the right hand of the poor, to save him from those that condemn his soul."

In other words, here is a summary of the way of the Lord as we have been discussing throughout the Psalms and within the Bible as a whole:

1. The Lord is our refuge.
2. The Lord will protect us.
3. The Lord will save us from the wicked.

But first, "Offer the sacrifices of righteousness, and put your trust in the LORD" (Psalm 4:5).

Lord, thank You for Your wisdom and teaching. It is a privilege to learn from You as Your humble servant. Amen.

Psalm 122: Our Feet Shall Stand within Thy Gates, O Jerusalem

> I was glad when they said unto me, Let us go into the house of the LORD. Our feet shall stand within thy gates, O Jerusalem. Jerusalem is builded as a city that is compact together: Whither the tribes go up, the tribes of the LORD, unto the testimony of Israel, to give thanks unto the name of the LORD. For there are set thrones of judgment, the thrones of the house of David. Pray for the peace of Jerusalem: they shall prosper that love thee. Peace be within thy walls, and prosperity within thy palaces. For my brethren and companions' sakes, I will now say, Peace be within thee. Because of the house of the LORD our God I will seek thy good.

Psalm 122 speaks of the temple of God and the city of Jerusalem. On the surface, it is a song of prayer to the house of the Lord, which is depicted in this psalm as the city of Jerusalem.

Now would be an excellent time to look a little further into Jerusalem, both historically as well as how it is referenced within the Bible.

Study: Jerusalem

A brief historical study of Jerusalem up until the time of David:

Historically, the first settlements in the area of what we know as Jerusalem happened around 6000 years ago, in 3500 BC, in what is known as the Chalcolithic period or the Copper Age. Then, 1000 years later, in 2500 BC, the area began seeing the first construction of houses, and 700 years after that, the first wall was built around what had become a rapidly increasing city during the Middle Bronze Age. It wasn't, however, until approximately 3500 years ago, in 1400 BC, during the Late Bronze Age, that the first mention of *Jerusalem* was written down as a word used to indicate the area.

Finally, in 1000 BC, which is 200 years after a hostile takeover of the city by the Canaanites, King David secured the area of Jerusalem and declared the city the capital city of the Jewish Kingdom.

It was during this reign of David and afterward that the Psalms were written, beginning around 3100 years ago. So, we can see that up until the time of David, the city we know as Jerusalem had been talked about and settled but was not formally declared as the Jewish capital until it was captured by David during his reign.

Over history, Jerusalem has also been called the city of God, the city of David, the promised land, and Zion.

1. Second Samuel 5:9, "So David dwelt in the fort, and called it the city of David. And David built a round about from Millo and inward."
2. Psalm 122:5, "For there are set thrones of judgment, the thrones of the house of David."

A brief biblical study of Jerusalem:

The meaning of the word Jerusalem is quite interesting. It is expressed from both the Greek *"Hierousalem"* and the Hebrew *"Yerushalayim"* to mean: "foundation of peace." In addition, the word "shalom" or "peace" comes from this word. Some who study the meaning of words have suggested that the first syllable, *"yeru,"* of the Hebrew spelling of Jerusalem, can mean either "to cast or throw" as in to cast peace (by God) or "wholeness" as in the "wholeness of peace." Both make sense because Jerusalem is the dwelling place of the Lord, as professed by God Himself:

1. Zechariah 8:3, "Thus saith the LORD; I am returned unto Zion, and will dwell in the midst of Jerusalem: and Jerusalem shall be called a city of truth; and the mountain of the

LORD of hosts the holy mountain."
2. Psalm 122:6, "Pray for the peace of Jerusalem: they shall prosper that love thee."

Jerusalem, the city that is compact together, began as a fort of David, which is a city contained within walls once known as the city of David. It is here that the thrones of judgment, the thrones of David, were contained. This is significant because in many places within the Bible, Jerusalem is set apart not only as the place of judgment from David but of the ultimate judgment of God:

1. Deuteronomy 17:8, "If there arise a matter too hard for thee in judgment, between blood and blood, between plea and plea, and between stroke and stroke, being matters of controversy within thy gates: then shalt thou arise, and get thee up into the place which the LORD thy God shall choose."
2. Second Chronicles 19:8, "Moreover in Jerusalem did Jehoshaphat set of Levites, and of the priests, and of the chief of the fathers of Israel, for the judgment of the LORD, and for controversies, when they returned to Jerusalem."
3. Luke 18:32, "Then he took unto him the twelve, and said unto them, Behold, we go up to Jerusalem, and all things that are written by the prophets concerning the Son of man shall be accomplished."

Jerusalem is the city by which the Lord has the final judgment. If a matter cannot be resolved satisfactorily by man, the Lord's judgment will come down on the issue in all matters.

1. Isaiah 2:3, "And many people shall go and say, Come ye, and let us go up to the mountain of the LORD, to the house of the God of Jacob; and he will teach us of his ways, and we will walk in his paths: for out of Zion shall go forth the law, and the word of the LORD from Jerusalem."

And thus, it is now, and thus it will be in the future. All matters of contention are adjudicated by the Lord as the final resolution.

> (And so terrible was the sight, that Moses said, I exceedingly fear and quake:) But ye are come unto mount Sion, and unto the city of the living God, the heavenly Jerusalem, and to an innumerable company of angels. To the general assembly and church of the firstborn, which are written in heaven, and to God the Judge of all, and to the spirits of just men made perfect.
>
> Hebrews 12:21–23

Throughout history, we can trace the judgment of the Lord through each and every final resolution, which puts a matter to rest—in both the small matters of our lives and of global matters. Make no mistake: everything has gone according to the will of God. At the end of the day, some judgments come swiftly, and some judgments take generations, eras, or eons. In fact, the final judgment of all things to come has been in the making since the dawn of time.

Revelation 16:5, "And I heard the angel of the waters say, Thou art righteous, O Lord, which art, and wast, and shalt be, because thou hast judged thus."

Biblically, not only is Jerusalem the city of peace, as its namesake suggests, but it is also the city in which God dwells and where the judgment of the Lord will be the final arbiter of justice in all matters, large and small, even unto the last days when a new Jerusalem will emerge according to New Testament accounts, particularly in Revelations:

> Him that overcometh will I make a pillar in the temple of my God, and he shall go no more out: and I will write upon him the name of my God, and the name of the city of my God, which is new Jerusalem, which cometh down out of heaven from my God: and I will write upon him my new name.
>
> Revelation 3:12

In that time, a new temple shall be made, and God, who will come down from heaven, shall dwell within this new Jerusalem, and He "shall go out no more." So, we can see that from very early on in the narrative of the Bible, the area of Jerusalem and the city itself has been and will be an important marker for the matters of the Holy Trinity of God.

And so it is, and so it shall be. I love You, Lord. You are amazing, O Lord, and our just judge for evermore. Amen!

Psalm 123: So Our Eyes Wait upon the Lord Our God

> Unto thee lift I up mine eyes, O thou that dwellest in the heavens. Behold, as the eyes of servants look unto the hand of their masters, and as the eyes of a maiden unto the hand of her mistress; so our eyes wait upon the LORD our God, until that he have mercy upon us. Have mercy upon us, O LORD, have mercy upon us: for we are exceedingly filled with contempt. Our soul is exceedingly filled with the scorning of those that are at ease, and with the contempt of the proud.

Verse 2, "Behold, as the eyes of servants look unto the hand of their masters, and as the eyes of a maiden unto the hand of her mistress; so our eyes wait upon the LORD our God, until that he has mercy upon us."

Psalm 123 is a reminder to not look elsewhere during difficult times or, indeed, anytime. Instead, have patience for the Lord to have mercy on you and your situation. In the meantime, keep your eyes fixed on the Lord.

Verse 4, "Our soul is exceedingly filled with the scorning of those that are at ease, and with the contempt of the proud."

It seems that this verse provides one of the ways our souls can express themselves in our difficult or trying times. We are prone to moving our attention toward those who are at ease and feeling scorn for their easy lives while we toil within our own lives. Perhaps we become filled with anxiety that others may have it easier than us, and a certain dread fills our minds. Or we look on, and perhaps judge, those we see as proud and begin to feel a certain contempt for them and their vanities.

Make no mistake, as Psalm 123 reminds us, these types of thoughts are merely distractions that take us out of our misery or hardship for the moment. We should try to avoid these states of the soul and move our attention back to the Lord.

Eventually, according to the will of God, your situation will end through the Lord's merciful intercession. As the great Saint Padre Pio said it best, "Seek the Lord: pray, hope, don't worry."

Patience brings understanding and humility. This is always one of the core values of those who walk with the Lord. We are to pray about our situation and give it up to the Lord where we gain hope in His mercy to see that the best outcome comes around, and in the meantime, we don't worry. Give it up to the Lord and let it go. This is the joyful path.

Worksheet: Give It to the Lord and Let It Go

Contemplate your life right now. Search your heart. Are there things going on that are causing you hardship or worry at the moment? List them here:

1. _____
2. _____
3. _____
4. _____
5. _____

What is your prayer for each of these worries? List them here:

1. _____
2. _____
3. _____
4. _____
5. _____

Now, make a plan on how you intend to let each one go to our Father and not worry about the outcome:

1. _____
2. _____
3. _____
4. _____
5. _____

Rest easy, and know that in His time, the Lord will have mercy on you and your situation. Keep your mind and heart on the hope this knowledge brings! Thank You, dear Father, for the wisdom contained in Psalm 123. We love You with all our hearts. Amen.

God loves you and is always working on your behalf to give you the best outcome that aligns with His will.

Psalm 124: Blessed Be the Lord, Who Hath Not Given Us as a Prey

If it had not been the LORD who was on our side, now may Israel say; If it had not been the LORD who was on our side, when men rose up against us: Then they had swallowed us up quick, when their wrath was kindled against us: Then the waters had overwhelmed us, the stream had gone over our soul: Then the proud waters had gone over our soul. Blessed be the LORD, who hath not given us as a prey to their teeth. Our soul is escaped as a bird out of the snare of the fowlers: the snare is broken, and we are escaped. Our help is in the name of the LORD, who made heaven and earth.

The Lord protects the souls of His children. In Psalm 124, David remarks what could have happened had the Lord not protected and saved Israel.

1. Men would have risen up against them and swallowed them quickly.
2. Their enemies' wrath would have been set on fire against them.
3. Their enemies' armies would be like waves of water that would have overwhelmed and drowned them.
4. The heat of the enemy's wrath and the overwhelming water would have produced hot steam, which would have harmed their soul.
5. Our souls would have been washed in the waters of the proud.

But because the Lord has protected him and his people (and protects us as well!), David makes these declarations in the end, "Our soul is escaped as a bird out of the snare of the fowlers: the snare is broken, and we are escaped. Our help is in the name of the LORD, who made heaven and earth" (verses 7–8).

In other words, the Lord will deliver His people from the snares and harm of those who hunt them. He has not and will not see His children become prey for the wicked. He will help them overcome adversity. One of the best things about our Father is that when He promises or even says something, it will come to fruition. Our Lord is that trustworthy and consistent. Amen

Worksheet: Times When We Were Delivered from Becoming Someone's Prey

There are going to be times in our lives when we may find ourselves on the receiving end of becoming prey to a person or company's deceptions or fraudulent behavior or even to someone with more evil and sinister intentions. Perhaps we are offered something too good to be true if we give financial information to someone or, even worse, we are targeted by someone who says they love us but who is a criminal using us for their gain. Whatever the situation, try to think of the times when you were preyed upon and could have had a much worse outcome, but in the end, you escaped with just a lesson (or even a hard lesson) learned.

_____

_____

_____

_____

_____

Now, imagine how your merciful Father in heaven protected you from falling fully victim to these evil intentions and situations. How did God protect you in the end and help you get out of the situation?

_____
_____
_____
_____
_____
_____
_____

Praise and glory are Thy name, O Most Holy Lord. The one who never changes!

Thank You for protecting us as we make our way down Your path.

Psalm 125: Do Good, O Lord, unto Those That Be Good

> They that trust in the LORD shall be as mount Zion, which cannot be removed, but abideth for ever. As the mountains are round about Jerusalem, so the LORD is round about his people from henceforth even for ever. For the rod of the wicked shall not rest upon the lot of the righteous; lest the righteous put forth their hands unto iniquity. Do good, O LORD, unto those that be good, and to them that are upright in their hearts. As for such as turn aside unto their crooked ways, the LORD shall lead them forth with the workers of iniquity: but peace shall be upon Israel.

The Lord will always protect the people who trust in Him and are righteous. Period. End of story. Psalm 125 is a simple reminder that those who trust in the Lord will not be forsaken by Him. God Himself will dwell around His people forever, and He will protect them against those who are wicked.

This reinforces the message that we found in Psalm 124 when we were shown how the Lord protected Israel and His people and how the outcomes of war could have been so much worse than they were. Psalm 125 discusses this concept further:

Verse 2, "As the mountains are round about Jerusalem, so the LORD is round about his people from henceforth even for ever."

In the end, we see once again that those who continue in their wicked and criminal ways will be led into the chaos of iniquity, but God shall lead His people into peace, "As for such as turn aside unto their crooked ways, the LORD shall lead them forth with the workers of iniquity: but peace shall be upon Israel" (verse 5).

He will always surround us with His help and protection. Always. Have faith. Thank You, Lord.

Psalm 126: They That Sow in Tears Shall Reap in Joy

> When the LORD turned again the captivity of Zion, we were like them that dream. Then was our mouth filled with laughter, and our tongue with singing: then said they among the heathen, The LORD hath done great things for them. The LORD hath done great things for us; whereof we are glad. Turn again our captivity, O LORD, as the streams in the south. They that sow in tears shall reap in joy. He that goeth forth and weepeth, bearing precious seed, shall doubtless come again with rejoicing, bringing his sheaves with him.

Psalm 126 is a reminder that God not only helps, consoles, and has mercy on those of His children who suffer, but when they come out of that season of suffering, He gives joyful reward and harvest to them.

Verse 6, "He that goeth forth and weepeth, bearing precious seed, shall doubtless come again with rejoicing, bringing his sheaves with him."

There are going to be times in our lives when we feel like we are captive to our circumstances. Imagine feeling like a prisoner in your own life during trying times and hardship. We all have them. There is suffering in life, and when we are there, it can feel like a lifetime of pain and helplessness. When we turn our thoughts to prayer and ask our Father to help us get through the tough times, or better yet, lean on God and trust Him to get us through them, eventually, there will be a break in the hardship. The day will come when it starts getting better.

Verse 1, "When the LORD turned again the captivity of Zion, we were like them in that dream."

In other words, when we are being freed from oppression and bondage (i.e., our suffering), it can feel like living in a dream. When the nightmare begins to shift into a dream, we may feel the shift, but somehow, it feels imagined. Eventually, the burden will lift, and "then was our mouth filled with laughter, and our tongue with singing" (verse 2).

As children of God, our faith in a season of hardship will always eventually lead to better and more joyful times, most of the time with some very good lessons learned.

Verse 5, "They that sow in tears shall reap in joy."

The Lord will raise His children from hardship to joy amid those who do not believe so that they will see what God has done for us. This is the way of God, not only to show those who do not believe how great and mighty He is but to encourage those who do not believe to put their trust in Him as well.

The Lord has brought us from tears to joy. Let us sing and give thanks!

Psalm 127: The Fruit of the Womb Is His Reward

> Except the LORD build the house, they labour in vain that build it: except the LORD keep the city, the watchman waketh but in vain. It is vain for you to rise up early, to sit up late, to eat the bread of sorrows: for so he giveth his beloved sleep. Lo, children are an heritage of the LORD: and the fruit of the womb is his reward. As arrows are in the hand of a mighty man; so are children of the youth. Happy is the man that hath his quiver full of them: they shall not be ashamed, but they shall speak with the enemies in the gate.

There are a few things of note happening in Psalm 127. Firstly, it is a reminder that when we do not include the Lord as a foundation for our lives, our homes, or even our cities and nations, then we are creating those things in vain.

Verse 1, "Except the LORD built the house, they labour in vain to build it: except the LORD keep the city, the watchman waketh but in vain."

One of the explanations of how this works is found in the Gospels when Jesus was talking to a great crowd during the Sermon on the Mount,

> Therefore whosoever heareth these sayings of mine, and doeth them, I will liken him unto a wise man, which built his house upon a rock: And the rain descended, and the floods came, and the winds blew, and beat upon that house; and it fell not: for it was founded upon a rock. And every one that heareth these sayings of mine, and doeth them not, shall be likened unto a foolish man, which built his house upon the sand: And the rain descended, and

the floods came, and the winds blew, and beat upon that house; and it fell: and great was the fall of it.

Matthew 7:24–27

It is the vanity of man who thinks his works alone are enough to keep his house or city healthy and in good working order, for it is only by the grace of God that all things exist. Without God, the house or city is built merely on sand, and eventually, it will crash down and perish. God sustains what man makes, and it is right and good to co-create with God as our partner.

When we lean on our Father in all things, not only are those things being built to stand the test of time, but as Psalm 127 reminds us, we will be given a reward. And what does this psalm show as the ultimate reward?

Verse 3, "Lo, children are an heritage of the LORD: and the fruit of the womb is his reward."

Generations and heritage are His reward and are frequently used as reward for having the Lord as the foundation of our lives, and the above verse of this psalm spells that out in no uncertain terms.

Here are a few more verses from early in the Bible that deliver this same message:

1. Genesis 33:5, "And he lifted up his eyes, and saw the women and the children …which God hath graciously given thy servant."
2. Genesis 48:4, "And said unto me, Behold, I will make thee fruitful, and multiply thee, and I will make of thee a multitude of people; and will give this land to thy seed after thee for an everlasting possession."
3. Joshua 24:3–4, "And I took your father Abraham from the other side of the flood, and led him throughout all the land of Canaan, and multiplied his seed, and gave him Isaac. And I gave unto Isaac Jacob and Esau: and I gave unto Esau mount Seir, to possess it; but Jacob and his children went down

into Egypt."

Right from the start, it is made clear that children and generations are one of the ultimate rewards for being a godly person or nation. Children are a reward from God for His faithful people. God can and will help His people multiply their populations as a reward. This can happen within a single family or a nation. Children are a blessing bestowed by God.*

At the same time, when a nation becomes barren, it is good to consider the spiritual health of the land. In modern times, there is talk of overpopulation and the need for population control. In many ways, this mindset is asking God to restrict His blessings on the world. For if God blesses His people with the reward of generations, what are we asking when we seek to limit the numbers in our generation? It's something to think about, at least.

Thank You, Lord, for blessing us with rewards for our faithfulness to and trust in You. Amen.

*(Note: Although God can create the miracle of birth for women who cannot bear children, this is not always His will for all families for a variety of reasons. If this is where you find yourself now, please pray for discernment and clarity for your specific situation.)

Psalm 128: Blessed Is Every One That Feareth the Lord

Blessed is every one that feareth the LORD; that walketh in his ways. For thou shalt eat the labour of thine hands: happy shalt thou be, and it shall be well with thee. Thy wife shall be as a fruitful vine by the sides of thine house: thy children like olive plants round about thy table. Behold, that thus shall the man be blessed that feareth the LORD. The LORD shall bless thee out of Zion: and thou shalt see the good of Jerusalem all the days of thy life. Yea, thou shalt see thy children's children, and peace upon Israel.

Psalm 128 advises us that when we have a reverential fear or piety for the Lord, and we walk in His ways, which are righteous, we will have the following:

1. Our work will keep us fed.
2. We will be happy.
3. We will be well.
4. We will have a productive household.
5. We will have children who will be fruitful.
6. We will be blessed.
7. All the days of our lives we will see the goodness of God's ways.
8. We will live to see generations of family.
9. We will see peace upon God's people.

In the Bible, it is important to remember that although Israel is a particular place on Earth, it is also a symbol for God's chosen people. In fact, Jacob, who was the grandson of Abraham, was renamed by God Himself to Israel, which means "one who struggles with God" or "God contends." And, in many ways, that makes anyone who contends with God a kind of Israel.

Throughout the Bible, Israel is used in many different ways and applies to different circumstances.

Study: God's Purpose for Israel Was Multifaceted

- To be a holy people, living according to His instructions.
- To serve as a witness to other nations, demonstrating God's character and faithfulness.
- To receive the Word of God and the promise of the Messiah.
- To exemplify how God works through imperfect people to accomplish His divine plan.

Keeping this in mind, Psalm 128 lets us know that "everyone that feareth the Lord" is blessed, and perhaps we, too, share in being a symbol of Israel in the eyes of God. In the end, when we walk in God's ways, we, too, will see peace be upon us during our lifetimes.

God is good to all His children. Thanks, and praised be Thy name, O holy and Most High! Amen!

Psalm 129: Many a Time Have They Afflicted Me from My Youth

> Many a time have they afflicted me from my youth, may Israel now say: Many a time have they afflicted me from my youth: yet they have not prevailed against me. The plowers plowed upon my back: they made long their furrows. The LORD is righteous: he hath cut asunder the cords of the wicked. Let them all be confounded and turned back that hate Zion. Let them be as the grass upon the housetops, which withereth afore it groweth up: Wherewith the mower filleth not his hand; nor he that bindeth sheaves his bosom. Neither do they which go by say, The blessing of the LORD be upon you: we bless you in the name of the LORD.

Once again, we are reminded in Psalm 129 that the Lord will protect the righteous. He will save His children from the wicked, and His people will always prevail against their enemies. By the end of this psalm, we understand that not only do the righteous prevail, but that the wicked and those who hate the principality of Zion will be rewarded with confusion, restrained growth, and lack of abundance and will not be blessed by God.

Throughout the length of our lives, we will be afflicted by the enemies of God. The world would want us to think that we are not in spiritual exchange in this life and that all is mere physical reality. This is the furthest from the truth. Many times, we will be afflicted by those who come against Israel and Zion; in other words, God's spiritual people and His dwelling places on Earth. But as this psalm states, "Many a time have they afflicted me from my youth: yet they have not prevailed against me" (verse 2).

Even from our youth, there will be those who will come for us both physically and spiritually. When we think about our spiritual development as a person, we can see that during various times in our lives—even in our youth—we have had to endure periods when we were being attacked for seemingly odd or irrelevant things: our looks, our job, the house we live in, our religious practice, etc. Sometimes, these attacks have been out of nowhere and vicious, and sometimes, they have been from the people we love and trust the most.

When we begin to consider these attacks in terms of spiritual development, we can see more clearly how the attacks affected us on a physical level, but even more so how we were affected in our spiritual and mental being. Perhaps we even decided to turn away from God as a result of one of these afflictions.

However, if we can manage to have patience and put our trust in God to see us through the trying times, we can also trace how our good Father protected us from the full brunt of the affliction and eventually brought us back to a place of peace. Afterall, He is our refuge and our protector.

Worksheet: Affliction

Affliction (noun): "Something that causes us pain and suffering."

Consider those times when you have been caused pain and suffering through an attack for whatever reason and how it affected you physically, mentally, and spiritually:

_____

_____

_____

_____

_____

Now, consider how you think God protected you from what could have been a far more devastating outcome:

_____

_____

_____

_____

_____

_____

What were some of the positive developments that came after the attack(s) that led you to a better place (spiritually, mentally, and physically) in life?

_____

_____

_____

_____

_____

_____

Dear Lord, although we are not immune to pain and suffering in this lifetime, I would like to thank You for using these difficult periods to show us Your kindness and mercy by turning all things that are meant for evil into good.

I glorify Your goodness for helping me in times of affliction. Love, Your faithful servant. Amen.

Psalm 130: If Thou, Lord, Shouldest Mark Iniquities, O Lord, Who Shall Stand?

> Out of the depths have I cried unto thee, O LORD. Lord, hear my voice: let thine ears be attentive to the voice of my supplications. If thou, LORD, shouldest mark iniquities, O Lord, who shall stand? But there is forgiveness with thee, that thou mayest be feared. I wait for the LORD, my soul doth wait, and in his word do I hope. My soul waiteth for the Lord more than they that watch for the morning: I say, more than they that watch for the morning. Let Israel hope in the LORD: for with the LORD there is mercy, and with him is plenteous redemption. And he shall redeem Israel from all his iniquities.

Psalm 130 is the prayer of someone who is feeling the pain of sin in the very depths of his soul.

Verse 1, "Out of the depths have I cried unto thee, O Lord."

There are going to be many times during our journey with God that we are going to feel unworthy of His love and forgiveness. Perhaps we are going through a confusing time in life and we imagine that every action we make is desperately wrong. Our sin and unworthiness are causing us to make horrible decisions, we think. We assume that it must be because we have offended God somewhere in our past or even in the present time that He is allowing us to fumble our lives. So, we beg God to hear us, "Lord, hear my voice: let thine ears be attentive to the voice of my supplications" (verse 2).

We become distressed in the humility of knowing that our lives, when we really think about them, have been littered with ungodly behavior, and there have been many times when we've forsaken God to pursue those things outside of His will. This is a perfectly normal thought to have. We know ourselves, and we know what we have done. We also know that we need God to help us, and feeling like we are out of the depths of our own lives causes us great pain and sorrow.

So, what does the author of Psalm 130 do? Verses 3 and 4 gives us the answer, "If thou, LORD, shouldest mark iniquities, O Lord, who shall stand? But there is forgiveness with thee, that thou mayest be feared."

In other words, the author remembers two very important things:

1. If God marked every sin of man as a reason to strike him down, then there would be no one left standing.
    a. God is merciful.
2. In His mercy, God gives forgiveness so that we may cultivate reverential fear of Him.
    a. God is forgiving.

In the end, there is hope. In many ways, the exercise of going through a soul wrenching season of feeling unworthy and desperate leads us to the realization, once again, that our God is merciful and forgiving.

Verse 5, "I wait for the LORD, my soul doth wait, and in his word do I hope."

He will help us out of our time of trouble, and we will be left with an even greater reverence for the goodness of our Father. We just need to wait it out.

"Let Israel hope in the LORD: for with the LORD there is mercy, and with him is plenteous redemption" (verse 7).

Psalm 131: Lord, My Heart Is Not Haughty, Nor My Eyes Lofty

> LORD, my heart is not haughty, nor mine eyes lofty: neither do I exercise myself in great matters, or in things too high for me. Surely I have behaved and quieted myself, as a child that is weaned of his mother: my soul is even as a weaned child. Let Israel hope in the LORD from henceforth and for ever.

In this world, there are those who imagine that their ways and pursuits are God-like. In their haughty and arrogant manner, they put themselves in the place of God and imagine that their ways are the best and greatest. At times, they even force others to comply with their worldview, where they are the most high and most knowledgeable leaders. In other words, they "exercise [themselves] in great matters, in and things that are too high for [them]" (verse 1).

But Psalm 131 reminds us not to do this.

Verse 2, "Surely I have behaved and quieted myself, as a child that is weaned of his mother; my soul is even as a weaned child."

In the realm of God, we are but children still young enough to be just weaned from the mother. The Lord is our Father; He will provide for us sustenance, and He will teach us. His role is Father, and we are His children. Imagine how ridiculous it would be for an infant who is just being weaned from their mother to think that their ways are sufficient to rule the world above the Father. Should the world be forced to comply with the desire of an infant? No one would take that seriously, and for good reason. Psalm 131 reminds us that our natural position or state as people is as a child and God as Father and all that entails.

The wise person leans into God for counsel and direction and finds hope in the Lord.

Verse 3, "Let Israel hope in the LORD from henceforth and for ever."

In other words, *trust* in the Lord and follow His ways. This is where our hope is now and evermore.

Thank You, Father, for guiding us as Your children so that we may enjoy a life filled with hope and all good things. Amen.

Psalm 132: Lord, Remember David, and All His Afflictions

LORD, remember David, and all his afflictions: How he sware unto the LORD, and vowed unto the mighty God of Jacob; Surely I will not come into the tabernacle of my house, nor go up into my bed; I will not give sleep to mine eyes, or slumber to mine eyelids, Until I find out a place for the LORD, an habitation for the mighty God of Jacob. Lo, we heard of it at Ephratah: we found it in the fields of the wood. We will go into his tabernacles: we will worship at his footstool. Arise, O LORD, into thy rest; thou, and the ark of thy strength. Let thy priests be clothed with righteousness; and let thy saints shout for joy. For thy servant David's sake turn not away the face of thine anointed. The LORD hath sworn in truth unto David; he will not turn from it; Of the fruit of thy body will I set upon thy throne. If thy children will keep my covenant and my testimony that I shall teach them, their children shall also sit upon thy throne for evermore. For the LORD hath chosen Zion; he hath desired it for his habitation. This is my rest for ever: here will I dwell; for I have desired it. I will abundantly bless her provision: I will satisfy her poor with bread. I will also clothe her priests with salvation: and her saints shall shout aloud for joy. There will I make the horn of David to bud: I have ordained a lamp for mine anointed. His enemies will I clothe with shame: but upon himself shall his crown flourish.

Psalm 132 reads as someone who is reminding God that David suffered afflictions for and made vows to Him so that one day he would find a holy habitation for the Lord. Very often within the Psalms the narrative goes back into the history of God's people to show that the current situation is a continuation of a situation that began years ago. In Psalm 132:6, we are reminded, "Lo, we heard of it at Ephratah: we found it in the fields of the wood."

Ephratah, which is either another name for Bethlehem itself or the district in which Bethlehem resides, is the place where David spent his youth and where he heard much about the ark of the covenant, although he never saw it till he found it long afterward at Kirjathjearim, which was also known as the city of the wood or the forest-town. In other words, Psalm 132 reminds us that David made good on his vow to God to bring His holy dwelling place into a habitation in the city of David (aka Jerusalem, aka Zion.)

Verses 13–14, "For the LORD hath chosen Zion; he hath desired it for his habitation. This is my rest for ever: here will I dwell; for I have desired it."

If the Lord desires something, you can be 100 percent sure that that thing will happen. For the all-powerful Father needs only to desire something, and it will happen.

Not only that, but God promised that if the children of God keep their covenant with Him and proclaim the testimony of His history, the line of David will sit upon the throne, "The LORD hath sworn in truth unto David; he will not turn from it; Of the fruit of thy body will I set upon thy throne" (verse 11).

You see, the Lord remembered the affliction of David and how David brought the throne of God to the holy temple. Our Lord is a Lord that remembers. He dwells among us and experiences our afflictions with us. When we can remain in covenant with Him, and when we praise Him in the congregation, we bring forth the fruits of His promises, and He will "abundantly bless her provision" (verse 15).

God has promised that His chosen people will never be eradicated from Earth for all time. And so it has been, and so it shall be. And these are some of the provisions that Psalm 132 indicates that the Lord will provide His people:

1. Bread for the poor.
2. He will clothe the priests with salvation.
3. His saints shall shout aloud for joy.
4. The horn of David shall bud.
   a. Horn of David is another name for the Messiah.
5. An ordained lamp will be available for His anointed.
6. His enemies will be clothed in shame.
7. But on those who are faithful, their crown will flourish.

In the end, everytime, it comes down to this: the enemies of God will be shamed and the faithful will flourish. This is not a vain promise. It is the truth and it will bear out for eternity.

Thank You, Lord. You are our provider and King! May we flourish in the light of Your anointing for now and evermore. Amen.

Psalm 133: It Is Good to Dwell Together in Brotherly Unity

> Behold, how good and how pleasant it is for brethren to dwell together in unity! It is like the precious ointment upon the head, that ran down upon the beard, even Aaron's beard: that went down to the skirts of his garments; As the dew of Hermon, and as the dew that descended upon the mountains of Zion: for there the LORD commanded the blessing, even life for evermore.

When we live together in brotherly love and unity and not in division, the Lord will command His blessing on those who are unified in loving kindness. Psalm 133 explains that living in brotherly love is like a precious ointment that blesses and gives peace to those who participate.

In other words, it could be said that unity and peaceful co-existence among brethren is a blessing from God. It is a grace given to those who participate. This suggests that this type of living is not natural to man and that in order to live in unity, we must be set aside by God from the true ways of the world, which are beastly and chaotic.

It is true that in society, we see many unified groups of like-minded souls. People who come together for a common cause. But how many of these groups continue to function entirely in brotherly love? It is something to think about. Anyone who has been part of a group has most likely seen division within the group regarding one issue or another. And, even worse, there are those divisions within groups that begin to sow the seeds of their ultimate destruction. Perhaps there are leaders and their followers who fight to come out on top. Maybe they begin using underhanded and fraudulent methods to defeat their opponents. Some groups even resort to criminality once the divisions take over.

Whatever way the divisions pop up within groups (and even within nations), we can see that full brotherly love and unity within groups of people is difficult at best and, at worst, impossible over time.

Occasionally, however, we encounter true unity and brotherly love within a group. Though it is rare, when we are introduced to these groups, we cannot help but see that the way of the group is pleasant and peaceful. The people tend to be humble and kind. It is always a joy to encounter these types of groups, for they are filled with hope and expansive potential. And this is no coincidence. Like Psalm 133 points out, when we find a way to live in true unity with one another, "As the dew of Hermon, and as the dew that descended upon the mountains of Zion: for there the LORD commanded the blessing, even life for evermore" (verse 3).

In other words, the Lord Himself commands His blessing on us—even forevermore. You see, to live in peaceful brotherly unity in this life is a blessing from on high and an indication of what life everlasting in heaven will be like. And like every other way of God, once achieved, it builds upon itself and continues to mount higher and become easier. To dwell in brotherly unity is a way of the saint and our ultimately blessed earthly existence.

Thank You, Lord. We pray that we shall find the courage to live in true unity and to continue to dwell in brotherly love while we walk together in this life and beyond. Amen.

Notes:

_____

_____

_____

_____

Psalm 134: Behold, Bless Ye the Lord, All Ye Servants of the Lord

> Behold, bless ye the LORD, all ye servants of the LORD, which by night stand in the house of the LORD. Lift up your hands in the sanctuary, and bless the LORD. The LORD that made heaven and earth bless thee out of Zion.

Bless ye the Lord. Psalm 134 is asking the servants of the Lord to bless His name in the holy places. When we are asked to praise the Lord, we understand that it means to vocally give glory and praise and thanks to the Lord for His mercy and generosity and loving kindness. However, when we are asked to bless the Lord, we are being asked to testify to the greatness of the Lord. By blessing the Lord, we proclaim that the Lord is Most High and seated above all else.

In this way, the word "bless" is very much like the word "esteem." To esteem means to respect and give admiration. But further still, as servants of the Lord, we know that all blessing comes from the Lord. As His children, we cannot possibly bless the one who blesses. Can a person bless anyone, yet alone the Lord? No, for God is the Lord and the arbiter of all blessings. God *is* blessings in much the same way that God is love.

So, in essence, when we are asked to bless the Lord, we are being asked to ask the Lord to bless Himself. We are bringing down the blessing of God and delivering it back to Him. This is a sign of our knowledge and understanding that we serve the one who, in actuality, truly deserves all blessing. Consider the child who asks his father to give him money. The father hands the child what was asked for, and then the child, in all humility, hands the money right back to the father. This is done as an act of honor to the father, for the child knows that without the father, there would be no money.

To bless the Lord is to give back all the blessings that we have been given in a show of deferment to the one who truly deserves all blessing. It is an act of true humility. It is right and good to "lift up your hands in the sanctuary, and bless the LORD" (verse 2).

Thanks and praise and blessing to You, Lord and master of all. Amen.

Notes:

Psalm 135: For the Lord Will Judge His People, and He Will Repent Himself Concerning His Servants

Praise ye the LORD. Praise ye the name of the LORD; praise him, O ye servants of the LORD. Ye that stand in the house of the LORD, in the courts of the house of our God, Praise the LORD; for the LORD is good: sing praises unto his name; for it is pleasant. For the LORD hath chosen Jacob unto himself, and Israel for his peculiar treasure. For I know that the LORD is great, and that our Lord is above all gods. Whatsoever the LORD pleased, that did he in heaven, and in earth, in the seas, and all deep places. He causeth the vapours to ascend from the ends of the earth; he maketh lightnings for the rain; he bringeth the wind out of his treasuries. Who smote the firstborn of Egypt, both of man and beast. Who sent tokens and wonders into the midst of thee, O Egypt, upon Pharaoh, and upon all his servants. Who smote great nations, and slew mighty kings; Sihon king of the Amorites, and Og king of Bashan, and all the kingdoms of Canaan: And gave their land for an heritage, an heritage unto Israel his people. Thy name, O LORD, endureth for ever; and thy memorial, O LORD, throughout all generations. For the LORD will judge his people, and he will repent himself concerning his servants. The idols of the heathen are silver and gold, the work of men's hands. They have mouths, but they speak not; eyes have they, but they see not; They have ears, but they hear not; neither is there any breath in their mouths. They that make them are like unto them: so is every one that trusteth in them. Bless the LORD,

> O house of Israel: bless the LORD, O house of Aaron: Bless the LORD, O house of Levi: ye that fear the LORD, bless the LORD. Blessed be the LORD out of Zion, which dwelleth at Jerusalem. Praise ye the LORD.

Verse 14, "For the LORD will judge his people, and he will repent himself concerning his servants."

In Psalm 135, it is acknowledged that the Lord will judge His people, but He can and does repent concerning His servants. In other words, He will judge His children and, at times, deliver His wrath; at other times, He will change His mind or repent concerning His wrath against them. This is another reminder that although the Father is all-powerful, He is also a loving Father, as well as a just judge.

There are times when He judges and delivers punishment for the offenses and crimes of men. Consider verse 10 from this psalm: the Lord "smote great nations, and slew mighty kings." In His wrath, the Lord brought down great nations and killed mighty kings. Not one nation nor king is great enough to be able to forgo the wrath of God. If God wants it so, it will happen. It is folly for us to think that we can use words, actions, or magic to bypass the wrath of God if His judgment has come down on the side of chastisement. And it can be even worse for those who hate God and live in iniquity,

> Thou shalt not bow down thyself to them, nor serve them: for I the LORD thy God am a jealous God, visiting the iniquity of the fathers upon the children unto the third and fourth generation of them that hate me.
>
> Exodus 20:5

God can and will bring down the hammer of His wrath hard on those who hate Him. That's the scary God that everyone is afraid of, and that seems to live in the back of the minds of those who do not know Him well.

However, now take, for instance, Zechariah 8:14–15,

> For thus saith the LORD of hosts; As I thought to punish you, when your fathers provoked me to wrath, saith the LORD of hosts, and I repented not: So again have I thought in these days to do well unto Jerusalem and to the house of Judah; fear ye not.

When it comes to His children, however, we can see in Zechariah that the Lord was provoked by the fathers and delivered His wrath and repented not. However, later on, "so again have I thought" (or in other words "re-thought") His wrath against His servants (aka His chosen people) who were now the sons of the fathers. This time, He thought "to do well unto Jerusalem." In other words, to the sons of the fathers of His wrath, the Lord has now thought to bless them. The Lord changed His wrath into blessings in the span of a generation and did well for the children.

There are times of wrath and times when God re-thinks His wrath and delivers mercy and blessings upon His children in faith.

It is wise for us to remember this as we move forward on our path with God. We should not fear chastisement but persevere, have patience, and stay on path, for there will come a time when our chastisement turns into blessing for those who serve Him. Fear not. Bless and praise His holy name during each season.

Verses 19–21,

> Bless the LORD, O house of Israel: bless the LORD, O house of Aaron: Bless the LORD, O house of Levi: ye that fear the LORD, bless the LORD. Blessed be the LORD out of Zion, which dwelleth at Jerusalem. Praise ye the LORD.

It is good to be reminded that our seasons of chastisement will eventually give way to our season of blessing. In Your holy name. Amen.

Psalm 136: For His Mercy Endureth Forever

O give thanks unto the LORD; for he is good: for his mercy endureth for ever. O give thanks unto the God of gods: for his mercy endureth for ever. O give thanks to the Lord of lords: for his mercy endureth for ever. To him who alone doeth great wonders: for his mercy endureth for ever. To him that by wisdom made the heavens: for his mercy endureth for ever. To him that stretched out the earth above the waters: for his mercy endureth for ever. To him that made great lights: for his mercy endureth for ever: The sun to rule by day: for his mercy endureth for ever: The moon and stars to rule by night: for his mercy endureth for ever. To him that smote Egypt in their firstborn: for his mercy endureth for ever: And brought out Israel from among them: for his mercy endureth for ever: With a strong hand, and with a stretched out arm: for his mercy endureth for ever. To him which divided the Red sea into parts: for his mercy endureth for ever: And made Israel to pass through the midst of it: for his mercy endureth for ever: But overthrew Pharaoh and his host in the Red sea: for his mercy endureth for ever. To him which led his people through the wilderness: for his mercy endureth for ever. To him which smote great kings: for his mercy endureth for ever: And slew famous kings: for his mercy endureth for ever: Sihon king of the Amorites: for his mercy endureth for ever: And Og the king of Bashan: for his mercy endureth for ever: And gave their land for an heritage: for his mercy endureth for ever: Even an heritage unto Israel his servant: for his mercy endureth for ever. Who remembered us in our low estate:

for his mercy endureth for ever: And hath redeemed us from our enemies: for his mercy endureth for ever. Who giveth food to all flesh: for his mercy endureth for ever. O give thanks unto the God of heaven: for his mercy endureth for ever.

Verse 1, "O give thanks unto the LORD; for he is good: for his mercy endureth for ever."

Psalm 136 is a litany of some of the times that God was merciful. It is interesting that this psalm begins with God as the creator and doer of wondrous things as a hat tip toward His merciful ways:

1. For Him alone does great wonders.
2. By wisdom, He made the heavens.
3. He stretched out the earth above the waters.
4. He made great lights.
5. He made the sun to rule the day.
6. He made the moon and stars to rule the night.

To have mercy implies that there is someone who is the benefactor of the mercy, but in Psalm 136, we see part of God's mercy is shown in the fact that He created the stars and the heavens. Could this psalm be recognizing that our all-merciful God created everything we see as an act of mercy toward us, His children?

In His infinite wisdom, God knew that we would need a place where we could ultimately be redeemed. He knew about the fall of man and what that would mean, and He created all we see as a mercy for man, as a place for us to get back on path and to end up in heaven with Him. You see, man was created for God to keep Him company and to glorify Him. Psalm 136 seems to imply that because He loves us so much, even from the beginning, He had mercy on us and gave us everything we would need so that we could find our way back to Him and away from our fallen nature. Ultimately, creation was God's plan to spend eternity with us, His beloved children.

He also shows us mercies while we walk the earth to let us know

He is merciful and to give us an idea of what that mercy looks like. In fact, the Bible itself could be seen as an epic story about how God loves us so much that even when we offend Him in our fallen nature, He will still be merciful.

Psalm 136 continues by discussing some of His more famous displays of mercy upon His chosen people:

1. He had mercy for His chosen people on the firstborn in Egypt.
2. He brought out Israel from among the Egyptians with a strong hand and stretched out arm.
3. He divided the Red Sea and made Israel pass through the midst of it.
4. He overthrew the Pharaoh and his army in the Red Sea.
5. He led His people through the wilderness.
6. He smote great kings, and He smote famous kings, including Sihon, king of the Amorites and Og, the Bashan king.
7. He gave a heritage to Israel, His servant.
8. He remembered Israel in her low estate.
9. He redeemed Israel from their enemies.
10. He gives food for all flesh.

The Lord, in His mercy, will provide for, protect, raise up, and defend His chosen people. Like it was in the ancient times, it is now. The ways of the Lord never change. He was, is, and forever will be merciful to His children.

Worksheet: God's Mercy in My Life

Think about your own life. What are some of the ways that God has shown mercy toward you and your family? If you can, try to come up with ten examples:

1. _____
2. _____
3. _____
4. _____
5. _____
6. _____
7. _____
8. _____
9. _____
10. _____

Thank You, O Lord, for Your continued mercy and grace in my life, the life of my loved ones, and in my country, and in our world. You are the eternal God of mercy. Amen.

The list of God's mercy in my life would look like this:

1. He dug me out of the pit my living put me in.
2. He restored my soul to be one of His children.
3. He forgave my sins.
4. By His grace and mercy, He sent two wonderful children for me to raise.
5. He provides food and shelter for my family.
6. He comforts us on our low days.
7. He is our joy on our high days.
8. He helped me clear out those who were enemies in my life.
9. He has sent good people into my life or returned the good

ones back to me.
10. He loves me despite my deficiency of goodness.
11. He is helping me to remain and grow in sanctity despite my sometimes lack of diligence.

(Definition of diligence: careful or persistent work or effort.)

12. Without God's mercy, I would be hopeless and in a low place, but His mercy raised me up. Thank You, my loving, merciful Father, my hope and joy.

Notes:

_____
_____
_____
_____
_____
_____
_____
_____
_____
_____
_____
_____
_____
_____
_____
_____

Psalm 137: By the Rivers of Babylon, There We Sat Down

By the rivers of Babylon, there we sat down, yea, we wept, when we remembered Zion. We hanged our harps upon the willows in the midst thereof. For there they that carried us away captive required of us a song; and they that wasted us required of us mirth, saying, Sing us one of the songs of Zion. How shall we sing the LORD'S song in a strange land? If I forget thee, O Jerusalem, let my right hand forget her cunning. If I do not remember thee, let my tongue cleave to the roof of my mouth; if I prefer not Jerusalem above my chief joy. Remember, O LORD, the children of Edom in the day of Jerusalem; who said, Rase it, rase it, even to the foundation thereof. O daughter of Babylon, who art to be destroyed; happy shall he be, that rewardeth thee as thou hast served us. Happy shall he be, that taketh and dasheth thy little ones against the stones.

Psalm 137 paints a chaotic picture of the chosen people of God being forced to sit on the banks of hell by the people of Babylon. While sitting there, in their torment, Israel laments that they do not forget the joy of Zion and her songs. In other words, the people of God implore God to help them keep His ways and the joy they bring in the midst of the terror they are now experiencing. However, in verse 3,

> For there that they carried us away captive required of us a song; and they that wasted us required of us mirth, saying, Sing us one of the songs of Zion. How shall we sing the LORD'S song in a strange land?

Babylon required that the sons and daughters of God who were being held captive in Babylon be merry and sing the songs of Zion. But how is it possible to sing the Lord's songs in the midst of what could be potentially hell? As Zion is the place where the Lord dwells among His people, so too is Babylon, where Satan dwells among his people. Is Babylon asking for songs to mock them? Furthermore, "If I forget thee, O Jerusalem, let my right hand forget her cunning. If I do not remember thee, let my tongue cleave to the roof of my mouth; if I prefer not Jerusalem above my chief joy" (verses 5–6).

One way that verses 5 and 6 can be interpreted is that the narrator is asking God to keep him from remembering Jerusalem so that he may not mock and ridicule it if he finds himself preferring the joys of the world (Babylon) over God's kingdom (heaven, Jerusalem). The ways of Babylon are insidious in this world and offer temptations that are hard to pass up.

But there is no just reward for the people of Babylon, "O daughter of Babylon, who art to be destroyed; happy shall he be, that rewardeth thee as thou hast served us. Happy shall he be, that taketh and dasheth thy little ones against the stones" (verses 8–9).

The kingdom of Babylon will be destroyed. These verses suggest that the people of God shall be happy to see the enemy's destruction and the annihilation of Babylon's children, which could easily be seen as the end of Babylon and the generations of her children. Babylon stops at her destruction, and God's people will witness it and be happy.

Study: Brief Biblical History of Babylon

Babylon was an ancient city in Mesopotamia that symbolized rebellion against God. It was founded by King Nimrod, who built the Tower of Babel to challenge God's authority.

> And Cush [grandson of Noah] begat Nimrod: he began to be a mighty one in the earth. He was a mighty hunter before the LORD: wherefore it is said, Even as Nimrod

the mighty hunter before the LORD. And the beginning of his kingdom was Babel, and Erech, and Accad, and Calneh, in the land of Shinar.

Genesis 10:8–10

Babel became the place where Babylon was established as a mighty city. The name of Babylon first appears in the Bible when the king of Assyria exiled the people of Israel and replaced them with Babylonians and other nations. Babylon later became a powerful empire that conquered Judah and destroyed Jerusalem and its temple.

Babylon is also a symbol of the way of the world's system and those who reject God's rule and His ways. Just as Zion symbolizes God's kingdom, Babylon symbolizes the enemy of God's kingdom.

Notes:

Psalm 138: The Lord Will Perfect That Which Concerneth Me

> I will praise thee with my whole heart: before the gods will I sing praise unto thee. I will worship toward thy holy temple, and praise thy name for thy lovingkindness and for thy truth: for thou hast magnified thy word above all thy name. In the day when I cried thou answeredst me, and strengthenedst me with strength in my soul. All the kings of the earth shall praise thee, O LORD, when they hear the words of thy mouth. Yea, they shall sing in the ways of the LORD: for great is the glory of the LORD. Though the LORD be high, yet hath he respect unto the lowly: but the proud he knoweth afar off. Though I walk in the midst of trouble, thou wilt revive me: thou shalt stretch forth thine hand against the wrath of mine enemies, and thy right hand shall save me. The LORD will perfect that which concerneth me: thy mercy, O LORD, endureth for ever: forsake not the works of thine own hands.

Psalm 138 is a song of praise from David to the Lord. He sings, "I will praise thee with my whole heart: before the gods will I sing praise unto thee" (verse 1). As the psalm continues, we are given a list of the reasons that David finds to "praise Thy name," and they include:

1. God's lovingkindness.
2. God's truth.
3. For answering him when he cried.
4. For strengthening his soul.
5. For the great glory of God.
6. For His respect of the lowly though the Lord be the Most High.

        a. God respects all of His children regardless of their rank in society.
    7. For not being close to the proud.
        a. On the other hand, a person who is proud and arrogant causes God to be distant.
    8. For reviving him when he was in the midst of trouble.
    9. For protecting him from the wrath of his enemies.
    10. For saving him with His right hand.
        a. David recognizes that it is the Lord who saves him and not his own hand.
    11. For perfecting those things that concern him.
        a. God perfects all our plans.
    12. For God's mercy.

In all things, David is recognizing that the Lord will be merciful, protective, and will perfect the plans of His children, whom He has created with His own hands. In the end, David implores the Lord to never take the works of His hands away from us!

Verse 8, "O LORD, endureth for ever: forsake not the works of thine own hands."

Once again, we see that David is being used as the archetype of all the children of God. Whatever David is praising the Lord for is available to all of us who have trust and hope in the Lord and who repent and follow His ways. We are all equal in God's eyes.

However, if we find ourselves filled with pride and imagine, in our arrogance, that we can do all things for ourselves and don't need God, then He will distance Himself from us. When God creates distance or forsakes us, we lose access to all the ways of God that David lists in this psalm, including His mercy, protection, and perfecting our lives.

Don't allow a false sense of superiority to cause you to lose the awesome power of God. Simply call on Him in all ways and *trust* Him with your life. It will be the best decision you ever make.

Our lives can and will be a much better version when we let God move us and we follow His plans.

Psalm 139: O Lord, Thou Hast Searched Me, and Known Me

O LORD, thou hast searched me, and known me. Thou knowest my downsitting and mine uprising, thou understandest my thought afar off. Thou compassest my path and my lying down, and art acquainted with all my ways. For there is not a word in my tongue, but, lo, O LORD, thou knowest it altogether. Thou hast beset me behind and before, and laid thine hand upon me. Such knowledge is too wonderful for me; it is high, I cannot attain unto it. Whither shall I go from thy spirit? or whither shall I flee from thy presence? If I ascend up into heaven, thou art there: if I make my bed in hell, behold, thou art there. If I take the wings of the morning, and dwell in the uttermost parts of the sea; Even there shall thy hand lead me, and thy right hand shall hold me. If I say, Surely the darkness shall cover me; even the night shall be light about me. Yea, the darkness hideth not from thee; but the night shineth as the day: the darkness and the light are both alike to thee. For thou hast possessed my reins: thou hast covered me in my mother's womb. I will praise thee; for I am fearfully and wonderfully made: marvellous are thy works; and that my soul knoweth right well. My substance was not hid from thee, when I was made in secret, and curiously wrought in the lowest parts of the earth. Thine eyes did see my substance, yet being unperfect; and in thy book all my members were written, which in continuance were fashioned, when as yet there was none of them. How precious also are thy thoughts unto me, O God! how great is the sum of them! If I should count them, they are more in number than the sand: when I awake, I am still with thee. Surely thou wilt slay the wicked, O

God: depart from me therefore, ye bloody men. For they speak against thee wickedly, and thine enemies take thy name in vain. Do not I hate them, O LORD, that hate thee? and am not I grieved with those that rise up against thee? I hate them with perfect hatred: I count them mine enemies. Search me, O God, and know my heart: try me, and know my thoughts: And see if there be any wicked way in me, and lead me in the way everlasting.

Psalm 139 is about how closely the Lord knows each one of His creatures and it is filled with deep wisdom and understanding. Even David acknowledges that what he is describing is beyond his own imagination to fully explain, "Such knowledge is too wonderful for me; it is high, I cannot attain unto it" (verse 6).

In modern vernacular, David is saying that knowing the true complexity and depth of knowledge of how God is intricately woven into our lives is above his pay grade. Even he cannot attain it fully. But this does not stop David from trying to convey this thought to those who willingly listen to it—which it is suggested that you do.

In the end, David implores God to search him, for he knows that our loving Father knows everything good in us and those things that are contrary to the ways of God.

Verse 23–24, "Search me, O God, and know my heart: try me, and know my thoughts: And see if there be any wicked way in me, and lead me in the way everlasting."

David wants God to know his true heart. He asks the Father to challenge and try him so that any evil in him can come to the surface so that God may continue to lead him in the ways of everlasting life.

It is so comforting and a source of inner strength for the children of God to know that our loving Father is with us at all times. For those who oppose the Lord and are His enemies? They may not feel the same way, but it is still a reality they will have to contend with.

Below, is a list of the ways David expresses how God searches us and knows us so that we, too, may possess this knowledge and, perhaps in our free time, contemplate it throughout our lives. It is praiseworthy knowledge to attain.

Study: How Does the Lord Search and Know Us?

1. He surrounds us at all times, as we are awake and when we rest.
2. He is acquainted with all our ways.
3. He knows what we speak.
4. He is close to us from behind and in front of us.
    a. He encompasses us.
5. He lays His hand on us.
6. If we ascend into heaven, He will be there.
7. He will be there if we are sent to hell.
8. Even if we try to escape Him by sailing off to the outermost part of the sea, He is there.
9. There is no escaping the presence of the Lord.
10. No matter where we go, the Lord's hand will hold us.
11. Even in the darkest night, the Lord will provide light.
12. The Lord has been with us even in the womb (verse 13).
    a. The Lord does not wait until we are born to be with us; He is with us in our pre-born state.
13. The Lord has made us wonderfully and fearfully.
    a. He made us to be wonderful beings and we are incorporated with reverential fear of Him while we are being constructed.
14. Our soul knows what is right and how marvelous God's works are.
15. From inside the womb, our soul has been made to know the wonderful ways of God.
    a. In other words, we are made to know and praise God from our conception.
16. The Lord was there when we were conceived, and the act was not hidden from Him, even when it happened in the

             lowest parts of the earth.
          a. Could this be a reference to conception during a violent or evil act?
          b. Even when we were conceived in the lowest parts, the act was not hidden from Him.
             i. Lowest parts as a reference to hell and hellish behavior (aka the pit).
      17. From the beginning, the Lord recognized us as imperfect.
      18. Yet, the Lord thinks of us as precious, always.
      19. The thoughts of us by the Lord number more than the grains of sand.
      20. He is always with us.

Psalm 139 paints the ultimate love story about God's all encompassing knowledge and love for us. Yes, all of us. He intricately knows all His children—even the ones who use their freewill to cut themselves off from Him.

For the past 139 psalms, we have been discussing ways in which we can have access to all of God's graces and ways in which we lose access. Psalm 139 reminds us that no matter which direction we have decided to go, God is there. God experiences each moment of our lives with us. He is that close to us. Though it may be difficult to comprehend, our Holy Father thinks about each one of us more times than all the grains of sand. He is that concerned with our being. No matter what you are doing, God is there. How does that make you feel?

In the end, the ultimate life question always comes down to this: Do you want God to be there when you are welcomed into heaven or when He watches you depart into hell?

It's a simple question with a simple solution: trust, believe, and have hope in God and follow His path and you, too, will be welcomed to the most glorious eternal feast with Him upon leaving your life on Earth. Praise His holy name! Thank You, Father!

Notes:

Psalm 140: Deliver me, O Lord, from the Evil Man

Deliver me, O LORD, from the evil man: preserve me from the violent man; Which imagine mischiefs in their heart; continually are they gathered together for war. They have sharpened their tongues like a serpent; adders' poison is under their lips. Selah. Keep me, O LORD, from the hands of the wicked; preserve me from the violent man; who have purposed to overthrow my goings. The proud have hid a snare for me, and cords; they have spread a net by the wayside; they have set gins for me. Selah. I said unto the LORD, Thou art my God: hear the voice of my supplications, O LORD. O GOD the Lord, the strength of my salvation, thou hast covered my head in the day of battle. Grant not, O LORD, the desires of the wicked: further not his wicked device; lest they exalt themselves. Selah. As for the head of those that compass me about, let the mischief of their own lips cover them. Let burning coals fall upon them: let them be cast into the fire; into deep pits, that they rise not up again. Let not an evil speaker be established in the earth: evil shall hunt the violent man to overthrow him. I know that the LORD will maintain the cause of the afflicted, and the right of the poor. Surely the righteous shall give thanks unto thy name: the upright shall dwell in thy presence.

Psalm 140 reads as a song asking God to protect us from the wicked and to remember the righteous when evil is upon them. Verse 1 sets us up for the following litany of evil that is present in our lives and in our world.

Verse 1, "Deliver me, O LORD, from the evil man: preserve me from the violent man."

The psalm then goes on to give a list of what we can encounter from evil and violent people:

1. They imagine mischief in their hearts.
2. They are continually gathered together for war.
3. They have sharpened their tongues like a serpent, perhaps by being deceptive and manipulating.
4. Adder's poison is under their lips—their words can kill the body, mind, or spirit of their enemy.
5. The hands of the wicked and violent have the purpose of overthrowing the goings of us.
    a. By physical restraint or violence.
    b. By getting in our good way.
6. The proud spread nets in wayside places to entrap us.
7. The proud have set gins or trays to cage us.

We ask God not to grant the desires of the wicked to further their wicked schemes, lest they think they are powerful and exalt themselves. Instead, like the author of this psalm, we ask that God:

1. Hear our supplications.
2. Cover our heads with the strength of God's salvation.
3. Let the words of mischief from the wicked bypass us and go back onto them.
4. Let burning coals fall upon them.
5. Let them be cast into the fire and the pit so they never get up again.
6. Let not an evil speaker be established on the earth.
7. Let the evil hunt the violent to overthrow them.
    a. In other words, let the evil and violent hunt each other instead of the righteous.
8. Maintain the cause of the afflicted and the rights of the poor.
9. See that the righteous shall give thanks unto God's name.
10. See that the upright shall dwell in God's presence.

Psalm 140 carries a common theme within the Psalms (as well as within the Bible itself). It is the theme of God turning the ways of the wicked and violence onto themselves. Letting evil fall for evil. As this psalm points out, it is right to ask that God forsake the righteous of evil and protect them, causing what the wicked want for the righteous to be turned back onto them.

In fact, one of the most famous of all verses in the Bible expresses this sentiment very clearly and in no uncertain terms,

> No weapon that is formed against thee shall prosper; and every tongue that shall rise against thee in judgment thou shalt condemn. This is the heritage of the servants of the LORD, and their righteousness is of me, saith the LORD.
>
> Isaiah 54:17

It is the heritage of the children of God to be protected in this way. Claim that, and do not fear. When we walk on the good path with our Father, He has promised this to us. Thank You, Father!

Your protection keeps us away from fear and in the hope of Your promises. Amen.

Psalm 141: Incline Not My Heart to Any Evil Thing

> LORD, I cry unto thee: make haste unto me; give ear unto my voice, when I cry unto thee. Let my prayer be set forth before thee as incense; and the lifting up of my hands as the evening sacrifice. Set a watch, O LORD, before my mouth; keep the door of my lips. Incline not my heart to any evil thing, to practise wicked works with men that work iniquity: and let me not eat of their dainties. Let the righteous smite me; it shall be a kindness: and let him reprove me; it shall be an excellent oil, which shall not break my head: for yet my prayer also shall be in their calamities. When their judges are overthrown in stony places, they shall hear my words; for they are sweet. Our bones are scattered at the grave's mouth, as when one cutteth and cleaveth wood upon the earth. But mine eyes are unto thee, O GOD the Lord: in thee is my trust; leave not my soul destitute. Keep me from the snares which they have laid for me, and the gins of the workers of iniquity. Let the wicked fall into their own nets, whilst that I withal escape.

In Psalm 141, David implores God to help keep him righteous in his words and deeds. Perhaps David was facing temptation or feeling powerless to his own desires when he wrote this because we can sense an urgency and desperation in his words.

Verse 1, "LORD, I cry unto thee: make haste unto me; give ear unto my voice, when I cry unto thee."

Instead of turning away, David acknowledges and welcomes the rebuke of those who are righteous to help keep him in line.

1. "Let the righteous smite me."

      a. Smite: using righteous anger/truth in such a manner that causes the subject to have an opening up of guilt of conscience in order to bring about a change of heart concerning their behavior.
2. "Let him reprove me."
      a. Reprove: to reprimand or censure.

David recognizes that this type of chastisement is actually a gift.

1. It is a kindness.
2. It is an excellent oil.

This psalm speaks to one of the core issues of our modern times. Currently, large swathes of the population not only do not welcome rebuke, but they actively reject, mock, and rebel against it. As a result, we can not help but see generations of people floundering through life in a state of depression, bitterness, and hatred. We have become a temptation-driven society rather than a society that seeks righteous living, and the conscience is well aware that these behaviors are unhelpful to living a life of joy.

Psalm 141 reminds us that when we are facing temptation or living in that lifestyle, we find ourselves in the center of two opposing forces:

1. Those who do not wish us well.
      a. They will lean into us in order to turn up the heat of temptation.
      b. They lay snares to weaken our resolve to remain on the right path.
2. Those who fight to keep us on path.
      a. Though they may chastise and rebuke us, their heart is in a good place, for they seek to strengthen our resolve against the temptation.

In other words, consternation is actually a kindness. It is an oil to bring our minds back to peace. When God sends these people to us, we should keep our eyes "unto thee, O GOD the Lord: in thee is [our] trust" that God will not leave our souls destitute (verse 8).

God's desire is always what is best for our souls, even when His (or the people He sends to us) chastisement might feel uncomfortable. The Father will never allow a temptation that is so great that we cannot escape it, and He promised that He will always provide an escape for us to turn from temptation. It is wise that when we find ourselves confronted with a situation that tempts us off-path, we find the escape route and use it. Sometimes, that escape route is simply hearing the truth of the righteous and following it back to the path that guarantees a more peaceful life.

Thank You, Lord, for Your wise ways and for loving us enough to kindly criticize the actions that we pursue when they threaten to take us off-path. Let us never be departed from You!

Psalm 142: No Man Cared for My Soul

I cried unto the LORD with my voice; with my voice unto the LORD did I make my supplication. I poured out my complaint before him; I shewed before him my trouble. When my spirit was overwhelmed within me, then thou knewest my path. In the way wherein I walked have they privily laid a snare for me. I looked on my right hand, and beheld, but there was no man that would know me: refuge failed me; no man cared for my soul. I cried unto thee, O LORD: I said, Thou art my refuge and my portion in the land of the living. Attend unto my cry; for I am brought very low: deliver me from my persecutors; for they are stronger than I. Bring my soul out of prison, that I may praise thy name: the righteous shall compass me about; for thou shalt deal bountifully with me.

Verse 4, "I looked on my right hand, and beheld, but there was no man that would know me: refuge failed me; no man cared for my soul."

David recognizes in Psalm 142 that when it comes down to it, man is alone in his very soul in this world. At the heart of it, even in our closest relationships, our souls cannot be cared for like the Lord cares for us. The Lord is our only true refuge away from the harshness and brutality of the world.

Verse 6, "Attend unto my cry; for I am brought very low: deliver me from my persecutors; for they are stronger than I."

There are going to be times in our lives when we are surrounded by hardship and trouble. During these times, we are going to feel weak and all alone against the overwhelming strength of our troubles. Our minds perceive that there is no way to overcome what lies ahead. We imagine that those who come against us are too strong for us to be victorious in our affliction. Even when we seek help from our friends and relations, we feel alone against our troubles.

Psalm 142 is here to remind us that with God on our right hand, we will find strength and rest within our souls to overcome everything. Even in our hardship, we can feel a supernatural protection and peace of mind when we lean in and trust our heavenly Father. In fact, in the end, our Lord is the only one who can fully release us from the prison of a soul in turmoil.

Verse 7, "Bring my soul out of prison, that I may praise thy name: the righteous shall compass me about; for thou shalt deal bountifully with me."

When we recognize that the Lord is the only true refuge of our souls and we learn to trust Him with our lives, He deals with us generously, and we are brought into places where others who take refuge in the Lord congregate. Being surrounded by other faithful people is part of godly bounty. Psalm 142 is here to remind us that we shall and will overcome every hardship with the help of our Father, and after all is said and done, He will bring us back to a place of bounty as a reward for our faith in Him. Thank You, Lord.

Help me to be surrounded by Your faithful as my soul finds refuge in Your love. Amen.

Psalm 143: Cause Me to Know the Way Wherein I Should Walk

Hear my prayer, O LORD, give ear to my supplications: in thy faithfulness answer me, and in thy righteousness. And enter not into judgment with thy servant: for in thy sight shall no man living be justified. For the enemy hath persecuted my soul; he hath smitten my life down to the ground; he hath made me to dwell in darkness, as those that have been long dead. Therefore is my spirit overwhelmed within me; my heart within me is desolate. I remember the days of old; I meditate on all thy works; I muse on the work of thy hands. I stretch forth my hands unto thee: my soul thirsteth after thee, as a thirsty land. Selah. Hear me speedily, O LORD: my spirit faileth: hide not thy face from me, lest I be like unto them that go down into the pit. Cause me to hear thy lovingkindness in the morning; for in thee do I trust: cause me to know the way wherein I should walk; for I lift up my soul unto thee. Deliver me, O LORD, from mine enemies: I flee unto thee to hide me. Teach me to do thy will; for thou art my God: thy spirit is good; lead me into the land of uprightness. Quicken me, O LORD, for thy name's sake: for thy righteousness' sake bring my soul out of trouble. And of thy mercy cut off mine enemies, and destroy all them that afflict my soul: for I am thy servant.

Throughout the Psalms, David asks for his prayers to be heard, and—boy—does he pray! He seems to pray about everything and on every occasion. He asks for what he needs at all times. David has faith that knows that even in his fallen nature as a man, the Lord our God will answer him. And this is why David and the other authors so desperately seek the help of the Lord throughout the Psalms.

Verse 8, "Cause me to hear thy lovingkindness in the morning; for in thee do I trust: cause me to know the way wherein I should walk; for I lift up my soul unto thee."

(Matthew 7:7, "Ask, and it shall be given you; seek, and ye shall find; knock, and it shall be opened unto you.")

The Lord listens to us in prayer, and He always answers us in the way that is best for our soul. He guides our lives if we allow our wills to follow Him in the steps that He shows us.

We can never ask for too much. Our trust in Him with the daily needs of our life is pleasing to the Lord. He wants to provide for us our best and greatest life. We are His children, and He is our Father. When we ask, He hears us and answers. Have faith and trust in Him for everything!

This is what it means to *trust in the Lord*.

When we ask, You will hear us, and You will answer without fail. I trust You to show me the way. Great are You, O Lord.

Psalm 144: How to Separate from Strange Children

Blessed be the LORD my strength, which teacheth my hands to war, and my fingers to fight: My goodness, and my fortress; my high tower, and my deliverer; my shield, and he in whom I trust; who subdueth my people under me. LORD, what is man, that thou takest knowledge of him! or the son of man, that thou makest account of him! Man is like to vanity: his days are as a shadow that passeth away. Bow thy heavens, O LORD, and come down: touch the mountains, and they shall smoke. Cast forth lightning, and scatter them: shoot out thine arrows, and destroy them. Send thine hand from above; rid me, and deliver me out of great waters, from the hand of strange children; Whose mouth speaketh vanity, and their right hand is a right hand of falsehood. I will sing a new song unto thee, O God: upon a psaltery and an instrument of ten strings will I sing praises unto thee. It is he that giveth salvation unto kings: who delivereth David his servant from the hurtful sword. Rid me, and deliver me from the hand of strange children, whose mouth speaketh vanity, and their right hand is a right hand of falsehood: That our sons may be as plants grown up in their youth; that our daughters may be as corner stones, polished after the similitude of a palace: That our garners may be full, affording all manner of store: that our sheep may bring forth thousands and ten thousands in our streets: That our oxen may be strong to labour; that there be no breaking in, nor going out; that there be no complaining in our streets. Happy is that people, that is in such a case: yea, happy is that people, whose God is the LORD.

In Psalm 144, David contemplates the people who surround him in his life and asks God to help him separate from those who worship strange gods and not the God of Abraham. We see this as a theme in other psalms and throughout the Bible. When the Bible points to "strange" people, it is essentially talking about people who worship earthly idols or demons. For instance:

1. Psalm 54:3, "For strangers are risen up against me, and oppressors seek after my soul: they have not set God before them. Selah."
2. Malachi 2:11, "Judah hath dealt treacherously, and an abomination is committed in Israel and in Jerusalem; for Judah hath profaned the holiness of the LORD which he loved, and hath married the daughter of a strange god."

And Psalm 144 is no different. Verses 7–8, 11 (emphasis added by the author) speak to this,

> Send thine hand from above; rid me, and deliver me out of great waters, from the hand of strange children; Whose mouth speaketh vanity, and their *right hand* is a right hand of falsehood. …Rid me, and deliver me from the hand of strange children, whose mouth speaketh vanity, and their right hand is a right hand of falsehood.

Generally, when we see the term "the right hand" in the Bible, it is speaking of being in a position of strength, protection, and support for a man or from God. Jesus sits at the right hand of God. God is at our right hand during times of distress and when we need His support. The right hand is significant within the context of the Bible as a place of support.

In Psalm 144, we see that the right hand of the "strange children" is a right hand of falsehood, or in other words, lies. David recognizes that the children who follow strange gods are being supported by lies. These strange children of false gods speak vanity and not truth. In this case, speaking vanity seems to mean self-serving and selfish (and in many cases in the Bible, vanity is another way of indicating someone who is wicked).

Yet, the children of the God of David—who have trust in the Lord and find strength in Him—have an inheritance coming to them. In Psalm 144, David asks God to rid his space of the children of strange gods so the people of Abraham may:

1. See their sons grow up in their youth.
2. The daughters may be cornerstones, polished in the fashion of a palace.
3. Have an abundance of food in store.
4. That their sheep will multiply to thousands and thousands.
5. That their oxen be strong in labor.
6. That there be no complaining in the streets.

The children of God who have separated themselves from the children of false gods are joyful people in all ways. This is a very good lesson of how we should use great discernment in who we allow to have in our lives. Our happiness depends on it. Thank You, Lord.

Worksheet: How Has God Encouraged You in Your Own Life?

Consider how God has encouraged and prompted you toward some people who turned out to be good for your life and how He helped separate and let go of those who were harming you.

_____

_____

_____

_____

_____

_____

_____

_____

_____

_____

_____

_____

_____

_____

_____

_____

_____

_____

_____

_____

My example: When I was born again unto the Lord, I started losing many people whom I had been close to for years. Some naturally fell away when our life purposes went in different directions. Others were remnants of my former life that I loved dearly, but upon gaining discernment, I realized they kept me bound in an unhealthy way. At the same time, I strengthened relationships with those who were also on their own good path and who supported and counseled me in ways that were good for my soul.

When you pray for discernment in an authentic manner, do not be surprised when you start to see things in terms of helping you stay on path versus just going along aimlessly. God truly does give you support and protection, for He knows what is best for you over the long run.

Thought: I am merely a traveler in this world, but I am not a part of this world.

Psalm 145: A Psalm of Praise

I will extol thee, my God, O king; and I will bless thy name for ever and ever. Every day will I bless thee; and I will praise thy name for ever and ever. Great is the LORD, and greatly to be praised; and his greatness is unsearchable. One generation shall praise thy works to another, and shall declare thy mighty acts. I will speak of the glorious honour of thy majesty, and of thy wondrous works. And men shall speak of the might of thy terrible acts: and I will declare thy greatness. They shall abundantly utter the memory of thy great goodness, and shall sing of thy righteousness. The LORD is gracious, and full of compassion; slow to anger, and of great mercy. The LORD is good to all: and his tender mercies are over all his works. All thy works shall praise thee, O LORD; and thy saints shall bless thee. They shall speak of the glory of thy kingdom, and talk of thy power; To make known to the sons of men his mighty acts, and the glorious majesty of his kingdom. Thy kingdom is an everlasting kingdom, and thy dominion endureth throughout all generations. The LORD upholdeth all that fall, and raiseth up all those that be bowed down. The eyes of all wait upon thee; and thou givest them their meat in due season. Thou openest thine hand, and satisfiest the desire of every living thing. The LORD is righteous in all his ways, and holy in all his works. The LORD is nigh unto all them that call upon him, to all that call upon him in truth. He will fulfil the desire of them that fear him: he also will hear their cry, and will save them. The LORD preserveth all them that love him: but all the wicked will he destroy. My mouth shall speak the praise of the LORD: and let all flesh bless his holy name for ever and ever.

Verses 2–3, "Every day will I bless thee; and I will praise thy name for ever and ever. Great is the LORD, and greatly to be praised; and his greatness is unsearchable."

The Lord's greatness is so vast that it encompasses everything we can comprehend and everything that we cannot even imagine! Please examine this list and spend a few moments contemplating the fullness of each of these attributes of our Father:

1. The Lord is gracious and full of compassion.
2. The Lord is slow to anger.
3. The Lord has great mercy.
4. The Lord is good to all.
5. His mercy is all over His works.
6. His kingdom is everlasting.
7. His dominion will last throughout all generations.
8. He holds those who fall.
9. He lifts up those who bow down.
10. He gives those who wait upon Him their meat in due season.
11. He satisfies the desires of all living creatures.
12. The Lord is in all ways righteous.
13. All His works are holy.
14. The Lord is available to all who call Him in truth.
15. He will fulfill the desire of those who fear (have reverential trust in) Him.

On the other hand:

1. All the wicked He will destroy.

In many ways, Psalm 145 presents a litany of all the ways we have been learning about the greatness of God throughout the entire book of Psalms. It cannot be more clear: Our Lord is filled with loving kindness and all goodness.

We are again reminded that His mercy, grace, and compassion is available to all, and those who have reverential trust and respect for Him will have access to all His goodness. But those who choose wickedness, He will destroy. Point, blank, period. It cannot be anymore clear than this, "The LORD preserveth all them that love him: but all the wicked will he destroy" (verse 20).

Remember: Choosing to be wicked means more than choosing to cut yourself off from God. It means cutting yourself off from His mercy and protection. At the end of the day, God will allow those who persist in a wicked life to be destroyed. But it's never too late to change course while we live.

Verse 18, "The LORD is nigh unto all them that call upon him, to all that call upon him in truth."

Trust and believe in the Lord with an honest and contrite heart and call unto Him. He will come close to you and bring you on path with Him. This is a promise God made to all mankind, and it shall always be that way because God keeps His promises.

Thank You for taking care of all living creatures. Your majesty is greater than anything we can ever imagine!

Let us pray for all our brothers and sisters to have open eyes and open hearts to You. In Christ's name. Amen.

Psalm 146: The Lord Loveth the Righteous...but the Way of the Wicked He Turneth Upside Down

Praise ye the LORD. Praise the LORD, O my soul. While I live will I praise the LORD: I will sing praises unto my God while I have any being. Put not your trust in princes, nor in the son of man, in whom there is no help. His breath goeth forth, he returneth to his earth; in that very day his thoughts perish. Happy is he that hath the God of Jacob for his help, whose hope is in the LORD his God: Which made heaven, and earth, the sea, and all that therein is: which keepeth truth for ever: Which executeth judgment for the oppressed: which giveth food to the hungry. The LORD looseth the prisoners: The LORD openeth the eyes of the blind: the LORD raiseth them that are bowed down: the LORD loveth the righteous: The LORD preserveth the strangers; he relieveth the fatherless and widow: but the way of the wicked he turneth upside down. The LORD shall reign for ever, even thy God, O Zion, unto all generations. Praise ye the LORD.

Once again, Psalm 146 is a reminder that the God of Jacob, which is our God, is beneficial to those who are righteous, and He does not help the wicked. In fact, in verse nine, not only does God not help the wicked, but He turneth the wicked upside down.

Study: Who Are the Wicked and What Do They Do?

Because the "wicked" are mentioned many times within the Psalms and throughout the Bible, perhaps now is a good time to remind us of some of the characteristics of who the wicked are and what they do:

1. God is angry with the wicked (Psalm 7:11).
2. The wicked shall be turned into hell (Psalm 9:17).
3. The wicked will not seek God (Psalm 10:4).
4. The wicked bend their bow, that they may shoot at the upright in heart (Psalm 11:2).
5. They borrow and do not pay back (Psalm 37:21).
6. The wicked has and is in great power (Psalm 37:35).
7. The wicked shall fall by his own wickedness (Psalm 141:10).
8. The wicked are driven away (Psalm 68:2).
9. The wicked flee even when no one pursues them (Proverbs 28:1).
10. The wicked are like a troubled sea (Isaiah 57:20).
11. They are corrupt and speak wickedly concerning oppression (Psalm 73:8).
12. The wicked fall into their own nets (Psalm 141:10).
13. Enemies in your mind are by wicked works (Colossians 1:21).
14. The dwelling place of the wicked will come to nothing (Job 8:22).

In more modern terms, we can observe that wicked people:

1. Enjoy the misfortune of others.
2. Have control problems.
3. Lie all the time.
4. Cause a righteous person to feel uneasy.
5. Mislead people.

6. Lack remorse.
7. Are cruel.
8. Lack responsibility.
9. Friends and family warn against them.
10. Make bad friends.
11. Dislike others who cannot help them.
12. Manipulate others.
13. Belittle people.
14. Create confusion and conflict.
15. Lead double lives.
16. Don't respect boundaries.

These are good lists to consider not only for discerning who someone is when they enter our lives but for inner contemplation as well. As difficult as it is to do, when we look within and expand our acceptance of who we truly are, we can work on and root out our own wicked habits and behaviors as we move forward on the righteous path. The pursuit of the righteous path is noble, but by no means is anyone perfect who is walking on it. There is always internal work to do. When we are children of God, He has promised us that we will be on a course that continuously mounts higher, and He will never push us back into the pit.

If we do fall, that will be a decision we make with our own free will. Once you are fully on the right path, falling way back into the pit takes an extreme and very conscious decision to abandon God. We may backslide occasionally, but as a child of God, He will always show us the way to return to the path that pleases Him the most. Even those who have fallen fully can come back by asking for help with a contrite heart and trust in Him who created us. As long as we are living in our bodies, there is hope. After our bodies die, then comes judgment.

Thank You, Lord, for Your mercy and kindness and for helping us to know who and what is wicked so we may avoid them and take care not to be like them. Your wisdom knows no bounds. Praise and glory to You, Most High God. Amen.

Notes:

Psalm 147: Praise Ye the Lord, for It Is Good to Sing Praises unto Our Lord!

Praise ye the LORD: for it is good to sing praises unto our God; for it is pleasant; and praise is comely. The LORD doth build up Jerusalem: he gathereth together the outcasts of Israel. He healeth the broken in heart, and bindeth up their wounds. He telleth the number of the stars; he calleth them all by their names. Great is our Lord, and of great power: his understanding is infinite. The LORD lifteth up the meek: he casteth the wicked down to the ground. Sing unto the LORD with thanksgiving; sing praise upon the harp unto our God: Who covereth the heaven with clouds, who prepareth rain for the earth, who maketh grass to grow upon the mountains. He giveth to the beast his food, and to the young ravens which cry. He delighteth not in the strength of the horse: he taketh not pleasure in the legs of a man. The LORD taketh pleasure in them that fear him, in those that hope in his mercy. Praise the LORD, O Jerusalem; praise thy God, O Zion. For he hath strengthened the bars of thy gates; he hath blessed thy children within thee. He maketh peace in thy borders, and filleth thee with the finest of the wheat. He sendeth forth his commandment upon earth: his word runneth very swiftly. He giveth snow like wool: he scattereth the hoarfrost like ashes. He casteth forth his ice like morsels: who can stand before his cold? He sendeth out his word, and melteth them: he causeth his wind to blow, and the waters flow. He sheweth his word unto Jacob, his statutes and his judgments unto Israel. He hath not dealt so with any nation: and as for his judgments, they have not known them. Praise ye the LORD.

As we come to faith and begin developing a deeper love and reverential trust in the Lord and witness for ourselves the power, mercy, and grace God provides, one cannot help but sing praises to Him.

Psalm 147 gives us even more reasons to praise God and expounds on why He is worth praising.

Praise the Lord list:

1. He builds up His nation of Israel.
2. Even the outcasts He brings together.
3. He heals broken hearts.
4. He binds closed the wounds of the heart.
5. He made His nation as high as the number of stars in the night sky.
6. He named all the seed of Abram for all generations.
7. The Lord has great power.
8. The Lord's understanding is infinite.
9. The Lord lifts up the meek.
10. The Lord casts down the wicked to the ground.
11. The Lord creates the weather that gives life to crops and all the plants.
12. He feeds all His creatures.
13. The Lord takes pleasure in those who give Him reverential trust.
14. The Lord takes pleasure in those who have hope in His mercy.
15. The Lord has strengthened the bars of the gates of His nations.
16. He blesses His children within the gates.
17. He makes peace between border nations.
18. He fills His nations with the finest crops.
19. When the Lord commands something, it happens very quickly.
20. He gives His creatures the means to stay warm.
21. He can cause cold to be unbearable, and He can melt the cold.
22. The wind blows, and the water flows because the Lord wills it.

23. He made a covenant with His nation and set them apart from other nations.

The Lord sets aside His children. He protects them and brings peace to them. He feeds them and clothes them. He uses His will to help them. All the fruits of the Lord are available to those who love and follow Him on the good path toward heaven.

But to the wicked, He casts them to the ground (verse 6).

It is important to recognize that the Lord is aware of those who fit the character of His children and those whom He deems as wicked, lest we think the wicked enjoy the fruits of His will. This is an important consideration for when we take an honest account of our own lives and where we stand. Take a moment to contemplate which path you are on at this time.

Are you on a righteous path or a wicked path, or are you trying to straddle both?

After we give our life to God and repent (or rethink) our lifestyles, we enter onto the good path, which then becomes a lifelong pursuit to stay on it joyfully. It is not easy in the beginning to let go of those habits we developed while riding quickly down the path that leads to destruction. At the time, many of those things gave us pleasure. The Psalms continuously remind us that the path that is paved in unhealthy, sinful pursuits (or wickedness) is the path that will lead to destruction. But the path that is perhaps more difficult, the path paved in good and righteous living, leads to refuge, rest, peace, joy, and the protection of the Most High creator. Knowing all of this and really understanding what it means is such a powerful tool for staying in faith and under the mantle of the Lord as we make our way up the path to eternal rest in heaven.

Are you making your way toward everlasting life in heaven, or are you firmly on the way to eternal death in hell? It's a question worth contemplating.

Which way are you going?

Psalm 148: Praise Ye the Lord. Praise Ye the Lord from the Heavens: Praise Him in the Heights

Praise ye the LORD. Praise ye the LORD from the heavens: praise him in the heights. Praise ye him, all his angels: praise ye him, all his hosts. Praise ye him, sun and moon: praise him, all ye stars of light. Praise him, ye heavens of heavens, and ye waters that be above the heavens. Let them praise the name of the LORD: for he commanded, and they were created. He hath also stablished them for ever and ever: he hath made a decree which shall not pass. Praise the LORD from the earth, ye dragons, and all deeps: Fire, and hail; snow, and vapour; stormy wind fulfilling his word: Mountains, and all hills; fruitful trees, and all cedars: Beasts, and all cattle; creeping things, and flying fowl: Kings of the earth, and all people; princes, and all judges of the earth: Both young men, and maidens; old men, and children: Let them praise the name of the LORD: for his name alone is excellent; his glory is above the earth and heaven. He also exalteth the horn of his people, the praise of all his saints; even of the children of Israel, a people near unto him. Praise ye the LORD.

The revelation of John in the book of Revelation, chapter 5, verse 13, is widely seen as a verse recognizing the universal adoration of the Lamb who is King at the time of the second coming of Christ and paints a picture of all of God's creatures praising Him upon His return:

And every creature which is in heaven, and on the earth, and under the earth, and such as are in the sea, all that are in them, heard I [John] saying, Blessing, and honour, and glory, and power, be unto him that sitteth upon the throne, and unto the Lamb for ever.

In many ways, Psalm 148 is an illustration of the time when Jesus Christ will once again appear to all during the time that marks the beginning of the end of all time (aka eternity). Even though this psalm was written many centuries before the revelations of John, it's almost as if this psalm gives us more details by listing specific creatures of the "every creature" in Revelation 5:13. These are some of the things that the author of Psalm 148 is talking about in verse 1 when illustrating all of God's creations that "praise ye the LORD. Praise ye the LORD from the heavens: praise him in the heights."

A list of some of God's creations that will praise Him:

- The angels.
- The sun and moon.
- The stars.
- The heavens and the water *above* the heavens.
- The dragons.
- Fire and hail.
- Snow and vapors.
- Stormy winds.
- Mountains and hills.
- Fruitful trees.
- All cedars.
- Beasts and cattle.
- Creeping things.
- Flying fowl.
- Kings of the earth.
- All people.
- Princes.
- Judges.
- Young men and maidens.
- Old men and children.

Psalm 148:13, "Let them praise the name of the LORD: for his name alone is excellent; His glory is above the earth and heaven."

During the miraculous second coming of the Messiah, God will exalt the horn of His people while we all sing praise to Him. God will, in return, honor those who will join Him in heaven as His saints, "a people near to Him."

What an amazing and joyful sight that will be! This is the ultimate *promise* of the Bible and, interestingly, is written all over the Psalms: *Persevere in your salvation, trust in the Lord and have hope in Him, and continue to sing praise to Him, and you will be exalted on the last day as all of creation gives God honor and praise.*

I'm really looking forward to that day! Are you?

Praise and glory and honor are Yours, Lord. Forever. Amen.

Notes:

Psalm 149: Sing unto the Lord a New Song!

> Praise ye the LORD. Sing unto the LORD a new song, and his praise in the congregation of saints. Let Israel rejoice in him that made him: let the children of Zion be joyful in their King. Let them praise his name in the dance: let them sing praises unto him with the timbrel and harp. For the LORD taketh pleasure in his people: he will beautify the meek with salvation. Let the saints be joyful in glory: let them sing aloud upon their beds. Let the high praises of God be in their mouth, and a twoedged sword in their hand; To execute vengeance upon the heathen, and punishments upon the people; To bind their kings with chains, and their nobles with fetters of iron; To execute upon them the judgment written: this honour have all his saints. Praise ye the LORD.

Psalm 149, at its core, appears to illustrate the virtues of singing praise to God by His people, who are described as saints. For the Lord takes pleasure in this. In fact, those who are meek and humble, the Lord will beautify with salvation.

1. The Lord made His people of Israel.
2. Let the children of Zion be joyful in their King.
3. Let the saints be joyful in glory.
4. They shall sing aloud in their beds.
5. Let the high praises of God be in their mouths and a double-edged sword in their hands.

The song of praise of the saints becomes a double-edged sword that will execute vengeance on those who do not call God their father. So mighty will the song of praise from His people be that it will bring joy to the saints who sing and, at the same time, issue punishment on behalf of the Most High to those who have no faith!

Verse 7, "To execute vengeance upon the heathen, and punishments upon the people."

According to Psalm 149, when the saints of God sing songs of praise in their congregation, this is also an act of vengeance of God that He uses to punish the non-believers and pagans.

If we compare this understanding of how songs of praise work in the realm of holy matters, imagine what vengeance will take place when all things sing praise to the King on the throne in heaven, as was illustrated in Psalm 148. The saints will be filled with joy, but those who chose a different path will find that these songs of praise are a punishment in an act of vengeance of God.

In many ways, this illustrates what we have learned about God throughout the Psalms. He is a gentle God. He gives us rest, refuge, and protection. He is merciful, kind, and full of grace. God is love in all ways. In fact, we find out in Psalm 149 that in His gentle and humble manner, He uses the beautiful sound of the song as a weapon of punishment. One of the ways God offers His vengeance is through songs of praise.

It makes sense when you contemplate it. We have all seen how some people wince at songs of praise, and it raises their ire. Sometimes, they become so uncomfortable that they leave the area where the songs are playing. This could be seen as an outward sign of feeling the vengeance of God. Perhaps now is a good time to look deeper into the term vengeance, what it is, and how it is presented within the context of the Bible.

Study: Vengeance

According to Dictionary.com, the term "vengeance" (noun) is defined as:

1. Infliction of injury, harm, humiliation, or the like on a person by another who has been harmed by that person.
2. Violent revenge.
3. An act or opportunity of inflicting such trouble:
   - To take one's vengeance.
   - The desire for revenge.
   - A man full of vengeance.
4. Obsolete: hurt; injury.
5. Obsolete: curse; imprecation.

What does the Bible say about vengeance?

1. Deuteronomy 32:35, "To me belongeth vengeance, and recompence; their foot shall slide in due time: for the day of their calamity is at hand, and the things that shall come upon them make haste."
   a. Recompense is defined as: "make amends to (someone) for loss or harm suffered; compensate."
2. Proverbs 6:34, "For jealousy is the rage of a man: therefore he will not spare in the day of vengeance."
   a. In other words, jealousy will cause a person to lash out in rage and become vengeful.
3. Isaiah 59:17–18, "For he put on righteousness as a breastplate, and an helmet of salvation upon his head; and he put on the garments of vengeance for clothing, and was clad with zeal as a cloke. According to their deeds, accordingly he will repay, fury to his adversaries, recompence to his enemies; to the islands he will repay recompence."
4. Ezekiel 25:14, "And I will lay my vengeance upon Edom by the hand of my people Israel: and they shall do in Edom according to mine anger and according to my fury; and they shall know my vengeance, saith the Lord GOD."

It is clear in the Bible that vengeance for misdeeds and wickedness will assuredly happen against the enemies of God and those who cause His people to suffer. God's righteous anger is very clear throughout the Bible, and though He be meek, the Most High is not without strength and purpose. However, it is also clear that God will repay those who have been afflicted and made to suffer, for our God is a just judge. But it is not up to us to act but to wait on the Lord.

Romans 12:19, "Dearly beloved, avenge not yourselves, but rather give place unto wrath: for it is written, Vengeance is mine; I will repay, saith the Lord."

It is right to have patience as we make our way up the good path. Even if our enemies surround us and are applying pressure, God's vengeance will be perfect and at the perfect time. Trust in the Lord. Amen.

All things will come around in God's time.

Psalm 150: Let Every Thing That Hath Breath Praise the Lord

> Praise ye the LORD. Praise God in his sanctuary: praise him in the firmament of his power. Praise him for his mighty acts: praise him according to his excellent greatness. Praise him with the sound of the trumpet: praise him with the psaltery and harp. Praise him with the timbrel and dance: praise him with stringed instruments and organs. Praise him upon the loud cymbals: praise him upon the high sounding cymbals. Let every thing that hath breath praise the LORD. Praise ye the LORD.

Psalm 150, which is the last psalm in the Bible, gives us a template of how to praise God. It is a fitting end to a book that lays out a very good case for all the wondrous things the Father does for His children and how we, His faithful, can find faith and keep it along the way, even in the midst of great peril and evil. Even when we are surrounded by the wicked who lay snares to take us down, get us off-path, and rejoice in our misery, the Psalms remind us that all is never lost and that He is our protection, rest, and refuge. We must trust in Him and surrender our ways for His ways, and great things can and will happen.

And so, Psalm 150 says, "Rejoice and praise!"

And where should we rejoice and praise?

In His sanctuary and in the firmament of His power. There are many indications of what the sanctuary is and where we may find it scattered throughout the Bible. If you would like to dive into the concept of sanctuary, it would be highly recommended for more depth, but by and large, a sanctuary, in broad terms, refers to a holy place wherein God dwells. So, Psalm 150 asks that we praise the Lord in a place reserved for God.

But what if we are unable to travel to a place outside our home or if we feel like praising God while we work or do chores? Because we have been told that the Lord is a sanctuary Himself and He provides refuge from this world, if we cannot get to a holy place reserved for God (aka a temple or church structure), we can praise Him in the place He dwells within our own being. In the place in our interior body where we meet God in prayer.

What are those things we should praise God for, according to Psalm 150?

1. His mighty acts.
2. His wondrous deeds.

In other words, recognize the wonderful things the Lord has done in our own lives and praise and thank Him. But also look around and acknowledge the great and mighty things the Lord has done outside ourselves as well.

Now would be a good time to list those wonderful things that God has done for you personally and some of your favorite creations of God.

List All the Wonderful Things of God

The wonderful things God has done for you and in your life:

_____

_____

_____

_____

_____

_____

Some of your favorite creations of God:

_____

_____

_____

_____

_____

_____

_____

_____

What are some of the ways we can praise God?

Psalm 150 makes it clear that using instruments, song, and dance are wonderful ways to praise Him. Song and music, in fact, are so important in praising the Most High that a book in the Bible is dedicated to songs or poems (or psalms) used in worship: the book of Psalms. The book we have been studying has enlightened us about some of the ways of our creator and His faithful children. At the end of it all, this beautiful book of Psalms reminds us for the final time: rejoice and sing praise to God, for He is mighty and wondrous.

Finally, who should praise God?

All things that breathe. It is such a powerful image that is formed when we contemplate that not only should we, the people who have been made in the image of God, praise Him, but that all the creatures of God give praise to Him as well. This means that those beings we normally consider to serve no real purpose but to be present and to eat and to play on or around are out there praising their creator as well.

Contemplation: Praise of All Things Created

"Let every thing that hath breath praise the LORD. Praise ye the LORD." (Psalm 150:6). It is highly recommended that the next time you are on a quiet path in nature, you consider that all of God's creations are singing praise to their creator. Try to hear the song. Use your eyes to see the praise. It makes for a very interesting walk the next time you are out in nature, enjoying the sounds and peaceful play of those beings that are around you.

Let every thing that hath breath praise the Lord. Praise ye the Lord.

(The very last verse of the book of Psalms) Hallelujah!

Printed in the USA
CPSIA information can be obtained
at www.ICGtesting.com
LVHW052044091224
798702LV00003B/3